PROBLEM-ORIENTED POLICING:
From Innovation to Mainstream

Johannes Knutsson

Editor

Crime Prevention Studies
Volume 15

Criminal Justice Press
Monsey, NY, USA

Willan Publishing
Devon, UK

CRIME PREVENTION STUDIES

Ronald V. Clarke, Series Editor

Crime Prevention Studies is an international book series dedicated to research on situational crime prevention and other initiatives to reduce opportunities for crime. Most volumes center on particular topics chosen by expert guest editors. The editors of each volume, in consultation with the series editor, commission the papers to be published and select peer reviewers.

Printed in the United States of America. No part of this book may be reproduced in any manner whatsoever without written permission, except for brief quotations embodied in critical articles and reviews. For information, contact Criminal Justice Press, Willow Tree Press Inc., P.O. Box 249, Monsey, NY 10952 U.S.A.

ISSN (series): 1065-7029
ISBN: 1-881798-37-2 (cloth)
ISBN: 1-881798-38-0 (paper)

CONTENTS

PREFACE

The idea for this book started with a conversation between Ron Clarke and me during a walk in Margaret River by the Sea, Australia, while bird watching. Inspired by scenery and birds, we discussed the state of policing. In particular, we discussed why problem-oriented policing, a sound way of conducting police business, is rarely implemented well. We found this question so troubling that we decided it would be worth convening a small meeting of experts to explore the various reasons for this state of affairs, and to find ways in which the problem-oriented approach could be brought more fully into the mainstream of policing.

Having agreed on that course of action, the next step was to get necessary funding. I was sure it would be possible to arrange a conference on the subject in Norway, since I was convinced that the newly appointed National Police Commissioner at the Norwegian Police Directorate, Ingelin Killengreen, would immediately realize the value of such a meeting. A week later, after a short meeting with her, she gave her full support.

This is the background to the invitations sent to Ron Clarke, John Eck, Graham Farrell, Herman Goldstein, Deborah Lamm Weisel, Gloria Laycock, Rana Sampson, Mike Scott, Nick Tilley and Michael Townsley to prepare the papers included in this book. These papers were discussed at a small conference at Kleivstua, just outside Oslo, between 21st and 24th April 2002, in magnificent surroundings, with the view from the hotel of fjords and snow-clad mountains. Just after the meeting, I had a final discussion with Ron Clarke at Ugglarp on the west coast of Sweden, where we did some more walking and bird watching. We concluded, with the presentations and discussions fresh in our memories, that the prospects were in fact promising for mainstreaming problem-oriented policing. However, it will take a strong, dedicated effort both from academics and police to realize the full potential of the approach.

Of all who have contributed to the book, I would especially like to thank Herman Goldstein for his continual insistance on improving the quality of policing and Ron Clarke for his help in bringing the idea of the book from initial conception into realization.

Johannes Knutsson
Research Director
The National Police Academy, Norway

FOREWORD

The development process in crime mirrors the development process in society. Likewise, the methods for preventing and combating crime mirror society as such. For many years, we have based our police methods on experience and common sense, and it is still as important as ever to take into account the police officer's practical knowledge and experience in regard to what works and what does not. On the other hand, it is equally important to realise that the police must be part of progress in general, and that it is necessary to make use of knowledge available — including knowledge based on empirical research. The police must play an active part in what has become a knowledge-based society. This is the only way in which we will be able to lay the foundations for a policing focused on crime prevention.

The organisational structures of the police vary at the international level. Besides, there are also considerable differences when it comes to the choice of police methods. Still, quite a few countries have reached the understanding that both the choice and development of methods should be based on research and scientific knowledge. Norway is one of the countries which, in recent years, has come to realise the importance of establishing a research milieu connected to the field of policing. Problem-oriented policing has become a central issue, and it has been emphasised in the Police Academy's education and training activities. This is of great importance to Norway, being a small country when it comes to population and having a modest amount of police officers as well as a low crime rate.

Problem-oriented policing has both succeeded and supplemented crime prevention and community policing as the main areas of interest and development for many years now. What all areas have in common is the understanding that the war against crime is not won by repressive measures and subsequent responses alone. Several countries have run successful projects, and have had good results. There may not be scientific documentary proof for all results. Still, there is a range of good — and concrete — examples showing that results are improved when the police make use of thorough knowledge and good analyses concerning the problems they are to solve, before measures are taken.

As the professional head of the Norwegian police I do believe that the problem-oriented approach is an efficient and workable method of policing. This is why the Norwegian National Police Directorate warmly supports the work initiated by the Research Department of the Norwegian National Police Academy. Correspondingly, we support the efforts now made in order to implement this work in the police students' training and education.

The idea for this book originated with the director of research at the Norwegian National Police Academy, Johannes Knutsson, and Professor Ronald V. Clarke of Rutgers University. All contributors are highly esteemed researchers on an international level. Some of them have, for years, been leading figures in the police research milieu. From a Norwegian point of view we are pleased to note that many Norwegian police officers are well acquainted with — and interested in — the work of these scholars.

I would like to thank Johannes Knutsson and Ronald V. Clarke for all their efforts, and moreover, to thank all the authors for responding to this initiative with valuable and very informative contributions. I am convinced that this book will be read — and applied. It will prove to be a useful tool in putting problem-oriented policing into practice.

Ingelin Killengreen
National Police Commissioner, Norway

INTRODUCTION

Johannes Knutsson
National Police Academy,
Norway

Problem-oriented policing (POP) is a police management philosophy that above all has come to be associated with Herman Goldstein. An important and influential article from the late 1970s introduced the concept and the principles behind it (Goldstein, 1979). In 1990, Goldstein published *Problem-Oriented Policing,* in which he described the approach in more detail. The main idea is to persuade police to move away from incident-driven policing by identifying the problems that lead citizens to call for assistance, and then to intervene in the mechanisms that cause the problems. Problems in this context are defined as: (1) a cluster of similar, related, or recurring incidents rather than a single incident, and (2) substantive community concerns. Goldstein made clear that problem-oriented policing is primarily a preventive approach, and that solutions are preferred that to a lesser extent, or preferably not at all, rely upon use of the criminal justice system.

In another important publication, Eck and Spelman (1987) reported a number of case studies using the approach, and introduced the acronym SARA to describe the four essential stages of a problem-oriented project: Scanning, Analysis, Response and Assessment (Eck and Spelman, 1987). Scanning means to identify, specify and describe specific problems. Analysis is the phase in which the causes of the problems are explored. Response refers to the search for tailor-made solutions to remove the causes of the problems and then the implementation of the selected responses. Assessment is the process in which the solutions are followed up to evaluate their implementation and effectiveness.

It can be misleading to perceive the process from problem identification to evaluation of effectiveness as following a predetermined sequence where analysis only takes place in the second phase. In fact, the process is iterative, with analysis going back and forth between the stages. For example, new information gained at the response

Crime Prevention Studies, vol. 15 (2003), pp. 1-11.

stage may require fresh analysis of determining conditions to be undertaken (see chapter by Clarke and Goldstein in this volume). In the United Kingdom an alternative to SARA is sometimes used — PROCTOR — that in a somewhat more modulated way describes the different stages and also underlines that analysis takes place throughout the whole process. PROCTOR signifies ".... PROblem, Cause, Tactic or Treatment, Output and Result" (Read and Tilley, 2000:11). To carry out a complete analysis of causes is an extremely demanding task that, however, is unnecessary in this context. It is sufficient to find factors that can be changed or manipulated — the so-called pinch-points.

Choice of response (Tactic or Treatment) also requires an analytical, creative approach. In addition, it is essential at this stage to have access to knowledge about methods that have been used successfully elsewhere when similar problems have been encountered. During the Output stage, the degree to which measures are implemented as planned, and the reception that they are given, are both explored. In the Result stage, an evaluation is conducted to discover if the expected effects have been achieved and if side effects have occurred. Evaluation is a demanding task that entails both data collection and rigorous analysis.

At a higher level of abstraction, problem-oriented policing may therefore be characterized as a much more analytic way of conducting police business than practiced hitherto. The goal is to get away from a reactive incident-driven mode in favour of a proactive and preventive way of conducting police business.

RECEPTION GIVEN TO PROBLEM-ORIENTED POLICING

The concept immediately aroused interest, and police forces in the United States, the United Kingdom and Scandinavia have adopted problem-oriented policing. Many projects, with varying degree of support from management, have been carried out by enthusiastic officers at the beat level. Some forces have also tried to implement a more complete realization of the idea. Central authorities (for example, the Home Office in the U.K., the National Police Board in Sweden and the National Police Directorate in Norway) and other organisations (for example, the Police Executive Research Forum in the United States) have also tried to stimulate police interest in problem-oriented policing.

In many places, more or less extensive courses for police officers on the principles and practice of problem-oriented policing have been given. For example, during basic training at the police academies in both Norway and Sweden, future officers are taught problem-oriented policing. The power of the good example has also been used to advocate and spread the approach. In the United States, the Police Executive Research Forum has arranged an annual conference on problem-oriented policing in San Diego every year since 1990. One of the main events consists of a competition — the Herman Goldstein Award — for the best problem-oriented policing projects. The award now attracts about 90 submissions each year. In United Kingdom a yearly conference — Brit PoP —has also been established, where the Tilley award is given to the best project. In Sweden, there has also been a national conference with a competition for the best problem-oriented policing project.

It was hoped that these competitions would encourage forces to duplicate the successes of others and that the concept would gradually diffuse, resulting eventually in a breakthrough in policing strategy. The original vision was, thus, that problem-oriented policing would permeate the police organization and that a radical shift in the policing paradigm would occur.

Extent of Implementation

Despite the welcome accorded to the concept by the police, hard questions soon began to be asked about the extent to which they were actually implementing it. Hardly any police force has adopted problem-oriented policing as its dominant strategy. The few exceptions could be counted on the fingers of one hand. The San Diego Police Department under Chief Jerry Sanders in the United States and the Lancashire Constabulary under Chief Constable Pauline Clare in the United Kingdom are such examples where genuine efforts to implement problem-oriented policing in the organization has taken place.

Other warning signs concerned the quality of the projects submitted for awards in both the United States and the United Kingdom. Many of these projects fall well below the depth and quality of work needed for successful problem-oriented policing interventions (Clarke, 1998; Scott and Clarke, 2000; Read and Tilley, 2000; Scott, 2000). Even Goldstein himself has sometimes shown signs of disappointment and frustration. The expected breakthrough has not occurred except in police rhetoric (see Goldstein's chapter in this book).

However, none of the early advocates of problem-oriented policing has questioned the basic idea. The disappointing implementation of problem-oriented policing is not thought to be evidence of "theory failure"; on the contrary, belief in the concept is still strong. Rather, it is a question of shortcomings in the implementation of problem-oriented policing.

Origins of this Book

If the concept is sound, the failures of implementation must be understood and corrected before the problem-oriented approach can assume its proper role in policing. Are the causes to be found in academia where the concept was originally developed, in lack of support from government or in the police service itself?

These questions were the starting-point for this book. The contributors, all of whom have considerable understanding of the problem-oriented approach and are among the foremost experts in the field, were asked to reflect on progress made to date and to think about ways of improving the implementation of the concept from whichever perspective they chose. In the event, their contributions range quite widely over a variety of topics concerned with ways of improving the number and quality of problem-oriented policing projects. These topics include:

- the receptivity of police managers and line officers (Goldstein, Townsley et al.);

- the willingness and capacity of police organizations to make necessary changes (Scott, Townsley et al.);

- the role of awards and importance of good case studies (Bullock and Tilley, Clarke and Goldstein, Sampson);

- the in-house expertise of police in crime analysis (Bullock and Tilley, Clarke and Goldstein, Goldstein, Lamm Weisel);

- the needed input and support from the research community in building a body of knowledge to support good practice (Eck, Goldstein, Scott);

- the need for police to become informed about relevant concepts from situational crime prevention and environmental criminology (Eck, Sampson, Scott);

- the experience of seeking to implement other evidence-based strategies such as repeat victimization (Laycock and Farrell);

- the level of support needed from governments (Goldstein, Laycock and Farrell); and

- the expectations of the wider community about the police role and function (Goldstein, Laycock and Farrell, Scott).

Complexity of the Enterprise

These topics were the focus of the meeting held in Norway to discuss the individual contributions. Perhaps the main conclusion that emerged was that the complexity of the problem-oriented approach has been greatly underestimated. Problem-oriented policing may be common sense, but it takes considerable experience, skill and technical knowledge to practice it. Reiss (1992) argues that only police organizations with considerable research capacity can be expected to implement problem-oriented policing in any thoroughgoing manner. It is a research- and evidence-based activity. It is not reasonable to expect all police to develop such a capacity or to develop it quickly. Nor is it reasonable to expect that police would move quickly to embrace such a radical shift in their traditional method of operating. Indeed, expectations concerning the time needed for the concept to be in everyday use have been wildly optimistic. Five, ten or even twenty years — depending on the country in question —is really a short time for a paradigm shift of this magnitude to occur.

Even if the police wished to move quickly to employ personnel with the necessary technical skills to implement the approach, the supply of such people with relevant training and experience is scarce. Education for this purpose hardly exists at universities or other institutions of higher education. Nor is it purely a question of technical skills, but also of attitudes. Researchers suited to this task must be willing to serve policy and practice, but an important part of criminological training at university institutions is to inculcate an independent and critical attitude toward government and the police. The pejorative term "administrative criminology" is sometimes used to characterize the type of criminology that is engaged in producing policy-relevant knowledge for government. It is assumed that this knowledge is "tainted" by the need to suit the interests of the establishment and is not pursued for the benefit of ordinary citizens (Young, 1988). To the contrary, police researchers should indeed have a critical, independent attitude. In fact, if they are properly to serve the police such an attitude, combined with unquestioned personal integrity, is of the utmost importance.

Nor is it well understood in university departments of criminology that knowledge about the "root" causes of criminality is of very limited relevance to everyday policing. The line of thought with most relevance to problem-oriented policing is found in the situational approach (see, e.g., Clarke, 1997). This criminological approach seeks to supplement the system of justice, not to provide a complete alternative. It also has a clear practical orientation by providing guidance about manipulating different situational factors to affect potential offenders' perceptions of criminal acts as more risky, more difficult and less rewarding. In this respect, situational crime prevention shares assumptions with the theoretical basis of policing — deterrence theory. Both share the assumption of humans as rational actors, even if there are nuances in this image (Cornish and Clarke, 1986; Clarke and Cornish, 2000; Sullivan, 2000).

However, many academic criminologists have objected to situational prevention on theoretical grounds. A common but faulty objection is that since (assumed) "root" causes are unaffected by situational measures, displacement of crime will of necessity occur. Many studies have shown this not to be true (Hesseling, 1994). An important tenet of the situational approach is that the opportunity structure for crime is a cause of criminality per se, and that by affecting the opportunity structure, crimes will be prevented in a true sense; thus explaining why displacement is not a necessary consequence of situational prevention.

Leaving aside the shortage of people with the relevant theoretical background, there is also a serious lack of people with the required analytic skills. Undertaking scanning and analysis at the level required for successful problem-oriented policing is a difficult and challenging task. It requires familiarity with different types of crime data and with a wide variety of statistical and mapping tools. During the last few years, crime mapping has developed very rapidly both in terms of theoretical knowledge and in software to assist analysis (see, e.g., Weisburd and McEwen, 1997), but training in crime mapping has lagged far behind in criminology departments. Finally, the ability to undertake rigorous impact studies is of the greatest importance, but this is also in short supply. Such studies make high demands on both methodological skills and research imagination, yet few researchers are being trained in evaluation methodology.

It is unclear if the technical capacity needed to support problem-oriented policing can build upon the crime analyst function that nowadays is increasingly found in many police departments. This function is gradually becoming more sophisticated as Geographic Information Systems (GIS) become more readily available. The uncertainty is created by the fact that crime analysts generally lack basic training in problem-oriented policing and primarily serve other tasks, like providing management with data for resource allocation or for media purposes. These day-to-day demands might make it impossible for crime analysts to provide the continuous analytic support needed for problem-oriented policing projects, and it might be necessary to create a specialized analytic capacity with personnel having specific competence in problem-oriented policing.

Given the difficult and demanding task that problem-oriented policing represents, it is also of vital importance to improve training of police officers. Normally courses are short, and it is not possible to get a sufficiently deep understanding after just a couple of days training. Considerable experimentation may be needed before a satisfactory curriculum and format is developed for longer courses of perhaps several weeks in duration. It is also imperative that management get more thorough training, since they have the ultimate responsibility for the activity. They must be well informed enough to know the level of commitment and the specific skills required to undertake a satisfactory problem-oriented project.

Problem Solving versus Problem-oriented Policing

A second conclusion reached at the meeting in Norway was that it is important to differentiate between problem-oriented policing in its proper sense and activities at beat level that are more accurately characterized as problem solving (Clarke, 1998). Problem solving signifies that officers have solved a persistent problem, perhaps in a creative and new way, but without undertaking a deep analysis (often because the problem was clear and evident), without undertaking a thorough analysis of its causes (one creative solution was perhaps enough), without requiring extensive and expensive measures (even if no one had come up with the idea before, it was simple to carry through), and without undertaking any formal assessment of the result (the problem was so evident and simple that its presence or absence was easy to observe).

It is of course important to encourage this kind of problem solving. It has always existed and has been carried out by officers who have sometimes been regarded as "oddballs," not engaged in "real" police work, by their colleagues. But problem solving, without the elements of SARA or PROCTOR, cannot be regarded as problem-oriented policing. Problem-oriented policing and problem solving go well together; they should both be encouraged, but should not be confused with each other.

The Capacity to Engage in Problem-oriented Policing

Finally the Norway meeting concluded that advocates had sometimes made the mistake of assuming that the primary and ultimate goal of the enterprise should be to make problem-oriented policing the dominant strategy for policing. Experience shows this to be unrealistic. Not only is the task too difficult, but also the police reject this goal. The more realistic alternative is for the police to develop the capacity, at least in the larger forces, to properly implement a small number — say three or four — problem-oriented projects each year. With a sufficient number of forces working in this way, knowledge about how to handle substantive problems that materially impact police resources would rapidly accumulate, though deliberate efforts to share the results of each department's work with the wider field would have to be made. If this were done, forces would learn from each other, thereby increasing progress for policing.

Cause for Optimism

In view of the disappointing progress to date in implementing problem-oriented policing, it may be a little surprising that the contributors to this book remain optimistic about the future of the concept. Apart from their belief in the inherent soundness of the concept, this optimism is grounded in the developments that have taken place in the past twenty years. Of particular importance is the growth in the body of knowledge on policing and crime prevention. Notwithstanding the urgent need for more case studies of problem-oriented policing, understanding about the effects of preventive measures and police tactics has grown considerably both in depth and breadth. During the last few decades of the 20th Century, many evaluations of crime preventive measures in general and, more specifically, of police tactics and interventions have been carried out. In this connection, compilations of research results are extremely important and helpful given that problem-oriented policing is an evidence-based activity. Examples of this are the anthologies of experiences of situational prevention in Scandinavia (Knutsson, 1998) and worldwide (Clarke, 1997). For police tactics, compilations by Sherman et al. (1997) and Bennett (1998) are available.

Despite the criticisms made above of the universities, there is now also available a supply of basic textbooks that are policy-relevant, some with a practical crime preventive orientation (e.g., Felson, 2002). At a more advanced level, books are available on evaluation research and methodology that focus on crime prevention (e.g., Pawson and Tilley, 1997). In these regards, conditions are far more favourable than just a few years ago.

An increasing number of tools and concepts have also been developed to help police undertake the complex functions entailed in problem-oriented policing. Concepts like SARA and PROCTOR have already been mentioned. The crime triangle (see Eck in this volume), developed from the routine activity theory (Cohen and Felson, 1979) is of great value in guiding problem-oriented policing projects. On a practical instructive level, the Office of Community Oriented Police

Services (COPS) in the United States Department of Justice has recently published a series of 20 guides for police officers on how to handle different types of problems. Just to give two examples, Guide number 1 is about assaults in and around bars (Scott, 2001) and number 4 is on drug dealing in privately-owned apartment complexes (Sampson, 2001). These guides are condensed literature reviews and summarize knowledge on how to decrease harm caused by the specific problems. In an extension of this effort, two other series of guides are planned: One will summarize knowledge on responses (for example, what is known about crackdowns or closed-circuit television), and the other will summarize knowledge about the use of various analytic tools (for example, how to do offender interviews or conduct a school crime-prevention-through-environmental-design survey). All these guides, and other relevant information, will be disseminated much more readily as a result of the development of the Internet.

Finally, changes that will likely assist problem-oriented policing have also occurred in government. In pace with more sophisticated management and audit styles, more emphasis is being placed on the need for evidence-led practice. Both nationally and at the local level, much more attention is being paid to performance indicators and evaluation. The training and education of police officers has also become more extensive and professional in the past few decades. In both Norway and Sweden, for example, basic training takes more than two years. Many large forces in the United States now require a college degree for newly employed officers. This means that there will be a growing number of well-educated officers with higher professional standards and expectations. Many of them will also be acquainted with the principles of problem-oriented policing. These developments in policing, in combination with more realistic expectations and a stronger theoretical foundation, make us believe that problem-oriented policing will become an integral part of doing police business in the future.

Address correspondence to: Johannes Knutsson, National Police Academy, PB 5027 Majorstua, 0301 Oslo, Norway. E-mail: <Johannes.knutsson@phs.no>.

REFERENCES

Bennett, T. (1999). "The Role of the Police in Preventing Crime." In: *Ungdom och kriminalitet. Justisdepartementets forskningskonferanse 11.-12. august 1998.* (PHS Forskning 1999:1.) Oslo: Politihøgskolen.

Clarke, R.V. (1998). "Defining Police Strategies: Problem-solving, Problem-oriented Policing and Community-oriented Policing." In: T. O'Connor Shelley and A.C. Grant (eds.), *Problem-oriented Policing: Crime-specific Problems, Critical Issues and Making POP Work.* Washington, DC: Police Executive Research Forum.

—— (1997). *Situational Crime Prevention: Successful Case Studies.* Monsey, NY: Criminal Justice Press.

—— and D. Cornish (2000). "Rational Choice." In: R. Paternoster and R. Bachman (eds.), *Explaining Crime and Criminals: Essays in Contemporary Criminological Theory.* Los Angeles, CA: Roxbury.

Cohen, L.E. and M. Felson (1979) "Social Change and Crime Trends: A Routine Activity Approach." *American Sociological Review* 44(4):588-608.

Cornish, D. and R.V. Clarke (1986). *The Reasoning Criminal – Rational Choice Perspectives on Offending.* New York: Springer Verlag.

Eck, J.E. and W. Spelman (1987). *Problem-Solving. Problem-Oriented Policing in Newport News.* Washington, DC: Police Executive Research Forum.

Felson, M. (2002). *Crime and Everyday Life.* Thousand Oaks, CA: Pine Forge Press.

Goldstein, H. (1990). *Problem-Oriented Policing.* New York: McGraw Hill.

—— (1979). "Improving Policing: A Problem-Oriented Approach." *Crime & Delinquency* 25(2):234–258.

Hesseling, R. (1994). "Displacement: A Review of the Empirical Literature." In: R.V. Clarke (ed.), *Crime Prevention Studies,* vol. 3. Monsey, NY: Criminal Justice Press.

Knutsson, J. (1998). "The Swedish Experience of Situational Crime Prevention." *Studies on Crime and Crime Prevention* 7(2):189-212.

Pawson, R. and N. Tilley (1997). *Realistic Evaluation.* London: Sage.

Read, T. and N. Tilley (2000). *Not Rocket Science? Problem-Solving and Crime Reduction.* (Crime Reduction Research Series Paper 6.) London, UK: Police Research Group, Home Office.

Reiss, A.J. (1992). "Police Organization in the 20th Century." In: M. Tonry and N. Morris (eds.), *Modern Policing.* (Crime and Justice Series, vol. 15.) Chicago, IL: University of Chicago Press.

Sampson, R. (2001). *Drug Dealing In Privately Owned Apartment Complexes.* (Problem-Oriented Guides for Police series, No. 4.) Washington, DC: Office of Community Oriented Policing Services, U.S. Department of Justice.

Scott, M.S. (2001). *Assaults in and Around Bars.* (Problem-Oriented Guides for Police Series, No. 1.) Washington, DC: Office of Community Oriented Policing Services, U.S. Department of Justice.

—— (2000). *Problem-Oriented Policing. Reflections on the First 20 Years.* Washington, DC: Office of Community Oriented Policing Services, U.S. Department of Justice.

—— and R.V. Clarke (2000). "A Review of Submissions for the Herman Goldstein Award for Excellence in Problem-oriented Policing." In: C. Sole Brito and E.E. Gatto (eds.), *Problem-Oriented Policing: Crime-Specific Problems, Critical Issues and Making POP Work,* vol. 3. Washington, DC: Police Executive Research Forum.

Sherman, L., D. Gottfredson, D. MacKenzie, J. Eck, P. Reuter and S. Bushway (1997). *Preventing Crime: What Works, What Doesn't, What's Promising.* Washington, DC: Office of Justice Programs, U.S. Department of Justice.

Sullivan, R.R. (2000). *Liberalism and Crime. The British Experience.* Maryland: Lexington Books.

Weisburd, D. and T. McEwen (1997). *Crime Mapping and Crime Prevention.* (Crime Prevention Studies, vol. 8.) Monsey, NY: Criminal Justice Press.

Young, J. (1988). "Radical Criminology in Britain: The Emergence of a Competing Paradigm." *British Journal of Criminology* 28(2):289-313.

ON FURTHER DEVELOPING PROBLEM-ORIENTED POLICING: THE MOST CRITICAL NEED, THE MAJOR IMPEDIMENTS, AND A PROPOSAL

by

Herman Goldstein
University of Wisconsin

Abstract: Problem-oriented policing is now a common term among police. Under the umbrella of the term, many commendable projects have been carried out — especially by street-level officers. Continued support for the concept is most likely explained, in part, by the self-evident nature of the central premise: police practices in responding to common problems that arise in the community should be informed by the best knowledge that can be acquired about those problems and about the effectiveness of various strategies for dealing with them. But many projects under the problem-oriented policing label are superficial, and examples of full implementation of the concept, as originally conceived, are rare. This paper argues that if problem-oriented policing is to advance beyond its current state of development and reach its greater potential, a much larger investment must be made within police agencies in conducting more in-depth, rigorous studies of pieces of police business, in implementing the results of these studies, and in the evaluation of implementation efforts. The paper identifies five major impediments in reaching this goal. A specific proposal to overcome some of these impediments is offered. By concentrating commitment and resources, the proposal is designed to create the leadership, skills and momentum to produce, within policing, a critical mass of high-quality studies that would: (1) inject a body of new knowledge into the overall field of policing of immediate value in upgrading practice; (2) serve as exemplars of the greater need; and (3) hopefully also serve to begin to build an institutional capacity to continue the effort.

INTRODUCTION

Almost 25 years have passed since problem-oriented policing was first conceptualized (Goldstein, 1979). In that period of time, the term itself has become a part of the vocabulary of modern-day policing. But the term has been used to describe a wide variety of initiatives, many of which bear little relationship to the original concept.

The purpose of this paper is to join with others in exploring the future development of problem-oriented policing. But given the many meanings now attributed to the term, it is important, at the beginning of such an endeavor, to be clear on what it is that we are trying to expand and grow. I turn first, therefore, in this paper, to a brief restatement of the concept and some reflections on implementation efforts. I then suggest a focus for future development.

As originally conceived, problem-oriented policing is an approach to policing in which each discrete piece of police business that the public expects the police to handle (referred to as a "problem") is subject to careful, in-depth study in hopes that what is learned about each problem will lead to discovering a new and more effective strategy for dealing with it. The concept places a high value on developing, within that strategy, new responses that are preventive in nature, that are not dependent on the use of the criminal justice system, and that draw on the potential contributions of other public agencies, the community, and the private sector. The concept carries a commitment to implementing the new strategy, rigorously evaluating its effectiveness, and subsequently reporting the results in ways that will benefit other police agencies and that will contribute to building a body of knowledge that supports good practice and ultimately, thereby, will also contribute toward the further professionalization of the police.

Analysis, study and evaluation are at the core of problem-oriented policing, not simply because they provide the factual basis for whatever strategies are adopted, but because, carried out adequately, they provide the license for sharing the results with the policing field. In its fuller development, adoption of the concept would have many implications for a police agency, its leadership, and its personnel (Goldstein, 1990). As originally set out, problem-oriented policing was described as a new way of thinking about policing: it introduces a thought process that could become the centerpiece around which all elements of police operations are organized. Specifically, the concept offers an integrated, coherent scheme for the delivery of services; for the recruitment, training and reward of police personnel; and, most especially, for making more effective use of police officers directly involved in providing routine services. This fleshed-out vision of the potential in problem-oriented policing remains strong, but it is not likely to be realized or, if tried, sustained without a strong commitment to analysis, study and evaluation. To the degree that police agencies have sought to implement changes that are at the periphery of problem-oriented policing without adopting its core, those efforts have often contributed to a diluted understanding of the original concept.

Fortunately, there is no need here to describe in detail the wide variety of adaptations and permutations that are now tied to the concept. Michael S. Scott, in an extraordinarily helpful and timely publication, has brought together a comprehensive description of developments under the problem-oriented policing umbrella (Scott, 2001). And he has performed the tedious job of sifting through them, separating the wheat from the chaff. Others have critiqued a more limited set of the initiatives with narrower objectives, but in equally helpful ways (Leigh et al., 1996, 1998; Clarke, 1998; and Read and Tilley, 2000). Each of these commentators concluded, as I have, that the vast percentage of the efforts to date, even when they contained some of the elements of the original concept, were nevertheless superficial. But each commentator acknowledged that substantial progress has been realized through these efforts, and, sharing in the sense that much more could be achieved, has suggested ways in which that potential might be more fully realized. With that potential as the focus of this paper, it is helpful to reflect anew, in a general way, on the efforts at implementation.

The Many Variations in Types of Problems, Analyses, and Evaluations: The Concept versus the Experience

As problem-oriented policing was originally conceived, it was assumed that the primary responsibility for identifying problems, analyzing them, developing new responses and testing them would rest with the management of police agencies (Goldstein, 1979; Goldstein and Susmilch, 1981). In large agencies, it was assumed that management would look to their research and planning units, newly energized and staffed, to develop the capacity to conduct in-depth analyses and to carry out the bulk of the work. It was contemplated that the problems would be sizeable — a collection of many similar incidents — usually occurring throughout the jurisdiction served or within a reasonably defined area. Examples would be the problem of the drinking-driver, the robbery of convenience stores, or theft from retail establishments.

Commenting on this formulation, Albert J. Reiss (1982:139) made this observation:

Were police to shift their concerns to these kinds of problems, the role of research for the police could change dramatically. The police would be no longer consumers of research but producers of it, and research would not be done primarily by outsiders but as a management operation. Moreover, the research and development department of a police organization might become as critical to its future as research and development are to other modern industrial and government agencies.

Early on, some police administrators and researchers concluded that the process of inquiry leading to new approaches had application throughout a police agency — all the way down to the officer on the beat (e.g., Taft, 1986; Eck and Spelman, 1987a, 1987b). They concluded that an officer who was authorized and encouraged to identify problems, analyze them, and develop creative tailor-made responses that increased police effectiveness could contribute a great deal toward improving the quality of policing. The logic was the same; that proactively addressing problems and the factors contributing to them made more sense than repeatedly responding reactively to the incidents that were the most overt manifestations of those problems. Problems, in this context, were usually viewed as persistently troubling situations — a collection of incidents involving the same behavior, locations, or individuals — loosely described, for example, as involving a specific apartment house, a specific playground, a specific group of disorderly children, or a specific drug dealer.

In this shift from addressing problems at the management level to addressing them at beat level, the quality of analysis and evaluation was destined to be much less exacting than originally contemplated. Officers have varying levels of skill in identifying and analyzing problems, and little relevant experience or training. The time and resources of officers are limited. Rigorous analysis is difficult, often impossible and, under many circumstances, not even appropriate.[1]

Nevertheless, the movement to encourage and empower officers to address problems they encountered, albeit in a somewhat looser fashion, had many attractions for the policing field. It promised greater effectiveness and a higher level of community satisfaction. It made better use of the time of police officers. It tapped their increasing levels of education and their latent talents, insights and commitment. It provided them with greater satisfaction in their work.[2]

The addressing of problems by officers working the streets gained so much momentum and, in relation to other reforms in policing, produced such positive results, that it was embraced by those who had advocated the original concept as an integral part of problem-oriented policing. The logic was simple and pragmatic. Given the enormous difficulty that was foreseen in gaining support for the more rigorous study of larger problems at higher levels in the police organization, initiatives that so closely paralleled the same thought process and that were so enthusiastically accepted should, it was argued, be endorsed. They were seen as an embryonic form of the more ambitious original concept. Weaknesses were understandable, it was argued, and should be tolerated. Appropriately nurtured, subsequent efforts, it was hoped, would be more refined and, through a "bottom-up" process, might ultimately lead to more exacting inquiries at the top of an agency. Additionally, the involvement of many police officers in addressing problems was seen as a potentially effective vehicle for changing the way in which an entire agency thought about its responsibilities and responded to them.

As a consequence, many of the efforts to support problem-oriented policing took the form of teaching problem solving to officers working the streets; to trying to instill support for problem-oriented policing into an entire police agency. The SARA model, so well known that it is often viewed as synonymous with problem-oriented policing, was itself designed, in part, to communicate the thought process to all ranks of police personnel. Scott summarizes the results of these efforts (Scott, 2001). He identifies some agencies that, over a period of time, largely as the result of a chief executive or a key staff person who "championed" the concept, made substantial progress in incorporating the concept into their way of regularly doing business. Among the agencies that distinguished themselves in this manner were those serving the cities of San Diego, Reno, Sacramento and Santa Ana in the United States; Edmonton in Canada; and Merseyside, Lancashire, Leicestershire and Thames Valley in the United Kingdom.

Over time, the volume of activity by rank-and-file officers in addressing problems has greatly overshadowed those relatively rare efforts on the part of management to address larger and more pervasive problems through in-depth studies. Indeed, in the eyes of many police practitioners, problem-oriented policing *is* beat-level "problem solving."

The best case studies that have emerged from the work of police officers are quite impressive, especially when related to other reforms and developments in policing (see Sampson and Scott, 2000). They take creative approaches to old problems, using non-traditional strategies, and go on, within the limitations of the officers involved, to demonstrate what they were able to achieve. The cases clearly confirm that there is indeed an enormous reservoir of talent, resourcefulness and commitment in street-level officers that has not been tapped. The best among these case studies have been appropriately recognized through a system of awards and, more recently, publication (U.S. National Institute of Justice, 2000, 2001a, 2001b).

And yet, measured against the need, the value of even these nationally recognized efforts is relatively modest. As noted in an earlier context, the best among them usually have major weaknesses — especially in the quality of analysis and in the evaluation of new strategies put in place. They are often the products of an intense effort by one or more especially motivated officers in an agency in which their work is an exception, in which other problems are not similarly addressed, and in which there is little involvement of top management. And both the projects and the work of the involved officers are often not sustained, with the result that the credibility of the case studies as exemplars is gradually eroded (Rojek, 2001).

As for the anticipated "bottom-up" benefits, there is little evidence that they are being realized. Without outside help, projects initiated by officers have not stimulated similar inquiries with regard to broader problems at higher levels in their respective agencies. With but a few exceptions, they do not seem to have propagated a substantial increase in the number of projects undertaken within an agency. Nor is there a discernible pattern in which projects, over time, have led to case studies with a higher quality of analysis or evaluation. Spectacular as the results of some officer-led projects have been, it is unrealistic to expect that these efforts alone carry sufficient force to meet the larger need.

The reasons for the limited growth of officers' efforts in addressing problems are rather apparent. Chiefs leave office. Agencies undergo changes in their orientation. Key people are promoted or reassigned. Individual officers are reassigned, or acquire less supportive supervisors, or are reigned-in or discouraged by other changes in their working environment. To my knowledge, there is no way in which to acquire an accurate measure of the volume and quality of current efforts. But based on a variety of informal measures, it is my impression that officer involvement in addressing problems in any depth has reached a plateau and may, in fact, be receding.

It does not follow from these observations that efforts to develop support among officers and throughout police agencies for problem-oriented policing should be abandoned. To the contrary, these efforts should be encouraged for all of the reasons cited earlier. The work of beat officers will continue to constitute an important part of the overall movement to implement problem-oriented policing. What these observations do say is that we cannot depend so heavily on those efforts to produce the benefits held out for in the original concept.

To energize and hasten the development of problem-oriented policing, the greatest current need, in my opinion, is to invest heavily in building a capacity into local policing to analyze discrete pieces of police business in depth and to carefully evaluate the effectiveness of alternative strategies for responding to them. Such an investment should continue to draw on the knowledge and experience of all police employees, but it will depend heavily, for its success, on the full engagement of the chief executive and management. And it will require, in one form or another, the acquisition of research skills that are not currently available within police agencies. The immediate goal should be to produce a good number of high-quality studies that constitute solid building blocks in expanding the body of knowledge relevant to the problems police must handle. With this objective in mind, the measure of success should be the quantity and quality of case studies completed, their dissemination, and their use, rather than indicators of the degree to which any one agency has institutionalized the processes associated with problem-oriented policing.

It is difficult to argue for such a bold investment in the absence of a greater number of cases drawn from the experience of recent years that (adequately studied, fully implemented and carefully evaluated) clearly demonstrate their value. The exhortation must continue to rest on the original arguments offered in support of problem-oriented policing. But as highlighted in the following section, those arguments, I believe, remain strong.

THE JUSTIFICATION FOR CONTINUING THE EFFORT

The Fundamental Underlying Premise: The Need To Build a Body of Knowledge in Support of Good Practice

The fundamental premise underlying the concept of problem-oriented policing is that police practices, in responding to common problems that arise in the community, should be informed by the best knowledge that can be acquired about the nature of those problems and about the effectiveness of various strategies for dealing with them.

This bare-bones premise — that operations should be informed by knowledge — is so elementary and so self-evident, that one feels apologetic in drawing attention to it. It is not an especially controversial proposition. It is certainly not radical. And it is not novel. Indeed, it is precisely for these reasons that problem-oriented policing strikes many people as just plain common sense. That is why, when newly explained to those in other endeavors (such as the business world) or to members of the community, the reaction is often one of disbelief:

"You mean to tell me that the police have not been doing that for all of these years?"

And yet, the premise has gained little acceptance in policing. Apart from what is reflected in the case studies in problem-oriented policing and the substantial rhetoric associated with the concept, there is no discernible, sustained and consistent effort *within* policing to make the basic premise that "knowledge informs practice" a routine part of professional policing. Considerable progress has been made in recent decades to upgrade policing through the recruitment of college-educated officers. Much progress has been made in modernizing police forces. But there remains a strong strain of anti-intellectual feelings in policing — a bias of sorts — that shuns connections with knowledge-building efforts and the use of that knowledge which has already been acquired. The police establishment, as a whole, has done little, especially when related to the need, to embody the notion that it should invest in developing a body of knowledge that can be used to drive the decisions police make in using their limited resources and authority.[3]

Veteran police will likely respond to this characterization defensively, and claim that it is an overstatement and too broad an indictment of their field. They will contend that they do indeed conduct studies; that they make extensive use of data, intelligence, and research in support of their daily operations. That is true.

Police do, for example, use a large body of forensic knowledge to assist them in the investigation of crime and in scientifically establishing the identification and culpability of offenders. They value the collection of facts in their reactive work in solving crimes. They gather intelligence in attempting to deal proactively with such problems as organized crime and, now, terrorism. In the management of their agencies, police use data to plan the use of their limited resources. In crime analysis, they use data to identify and apprehend offenders and to analyze patterns of crime — including the use of geographic information systems (GIS). And most recently, in meetings making intensive use of computer statistics (Compstat programs), they are increasingly using internally developed data to strategize field operations and to hold their officers to a higher level of accountability.

Important as all of these efforts are to make use of forensic knowledge, information, intelligence and internally produced data, they do not involve using the kind of knowledge contemplated in problem-oriented policing. Taken together, the results of these efforts do not constitute a body of knowledge about the problems police are routinely expected to handle and about the effectiveness of various strategies for dealing with them. Police, for example, daily handle large volumes of cases involving concerns about noise, vehicle theft, and assaults in bars. But they make little use of in-depth knowledge about the nature of these specific behaviors and the effectiveness of methods for either preventing or responding to them. If police are asked to explain their practices for dealing with most such substantive problems, they will rarely articulate a uniform, coherent agency-wide strategy. And even if it appears that there is a consensus on a response, it is rare that the agreed-upon strategy would have been validated by in-depth study.

The norm, with regard to most problems handled by the police, is that their response is generic. It takes the form of patrolling, investigating, arresting, and prosecuting, without detailed regard to the specific nature of the problem they are seeking to impact and without benefit of rigorously derived knowledge about the effectiveness of what they do. And when confronted by a crisis, the response is too often, on examination, largely cosmetic, designed as a show of force that has the effect of temporarily reducing the most overt manifestations of a problem and, thereby, temporarily relieving public pressures to do something about it.

There are some recent and important exceptions to this overall pattern. Police can appropriately cite the relatively new forms of response to sexual assaults, domestic violence, child abuse, and those experiencing some form of mental illness. It is hard to separate how much of the initiative for newly addressing these problems originated with the police and how much with researchers. The work on domestic violence, much of it carried out by Lawrence Sherman and colleagues, is most extensive and most closely parallels the kind of endeavor contemplated in problem-oriented policing (Sherman, 1998). Some of the underlying research relating to the four problems commendably engaged police personnel, but, for the most part, the bulk of the research was conducted outside police agencies. A blend of social and political movements that sought to redefine public attitudes toward these problems stimulated much of the research and pressured the police into making use of it.

More recent is the recent case study on gun violence among youth by the Boston Police Department and researchers at Harvard's Kennedy School. This study was initiated as a problem-oriented policing project and stands as one of the best examples of not only how such a project can inform police practice, but also how police and researchers can enter into a productive relationship (Kennedy, 1997; Braga et al., 2001).

Another major exception is all of the work done on domestic abuse, burglary and car crime — primarily in the United Kingdom — in which the focus has been on repeat victimization. In a relatively short period of time, a good number of experiments have been conducted and evaluated. Based on that work, the analysis of repeat victimization has emerged as an essential, powerful analytical tool in studying the police response to any problem, and in formulating new, more effective responses (Pease, 1998). Especially noteworthy is the effort that has been made to translate the research for use by police personnel (Bridgeman and Hobbs, 1997). Most significant, perhaps, is that the strength of the recommendations growing out of these studies has resulted in their adoption being made a formal measure of police performance in all of the U.K.

When an exhaustive literature search is made, one finds an impressive list of problem-focused studies that clearly constitutes a body of knowledge regarding problems commonly handled by the police. A large number of these are studies in situational crime prevention, the field of criminology that is most relevant to problem-oriented policing (Clarke, 1997). Many of these case studies are conveniently collected in the series of volumes, now numbering 14, published as *Crime Prevention Studies*. The crime prevention and research staff of the Home Office in the United Kingdom has, over the past several decades, produced an extraordinarily rich accumulation of studies on specific pieces of police business. Scott, in his recent monograph, has included many of these studies and others in an effort to begin to catalogue relevant work on specific problems (Scott, 2001:Appendix B).

It is regrettable that, at least in the United States, this literature is rarely used by the police.[4] Access by practitioners is admittedly often difficult. One gets the impression that the police, if they do have access to the studies, feel that they are of limited value to them; that the studies do not connect with their perspectives, interests, language, and practical needs. That felt disconnection stems, in part, from the fact that a good number of the studies were conducted from outside police agencies, without making full use of police data and insights, and without engaging police personnel. We have learned that studies conducted within police agencies not only benefit from the rich sources of available data and the insights of operating personnel; they better connect with the interests and perspectives of police personnel (e.g., Goldstein and Susmilch, 1982; Clarke and Goldstein, 2002, 2003). But, in the end, the strongest explanation for the limited familiarity of the police with these studies is most likely that there has been no tradition within policing to seek out such knowledge and to make use of it.

The current lack of a connection between available research and the police use of that research in the U.S. highlights the importance of the recent project to produce 19 guides for the police, each of which addresses a common problem.[5] By sorting through all of the research relevant to each problem, synthesizing the most significant points, and reporting those findings in a context and in terms relevant to the police, the authors have made the needed connection. They bridge the present gap by making the existing literature relevant and accessible to the police. The guides persuasively demonstrate the value in drawing on already existing knowledge. They invite both police and researchers to emulate the effort relative to other problems. And, through the questions that are posed and the pattern by which problems are analyzed, the guides will hopefully stimulate the development of new knowledge as well. If this works, the guides will have served as the vehicle for making a significant start on building a body of knowledge that, while previously available in somewhat scattered form, can more clearly be identified as connected to the police — as informing police decision making. Simultaneously, of course, the guides will provide a big boost to the continuing efforts of police officers up through the ranks of management to examine the problems addressed by the guides as they arise in their respective communities. Much of the work, in reviewing existing literature and in framing their local analysis, will have been done for them.

The Need for a New Framework for Remedying the Infirmities in the Current-Day Arrangements for Policing and in the Police Institution

A second important reason that problem-oriented policing warrants development is its potential for providing a coherent framework for achieving true reform in policing. Going beyond the building of a body of knowledge, the various elements that together constitute the fuller concept of problem-oriented policing are interwoven with the complex dynamics of policing and the intricacies of the police institution — complexities that are not generally recognized nor widely understood.

To the average citizen, the police function seems straightforward and, except for the intrigue associated with some detective work, rather mundane. But a foray into the dynamics of policing — especially in large, congested and diverse urban areas — rapidly reveals that policing is an incredibly complex business. The police function is ill defined. Demands on the police are often in conflict. The police are commonly thought to be omnipotent, but are in fact extremely limited. Public expectations exceed both available resources and authority. As a result, police are frequently pressured into stretching their authority in order to get things done, thereby increasing the potential for abuse. Police are assumed to operate based on highly specific laws and guidelines, but in fact exercise enormous discretion. They must take risks all of the time, but no allowance is made for error. Police are thought to be in control of their workload, but it is the citizenry, through their use of 911, that has the strongest influence on the use of police resources.

These conflicts bedevil policing as an institution. They account for the fact that the police often feel overextended. They eat away at the integrity of police operations. Stripped of the mythology and pumped-up popular image of the police, one could persuasively argue that the police job, as formally defined, is impossible of achievement.[6]

Police succeed as well as they do because they have, over the years, made an endless number of accommodations. They improvise. They take many shortcuts. And they often resort to "bluff," hoping that their authority is not challenged and their true capacity is not revealed. The police should not be forced to be devious, disingenuous, or circuitous in carrying out that which is formally required of them. They ought not to have to operate sub rosa. The fact that they must do so, sometimes euphemistically referred to as "the art of policing," is acknowledged by most practicing, reflective police in moments of candor.

With such imperfect working conditions, it should not come as a surprise that, with monotonous regularity, shortcomings in policing surface: allegations of inefficiency, abuse of authority, corruption, negligence or incompetence. And with equally monotonous regularity, shotgun remedies are proposed from a standard litany of so-called reforms: more personnel, more training, improved equipment and technology, new leadership, or more civilian oversight. But few of these reforms reach and affect the underlying infirmities. They do not get at the fact that something is inherently wrong and often lacking in the arrangements by which we expect the police to operate.

Remedying some of these infirmities was as much a goal in formulating problem-oriented policing as meeting the basic need to inform police operations. The two needs are inextricably interrelated. The absence of a strong body of knowledge supporting policing contributes to many of the cited conflicts; and, in reverse, the pressure to live with these conflicts contributes to blinding the police to the importance of developing that body of knowledge.

The gradual acquisition of knowledge to inform police operations would contribute to honing the arrangements currently in place that shape modern day policing. Here are a few examples of the potential:

- Insight into a specific problem makes it possible to more clearly define the police role vis-à-vis that problem, thereby reducing unrealistic public expectations and increasing the likelihood that the police can meet agreed upon goals.

- Knowledge about a problem leads to identifying new strategies for dealing with the problem that could prevent it in the first instance, thereby reducing police workload and increasing effectiveness and citizen satisfaction.

- A wide range of new strategies for dealing with problems reduces the over-dependence currently placed on the criminal justice system, thereby reducing the potential for abuse of police authority, increasing police effectiveness, and providing greater satisfaction to both the police and those served.

- The compilation of hard data about a problem often leads to identifying others in the public and private sector who may be in a better position to prevent or deal with the problem, and is useful in persuading such parties to assume a greater role, thereby reducing the burden on the police while increasing effectiveness in dealing with the problem.

- The design of specific strategies for dealing with specific problems, including the identification of those in the best position to implement those strategies, provides specific guidance for building partnerships, thereby reducing the ambiguities now commonly associated with the concept of community policing.

These potential benefits are but illustrative of the inter-relationship of these two needs — how study of specific pieces of police business can contribute to remedying some of the systemic infirmities in policing, and vice versa. The full range of possible benefits is described elsewhere (Goldstein, 1990, 1993; Scott, 2001). If police can succeed in refining their operations relative to a highly specific problem and, in the course of doing that

- define expectations more realistically;

- make better use of their resources;

- develop new strategies that are more effective;

- give a higher priority to prevention;

- depend less on the criminal law; and

- engage others;

they can — over time — reshape their overall function in ways that will eliminate many of the current conflicts inherent in their operations. They can make their organizations more internally coherent. And they can thereby increase the likelihood that they can carry out their function in a straightforward, forthright and, most importantly, effective manner. It should be possible for the police — in all aspects of their work — to act legally, honestly and openly. It is this potential, so important to the quality of policing in a democracy, that fuels the desire for further progress.

THE FIVE MAJOR IMPEDIMENTS AND SOME THOUGHTS ON PENETRATING THEM

Those who have worked on any aspect of the development of problem-oriented policing can contribute a long list of difficulties that they encountered, both in tackling a specific problem and, more broadly, in trying to develop a commitment to the concept within a police agency. Because the list is so long, there is need to sort through the most common complaints, separating substantial difficulties from the petty; the bigger barriers from those that are only manifestations of those barriers; and universal impediments from those that are specific to a given agency or locale. After much squeezing and culling, I have identified five major concerns. But even these are interconnected. Developing a way in which to address, at least partially, one or two of them will not be enough. Progress requires some movement in addressing all of them.

(1) The Absence of a Long-Term Commitment on the Part of Police Leaders To Strengthening Policing and the Police as an Institution

Problem-oriented policing has always contemplated building, within police agencies, an *internal capacity* to examine specific types of crime and disorder. The assumption is that the police themselves — along with community members — are in the best position, in the first instance, to identify problems warranting study. They have extraordinary insights into problems that often go untapped by outside researchers. Commenting on the potential value in policing of applied research conducted by practitioners, Bittner (1990:378) drew on the experiences in other fields in observing:

> The discoveries that led to the conquest of the so-called infectious diseases were not made by the faculties of the schools of medicine at university centers, bur rather in the laboratories of public health physicians who had the noble, but quite practical, task of keeping people from getting sick and making them well when they did get sick.

The police have easier and direct access to relevant data. Their involvement can greatly expedite an inquiry if, as is contemplated, they develop a sense of ownership of both the problem and a potentially more effective response. And while studies conducted outside policing, perhaps even with police cooperation, are of great value in support of such efforts, such studies will simply sit on library shelves unless police make use of them. Implementation of the results of a study, in particular, requires the full engagement of the police. The likelihood of meeting that need is greatly enhanced if the police are involved from the outset.

Developing this capacity within policing places heavy demands on police leadership. It requires, initially, that the chief executive of an agency fully understands the rationale behind problem-oriented policing and be committed to it. As Scott has pointed out, the police agencies that have made the greatest progress in experimenting with problem-oriented policing had top executives who championed the concept (Scott, 2001).

Such dedication requires a strong commitment up front to the importance of carefully analyzing problems. It requires an appropriate allocation of resources. It requires protecting those personnel engaged in detailed analysis from the demands of daily operations. It requires patience, because each in-depth study may take a substantial amount of time. It requires that those conducting a study and implementing its results have easy access to top executives for reviewing their recommendations. And, if approved, it requires that these staff members have their backing in gaining both internal and external support for implementation. Moreover, there is an altruistic element involved. The investment of one agency in the study of a problem should be seen as having the potential for contributing to a body of knowledge that will benefit other police agencies as well. That benefit may require defending an investment of resources beyond what the agency can justify for its own needs.

These requirements of police leadership are in sharp conflict with the culture of police agencies and, specifically, with the demands being made on police executives today. Even the most outstanding current police executives would have trouble meeting them. Police and, it follows, their leaders, are under extraordinary pressure in these times to respond most directly to the urgent concerns of the moment — be it a serious crime that awaits clearance, a crime wave that is generating widespread fears, or a much larger and amorphous threat such as, most recently, terrorism. This is certainly not a new phenomenon. It is inherent in the emergency nature of police service. Police are committed to focusing on the here and now — maintaining a readiness to respond quickly to the next unpredictable crisis. That gets highest priority. And that mindset affects the entire institution, including the chief executive whose support for any long-term planning — for the agency and for the policing field — is most crucial.

Beyond this common characteristic of police institutions, police executives, more recently, seem to be increasingly engaged in handling administrative problems that rise to the level of a crisis for their agency and that require fixing: e.g., allegations of abuse or corruption; questionable use of deadly force; allegations of racial profiling; complaints of unanswered calls or slow responses. The majority of a police administrator's time is consumed in matters relating to the management of his or her personnel. One indication of the increased pressures on police administrators in recent years is evidenced in the sharp reduction in their tenure. It was reported in 1998 that, based on a survey of chiefs in cities and counties with a population over 50,000, the average tenure of the survey respondents' predecessors was 4.93 years.[7] That is a very short time in which to establish oneself in office, take on the most pressing crises, and also commit to bringing about constructive change, let alone make long-term investments in study and research that *may* produce demonstrable results some time down the line. Moreover, the citizenry and both elective and appointed officials to whom police chiefs are accountable have little awareness of the need for long-term thinking in policing. They tend to give greater support to the chief who is likely to endorse familiar and immediate responses to problems, even though the responses may be of questionable value.

In this highly pressured environment, it is no wonder that a plea for more intensive study of common problems is resisted or, at best, gets low priority. Appeals for building in a capacity for internal research are seen as having an "ivory tower" quality to them — as somewhat amorphous, uncertain in their value, and consuming of both time and resources. Given this atmosphere, it is understandable why there has been so much more support for street-level "problem solving" by beat officers. It is an exercise that tends to be discrete, limited in its implications, and requiring much less in the way of time and resources, and much less personal attention by police managers. Many are content to provide some general agency-wide encouragement for beat-level problem solving without making any adjustment in their own routines.

Given the formidable, perplexing nature of this situation, it is unlikely that appeals alone will produce much progress. And yet there are a good number of chief executives in policing who see the value in deeply probing specific problems and who would become engaged if they were provided with sufficient funds to hire staff with the technical skills required to help conduct the needed studies. The likelihood of their doing so would be further increased if involvement was not conditioned, from the outset, on their taking on the much more ambitious, albeit desirable, effort to change the nature of their entire organization; if the more modest, immediate goal — in order to get going — was limited to addressing only one, two or three, at most, substantial problems in a restricted period of time. The design of such a program would obviously need to be integrated with measures to meet other current impediments to which I now turn.

(2) The Lack of Skills Within a Police Agency That Are Required To Analyze Problems and To Evaluate Strategies for Dealing with Those Problems

In popular accounts of policing, the police are commonly portrayed as highly analytical. Successful detectives — in novels, in the movies, in TV serials, and, indeed, in real life — engage in sound reasoning, are resourceful, exploit all possible sources of information, ask all of the right questions, and are precise and rigorous in putting a case together. Striking as these well-honed analytical skills are in the context of solving crimes and apprehending offenders, there is little transfer of them to the management of police agencies — to the analysis of the behavioral problems that constitute police business and to the evaluation of strategies for dealing with them.

Many police agencies of sufficient size have, over the past half-century, established units or designated individuals to engage in research, planning, and crime analysis. The scope and quality of the work of these units is quite uneven. Some are unfortunately relegated to performing rather mundane administrative and clerical tasks in support of an agency's operations. Most analyze crime patterns and seek to identify the offenders responsible for them. The best among them, buoyed by advances in the use of computerized data and in crime mapping, are now quite sophisticated in their operations. They go well beyond helping operating officers in identifying offenders. They study crime patterns as a basis for allocating personnel, for selecting strategies for dealing with these patterns, and for achieving greater accountability in the organization. But even the most advanced of the crime analysis efforts have not extended their work to analyzing in depth (as contemplated in the context of problem-oriented policing) the common problems that the police are required to handle. Nor have their efforts extended to evaluating police strategies in responding to these problems.

To study management-level problems in depth, police agencies must have one or more individuals on their staff, depending on their size, who have the needed advanced research skills.[8] Such staff must be trained in research methodology; be comfortable collecting and analyzing data from various sources; be familiar with criminological theories; be understanding of the complexities and dynamics of police operations; and have familiarity with — or have easy access to — the literature accumulated to date on problems handled by the police. They must also have some strong personality traits. Contrary to a widespread image, digging into a specific problem in depth can be very hard work. It requires patience, tenacity, and a sharp mind. Organizationally, it is important that such staff be insulated from the very intense pressures, within a police agency, to get involved in meeting daily operational needs.

Two quite different views exist on how best to build this capacity. One argues for augmenting the skills of the best of the existing cadre of crime analysts. The other, against the background of the strongly ingrained, more limited focus of crime analysis, argues for making a clean break from that job classification — for creating a newly defined position of problem analyst. This, it is contended, would stress the novelty of the position and the very distinct new contribution that such a staff person would be expected to make to the capacity of a police agency to examine and evaluate its response to those matters the public expects it to handle.

However the need is met, given the past history and unique culture of police agencies, it is important that those selected to meet this newly defined function have the personal skills that enable them to build a constructive relationship with police officers. Such a person must respect the contribution police can make to a critical analysis of pieces of police business while, at the same time, be capable of working diplomatically to introduce police to the methodology involved in conducting such an analysis. And wherever the job is placed in the organization, it is important that the person filling the newly defined role has easy access to the chief executive of the agency and be fully informed regarding the management of the agency. Maintaining that access and introducing new skills into police management while relating to all ranks of officers and their pragmatic concerns requires a high degree of humility and tact.

Ultimately, in the development of this capacity, an agency would require a staff that, in its size, would be proportional to the size of the agency and the jurisdiction it serves. And even a single problem analyst would require clerical support lest the analyst get bogged down in routine, mundane tasks. Looking to the future, as distinct from the most immediate needs in getting going, it is not unreasonable to argue that a police agency should have no less than one program analyst and appropriate support for every 500 employees; that the return on the investment in those 500 employees would be heavily dependent on the contribution that the analyst makes to assuring that they achieve the greatest effectiveness in dealing with the problems they are called on to handle.

(3) The Lack of A Clear Academic Connection

A natural inclination, when one identifies the need for specially trained problem analysts, is to look to the universities and colleges to produce them. Likewise, when one decries the absence of a sufficiently strong body of knowledge to support policing, one tends to turn to academia for help in producing it.

Given the volume and variety of work that has been done by academics and other researchers on crime and on the police, it would be foolhardy, within the limits of this paper, to assess the relevance of that work to the needs that have been identified here. For purposes of this paper, it will suffice to make two broad observations: (1) From among the universe of studies, only a small percentage have focused specifically on researching problems that the police routinely handle and on the way in which those problems present themselves to the police. Among these studies, even fewer focus on strategies for responding to those problems and, particularly, on the relative effectiveness of those strategies. (2) An array of complex issues in the relationships between practitioners and academics and other researchers impede initiating more such studies. These same issues greatly limit the use of that knowledge which has already been acquired.

The most relevant work has been produced by a small number of researchers (located not just in universities, but in government research units as well), many of whom now identify themselves as environmental criminologists. The relevance of their work to the needs identified in this paper stems from their focus on controlling crime rather than on just dealing with the criminal; from their emphasis on prevention rather than just apprehension; and from their efforts to understand the circumstances that give rise to specific crimes and how those circumstances might be changed so as to reduce the opportunity to commit them (Clarke, 1997).

While the volume of scholarship relevant to the needs identified in this paper is comparatively small, it is clear that the volume nevertheless already exceeds the capacity and willingness of practitioners and policy makers to make use of it. Happily, environmental criminologists are increasingly struggling with the difficulty of transferring already available knowledge to practitioners and policy makers (Tilley and Laycock, 2000; Laycock, 2002; Ekblom, 2002).

The most critical needs, up front, are: (1) to increase the number of academics willing to study the problems of concern to the police and willing to work on the development of the methodologies for doing so; (2) to increase the number of practitioners who are willing to engage with academics involved in this work and to open their agencies to research; and (3) to develop university-level training for students interested in a career working within the police field in the newly defined position of problem analyst.[9]

Thoughts about filling these needs bring to the surface the sensitivities that have long strained the relationship between police practitioners and academics or researchers based outside universities. Many of these tensions stem from factors inherent in their respective working environments. Academics and other researchers, by the very nature of their job, are accustomed to conducting unrestricted explorations, to experimentation, and to producing negative as well as positive results. Police work in an environment that is highly controlled (by law and by the citizenry), that involves the use of government authority, and that allows for very little risk taking. In many ways, these characteristics place the two occupations at opposite ends of a scale. It is no wonder that the personalities of those drawn to the two occupations often get in the way of a productive relationship. Many academics are arrogant in their relationships with the police. They are disdainful or least condescending. And many police view academics with equal scorn — as "egg-heads" — overly theoretical and disconnected from the real world in which the police work.

Establishing new and more productive relationships will require greater flexibility and openness on the part of both parties. The police must recognize that quality research takes time and patience. It requires challenging established practices and strongly held views. It must be objective, requiring facts to support conclusions. It may take researchers down paths that turn out to be dead ends. It may produce results that could be interpreted as critical of past and current operations. It may experiment with new strategies that fail. That is the very nature of research.

Researchers, on the other hand, cannot be condescending in their relationships with the police. They must demonstrate a healthy respect for the expertise and knowledge which the police possess, but which they tend not, on their own, to express. They must demonstrate that they have a genuine interest in helping the police to be more effective, acknowledging that while publication is an essential element for both researchers and the police in the building of knowledge, it is not the end-all that it is often made out to be. They must use good judgment in the selection of research methodologies and in standards of proof, adequate to produce credible results but not disproportionately demanding, given the limits on the data that can be acquired and the sometimes rough nature of the problem being studied or the strategy being evaluated. And researchers must be sensitive to their own limitations — aware that, while their work is exacting and must meet agreed-upon standards, it is not usually as scientific as some would claim. They ought not to oversell their product.[10]

A good number of academics and researchers have, over the years, worked closely and productively in partnerships with the police in examining specific problems. By way of illustration, one can cite the work of: Morton Bard in New York City; Hans Toch and Douglas Grant in Oakland; John Eck and William Spelman in Newport News and Eck in numerous other cities thereafter; Lawrence Sherman in Minneapolis, Milwaukee and Indianapolis; David Kennedy and Anthony Braga in Boston; Ken Pease and Sylvia Chenery in Huddersfield; Malcolm Sparrow in several federal agencies in the U.S. and Ronald Clarke and Goldstein in Charlotte (Bard, 1970; Toch and Grant, 1991; Eck and Spelman, 1987b; Sherman et al., 1984, 1991; Kennedy, 1999; Braga et al., 2001; Chenery et al., 1997; Sparrow, 1994; Clarke and Goldstein, 2002, and this volume). Many of the projects that examined specific problems by the Police Research Group in the Home Office, and its successor, the Policing and Reducing Crime Unit, were undertaken as collaborations between researchers and police. Some of these partnerships resulted in the publication of a joint paper, acknowledging the degree of police involvement. Given the value derived from these partnerships, it would be useful to subject them to careful examination so that future collaborations between police practitioners and researchers based outside police agencies — committed to studying pieces of police business — might benefit.[11]

(4) The Absence of Informed Outside Pressures

Given the absence of a stronger initiative from within police agencies to make greater use of new knowledge to inform police practice, it has been observed that it will take pressure from outside police agencies to get them to do so. But there is little reason to believe that the public is sufficiently informed about policing to bring such pressures to bear — to know what they should be pressuring for or even what questions they should be asking.

The public as a whole is woefully ignorant about the nature of the police function and the capacity of the police. It has little knowledge of the legal limits under which the police operate — limits to which we assign a high value in a democracy. A prevalent perception in American society is that policing is very simple and straightforward — that, more than any other quality, it calls for determination and courage in moving aggressively against those who misbehave. So when an especially vicious crime is committed or when crime seems to have gotten out of control in a given area, the pressure to "do something" usually translates into support for simplistic measures that are often highly visible and somewhat dramatic. While some even call them cosmetic, they may in fact have an immediate reassuring effect. But they rarely have a lasting impact on the problem and inevitably consume substantial resources. Among the most common measures is simply the assignment of more police officers to a given area. Another is the more aggressive practice of conducting "sweeps" — making a strong police presence felt by challenging those in a given area and making large numbers of arrests. There may be some aspects to these operations that are dysfunctional. Sweeps, for example, by virtue of their less discriminate nature, often create a fertile ground for police to exceed their authority. They are among the most common sources of increased hostility toward the police, especially when used in minority communities. And yet, these responses are adopted despite their high monetary costs, the diversion of personnel from other programs, and their potentially negative side effects.

Much of the support for traditional responses stems simply from the fact that no one in the police agency or the community has analyzed the problem in depth and offered a better alternative for dealing with it. The remedy for the poorly informed pressures brought to bear on the police is for the police to offer carefully crafted responses that are potentially more effective and that cause no collateral damage. If the police do not undertake this task, it is hard to imagine who will do the job. And in the absence of getting that job done, the police will continue to be relegated to an awkward cycle in which uninformed pressures pervert the police as an institution.

Experience to date in problem-oriented policing offers many examples of situations in which a community that is presented with the results of careful study and hard facts in support of a proposed solution will join in support of that solution. Good, rigorously developed data, carefully presented, can be very powerful in altering public attitudes and pressures. Affected citizens can become an important force in support of good practice. To get to that point, however, one needs a blend of factors: police leadership that will support careful study; staff members capable of conducting such a study and producing clear and persuasive results; and, of course, a citizenry and their elected representatives and leaders who are open to new and creative ways in which to respond to their needs.

(5) The Lack of Financial Support

For a police agency to hire one or more problem analysts will require funds. And to free police officers from other duties so that they can join in working on specific problems will also involve some costs. In the current milieu, most police executives would resist these new costs. In the intense competition for police resources, a police chief is hard pressed to create any positions that take funds, officers or other existing staff away from the established programs aimed at providing basic services in the field. Given the nature of public demands on the police, a police executive can more easily be persuaded to assign officers to an admittedly mindless and unproductive assignment than to set aside less costly resources to support rigorous inquiry into the agency's effectiveness. Admittedly, a proposal for such a novel set-aside does suffer — in this period in the development of problem-oriented policing — from an insufficient number of cases that clearly demonstrate, in concrete terms, its potential value.

Making the case to use scarce funds to develop an internal research capacity is made even more difficult because, in smaller agencies, the size of the commitment might appear to be out of proportion to what the agency itself might gain from such an exploration. A police agency of several hundred officers, for example, might see the value in better understanding the problem of theft from storage warehouses, but might conclude that the investment required for such a study would be out of proportion to the gains likely to be realized for that particular agency and jurisdiction. That conclusion, however, ignores how a study of one problem, undertaken by one agency, might then benefit numerous other agencies. Such sharing and building of knowledge is a key element in problem-oriented policing.

The strength of the argument for needed funding flows largely from the difficulty in defending the current situation. Policing is one of the largest and most important functions of government. In the United States alone, it is reported that state and local police agencies have over 800,000 employees (U.S. Bureau of Criminal Justice Statistics, 2000). If there currently are, among these thousands, employees who, with appropriate training, are assigned full-time to the specific job of studying the problems the police are routinely called on to handle and to evaluating their effectiveness, that number is minuscule. This means that large police agencies, with thousands of employees, do not routinely have individuals on their respective staffs, insulated from the pressures of day-to-day operations, whose full-time job it is, through study and evaluation of their routine business, to provide guidance to management on the most effective means by which those agencies can respond to pieces of their business.[12]

When all else fails in looking for financial backing to fill critical needs in government, it has become common, at least in the U.S., to seek federal support. But there are several factors that make a special case for such support in meeting the specific needs outlined here.

In the federal system in the U.S., there has long been a strong belief that policing should be a function of local government. Federal involvement and control has been resisted. The role of federal and state agencies has, nevertheless, increased rapidly in the past half century, largely in response to perceived needs relating to drugs. At the same time, the federal government's involvement in matters relating to local policing has moved from sponsoring research and funding very targeted initiatives (often experimental) to providing large sums for the hiring of personnel and the purchase of technology and equipment. And yet, in assuming this more expansive role, the federal government still resorts to a carrot and stick approach that is intended to stimulate certain types of change without taking on the total cost of that change. And at least in the pronouncements that are made, political leaders continue to express a strong reluctance to increase federal control over local police operations. Many would argue — liberals and conservatives alike — that the federal government has already exceeded its appropriate role.

In this sensitive framework of federal, state and local relationships vis-à-vis policing, a program that equips local police to essentially think more for themselves — to engage in explorations that will improve their own know-how — appears to be an ideal candidate for federal funding. It would meet a critical need that has enormous potential for improving local policing without exerting any new controls over how that policing is carried out. (With appropriate adjustments for the variety of different relationships, the pattern may have some relevance for other countries as well where policing is mostly decentralized.) Such a program would not only allow local police to get a start on studying, revising and evaluating their response to common problems; it would serve as an incentive for them to do so. It would have the potential for multiplying such efforts, once they gain a foothold and some momentum. And it would appropriately compensate agencies for those benefits of their work that might accrue to individuals living well beyond their borders. Carefully designed, the program could produce a "big bang for the buck." It could have a positive influence on the quality of policing in the U.S. far in excess of the influence of other larger and much more costly programs that have involved substantial federal outlays for personnel, technology and other equipment.

The hiring of problem analysts and the establishment of research units within local police agencies are at the core of an effort to develop the capacity of those agencies to improve the effectiveness of their operations. It follows that highest priority would attach to the funding of such positions and units. But there will be other related costs for recruiting and training program analysts; recruiting and developing academic staff capable of expanding the academic component needed to support their efforts; cultivating, at least initially, the case studies that are undertaken; publishing the results; and engaging police executives in the process. These elements of a larger program are, like the creation of problem analyst positions, appropriate candidates for federal support.

A federal program in the U.S. to support these needs would not be a novel undertaking for the federal government. To the contrary, policing should be seen as a "Johnny-come lately," belatedly surfacing some long-neglected critical needs and seeking to have these needs met with the help of strategies that, with federal resources, have proved successful and are now routine in many fields. In a multitude of ways, the federal government has played a critical role — a role that only it can play — in advancing efforts to build and disseminate new knowledge in such fields as medicine and the other sciences. It has done the same in engineering, in agriculture, in public health, in education, and in traffic safety. To stimulate advances in these and numerous other fields, federal agencies sponsor scholarships and fellowship programs, stipends for faculty development, university-affiliated or freestanding research institutes, and research and training programs of various kinds. A program to build a knowledge base with regard to the problems local police are expected to handle in the United States will require similar support.

A PROPOSAL

At the outset of this paper, it was argued that the great need at this time, in seeking to further develop the concept of problem-oriented policing, is to encourage more explorations of pieces of police business of the type contemplated when the concept was first proposed. As a minimum, such studies would:

- be conducted within a police agency;

- focus on a discrete common problem arising in the community that is of some magnitude (volume/geography);

- fully engage the chief executive and management of the police agency;

- make use of the skills of a person with special training in research methodology;

- analyze the problem in depth, including a review of all relevant literature;

- weigh the potential value of a broad range of alternative responses, with a high priority on prevention and on decreasing dependence on the use of the criminal law;

- implement a new response strategy;

- rigorously evaluate the results of that implementation; and

- disseminate the results for use by other police agencies.

Acknowledging that some of the original arguments for addressing problems in this way might have become blurred over the years (or are even in danger of being lost), the third section of this paper summarized, with a fresh perspective, the rationale behind problem-oriented policing and the rationale for continuing to work on developing the concept. The next section identified five of the major impediments that have been encountered, and offered some thoughts on how progress might nevertheless be realized.

It is tempting to synthesize those thoughts here and offer a broad, new agenda for development of problem-oriented policing, exhorting a large, diverse audience to take action on those pieces of the agenda that they are in a position to adopt. I choose, instead, to offer a highly specific and relatively modest proposal. It is shaped by a fresh awareness of the formidable difficulties that have been experienced in seeking to implement problem-oriented policing, having identified and explored those difficulties here. Its purpose is to launch an initiative in policing that would: (1) more clearly demonstrate the value of addressing specific problems; and (2) gradually, thereby, create a critical mass of significant projects that, by virtue of their own power and self-evident value, would hopefully be widely emulated and ultimately achieve broader change.

The strategy of this proposal, as distinct from the substantive work on problems that it would entail, rests on the observation that efforts to implement problem-oriented policing to date have been too diffuse. The concept of problem-oriented was, in a variety of ways, broadcast to the entire field of policing. Police were — through various publications, training programs, and conferences — exhorted to adopt it. Some agencies, some chief executives, and mostly, some beat-level officers picked up on the concept and, with varying interpretations, intensity and success, sought to implement it. When their experiences were collected in one place, as Sampson and Scott (2000) did in their collection of case studies and as Scott (2001) did in reflecting on the first 20 years, they constitute an impressive story. But when viewed in the context of the overall field of policing, these efforts appear widely scattered among (and even within) agencies and limited in their impact to the local problems that were addressed. With the passage of time and changes in administration, it is increasingly difficult to point with confidence to a single agency in which there is a continuing concentration of high quality work in addressing pieces of its business. In exploring ways in which to develop problem-oriented policing, the need is not only to concentrate on conducting more in-depth management-level studies having all of the minimum elements identified above, but to do so in a way that creates a *critical mass* of such studies and evaluations.

The locus of such a concentration should be a center that is either university-affiliated or freestanding; either physical or virtual. Its life ought not to depend on strong attachments to one or more specific police agencies, given the frequent changes that occur in the management and priorities of those agencies. The basis for affiliation with the center for both practitioners and researchers should be their commitment to the central goal of the center in promoting quality research on substantive problems confronted by the police. The program proposed here for such a center is based on the experience in the United States, with which the author is most familiar, but could be adapted, with some adjustments to local circumstances and scale, to other countries as well. I would envisage the following as the key elements in an initial five-year program for such a center. (Obviously, the numbers and timeframe are not cast in concrete.)

- The recruitment, each year, of 10 individuals (from universities, from the private sector, or from within police agencies — including from among the most highly qualified of present crime analysts) to receive specially developed training of approximately three to six months' duration (depending on prior experience) in the knowledge and skills required of problem analysts. It would be necessary to cover the cost of the training and to provide a stipend to the participants.

- The preparation of the materials required to teach such a course, and the preparation of a manual that trained problem analysts could subsequently use as a guide in examining a specific problem.

- The identification, each year, of 10 police executives who endorse the value to their agencies, their communities and the policing field in conducting studies of the type contemplated. They would be asked, in exchange for having a trained, fully-subsidized problem analyst made available to them, to commit themselves to providing the full support of their agencies in conducting the study of from one to three problems; in implementing a new response to those problems; and in evaluating the effectiveness of the response. If selected, the chief executives, themselves, would be expected, at the outset, to participate in a seminar, organized by the center, that is designed to explore in depth the elements of problem-oriented policing, the partnership to which they were committing themselves, and, in specific terms, what would be expected of them.

- The pairing of a problem analyst to a police agency for a minimum commitment of two years, recognizing that not all individual projects would take that period of time; that they might study an additional problem or move on to another agency.

- The monitoring of each such effort, providing technical and other forms of support, and setting standards for each project. It is envisaged that center staff would be involved in each stage of the project in each community, conferring frequently with department members and the problem analyst, and in promoting the sharing of experiences between and among analysts.

- The publication of the results of each project in ways that are designed to reach a broad audience of police practitioners, thereby sharing the knowledge acquired about specific problems and the results of experimenting with new responses, but also serving to promote similar examinations of other problems confronted by the police.

- The development of an outreach program — to mayors, city managers, judges, prosecutors, advocacy groups, business interests, and others — using the results of the overall project to demonstrate how rigorous study can contribute not only to improved police practice, but to remedying many of the current infirmities in policing — thereby creating a constituency for police services that is better equipped to assert its expectations of the police.

- The facilitation of future pairings between experienced problem analysts and those police agencies that recognize the demonstrated value of their work and who want to undertake projects on their own, thereby encouraging the establishment within police agencies of a continuing, institutionalized capacity to conduct such analyses and evaluations.

- The continued synthesizing of existing literature on common problems — the process established by the Problem-Oriented Guides for Police Project — with the objective of making such information conveniently available to the whole field of policing and, in the process, identifying problems most critically in need of new work that could appropriately be made the subject of study in one of the center-sponsored partnerships.

- The design of a program that seeks to identify present faculty in colleges and universities and those newly entering the academic world who have the qualifications and interest in developing a commitment to research and teaching in this area. This could be implemented through the sponsorship of summer seminars that introduce the candidates to research within policing; cover the work of the center; and offer incentives in the form of stipends to participants.

Like all model programs, one ought not to anticipate a success rate of 100%. Much can go wrong. Some of the investment will not yield a return. But if, for example, each agency studied only one problem and only half of the problems examined produce solid results, the field of policing in the U.S. would have exhaustively examined 25 different pieces of its business in a period of five years. A substantial percentage of those studies would most likely identify practices that are more effective than the practices now currently employed. Through dissemination of the results, the benefits would be realized not just in the one agency doing the study, but potentially in all police agencies.

The budget for such a model program — which would total several million dollars a year — would appear to some to be overwhelming. But that amount is modest — even paltry — when related to:

- the costs of providing police services throughout the nation,

- the costs to the victims of specific forms of crime,

- the costs of massive federal programs launched to improve local policing, or

- the costs of federal programs designed to promote similar development in other areas of government concern.

Improvements in policing — a government function so vital to the quality of life in a democracy — will not come about by simply increasing the numbers of police and by augmenting and modernizing the equipment they use. We need to invest proportionately and more heavily in thinking — in an organized, systematic and sustained way

— about what it is that the police are called on to do — and how they should do it.

Address correspondence to: Herman Goldstein, University of Wisconsin, 606 Law Building, 975 Bascom Mall, Madison, WI 53076 USA. E-mail: <hgold@facstaff.wisc.edu>.

REFERENCES

Bard, M. (1970). *Training Police as Specialists in Family Crisis Intervention.* Washington, DC: U.S. Government Printing Office.

Bittner, E. (1990). *Aspects of Police Work.* Boston, MA: Northeastern University Press.

Braga, A., D. Kennedy, E. Waring, and A. Piehl (2001) "Problem-Oriented Policing, Deterrence, and Youth Violence: An Evaluation of Boston's Operation Ceasefire." *Journal of Research in Crime and Delinquency* 38(3):195-225.

Bridgeman C. and L. Hobbs (1997). *Preventing Repeat Victimisation: The Police Officer's Guide.* London, UK: Home Office Police Research Group.

Brodeur, J. (1998). "Tailor-Made Policing: A Conceptual Investigation." In: J. Brodeur (ed.), *How To Recognize Good Policing: Problems and Issues.* Washington, DC: Police Executive Research Forum and Sage Publications.

Chenery, S., J. Holt and K. Pease (1997). *Biting Back II: Reducing Repeat Victimisation in Huddersfield.* (Crime Detection and Prevention Series, Paper No. 82.) London, UK: Home Office Research Group.

Clarke, R. (1998). "Defining Police Strategies: Problem-Solving, Problem-Oriented Policing and Community-Oriented Policing." In: T. O'Connor Shelley and A. Grant (eds.), *Problem-Oriented Policing: Crime-Specific Problems, Critical Issues and Making POP Work.* Washington, DC: Police Executive Research Forum.

—— (1997). *Situational Crime Prevention: Successful Case Studies* (2nd ed.). Monsey, NY: Criminal Justice Press.

—— and H. Goldstein (2002). "Reducing Theft at Construction Sites: Lessons From a Problem-Oriented Project." In: N. Tilley (ed.), *Analysis for Crime Prevention.* (Crime Prevention Studies, vol. 13.) Monsey, NY: Criminal Justice Press.

Ekblom, P. (2002). "From the Source to the Mainstream is Uphill: The Challenge of Transferring Knowledge of Crime Prevention Through Replication, Innovation and Anticipation." In: N. Tilley (ed.), *Analysis for Crime Prevention*. (Crime Prevention Studies, vol. 13). Monsey, NY: Criminal Justice Press.

Eck, J. and W. Spelman (1987a). "Who Ya Gonna Call? The Police as Problem-Busters." *Crime & Delinquency* 33(1):31-52.

—— (1987b). *Problem-Solving: Problem-Oriented Policing in Newport News.* Washington, DC: Police Executive Research Forum.

Geller, W. (1997). "Suppose We Were Really Serious About Police Departments Becoming 'Learning Organizations'?" *National Institute of Justice Journal* (December):2-7.

Goldstein, H. (1993). "Confronting the Complexity of the Policing Function." In: L. Ohlin and F. Remington (eds.), *Discretion in Criminal Justice: The Tension Between Individualization and Uniformity.* Albany, NY: State University of New York Press.

—— (1990). *Problem-Oriented Policing.* New York, NY: McGraw Hill. (Also published in hard-cover by Temple University Press.)

—— (1979). "Improving Policing: A Problem-Oriented Approach." *Crime & Delinquency* 25(2):236-258.

—— (1977). *Policing a Free Society.* Cambridge, MA: Ballinger Publishing.

—— and C. Susmilch (1982). "Experimenting With the Problem-Oriented Approach to Improving Police Service: A Report and Some Reflections on Two Case Studies." (Volume 4 of the Project on Development of a Problem-Oriented Approach to Improving Police Service.) Madison, WI: University of Wisconsin Law School.

—— and C. Susmilch (1981). "The Problem-Oriented Approach to Improving Police Service: A Description of the Project and an Elaboration of the Concept." (Volume 1 of the Project on Development of a Problem-Oriented Approach to Improving Police Service.) Madison, WI: University of Wisconsin Law School.

Kennedy, D. (1999). "Research for Problem-Solving and the New Collaborations." In: *Viewing Crime and Justice From a Collaborative Perspective: Plenary Papers of the 1998 Conference on Criminal Justice Research and Evaluation.* Washington, DC: National Institute of Justice, U.S. Department of Justice.

—— (1997). "Pulling Levers: Chronic Offenders, High-Crime Settings, and a Theory of Prevention." *Valpariso University Law Review* 31:449-484.

Laycock, G. (2002). "Methodological Issues in Working With Policy Advisers and Practitioners." In: N. Tilley (ed.), *Analysis for Crime Prevention.* (Crime Prevention Studies, vol. 13.) Monsey, NY: Criminal Justice Press.

Leigh, A., T. Read and N. Tilley (1998). *Brit POP II: Problem-Oriented Policing in Practice*. (Police Research Series, Paper No. 93.) London, UK: Home Office Policing and Reducing Crime Unit.

—— (1996). *Problem-Oriented Policing: Brit POP*. (Crime Detection and Prevention Series, Paper No. 75.) London, UK: Home Office Police Research Group.

Pease, K. (1998). *Repeat Victimisation: Taking Stock*. (Crime Detection and Prevention Series. Paper No. 90.) London, UK: Home Office Policing and Reducing Crime Unit.

Read, T. and N. Tilley (2000). *Not Rocket Science? Problem-solving and Crime Reduction*. (Crime Reduction Research Series, Paper No. 6.) London, UK: Home Office Policing and Reducing Crime Unit.

Reiss, A. (1982). "Forecasting the Role of the Police and the Role of the Police in Social Forecasting." In: R. Donelan (ed.), *The Maintenance of Order in Society*. Ottawa, CAN: University of Toronto.

Rojek, J. (2001). "A Decade of Excellence in Problem-Oriented Policing Characteristics of the Goldstein Award Winners." Presentation at the Academy of Criminal Justice Sciences, Washington, DC (April 6, 2001).

Sampson, R. and M. Scott (2000). *Tackling Crime and Other Public-Safety Problems: Case Studies in Problem-Solving*. Washington, DC: Office of Community-Oriented Policing Services, U.S. Department of Justice.

Scott, M. (2001) *Problem-Oriented Policing: Reflections on the First 20 Years*. Washington, DC: Office of Community-Oriented Policing Services, U.S. Department of Justice.

Sherman, L. (1998). *Evidence-Based Policing*. (Ideas in American Policing series.) Washington, DC: Police Foundation.

—— J. Schmidt, D. Rogan, P. Gartin, E. Cohn, D. Collins and A. Bacich (1991). "From Initial Deterrence to Long-Term Escalation: Short-Custody Arrest for Poverty Ghetto Domestic Violence." *Criminology* 29(4):821-850.

—— and R. Berk (1984). "The Specific Deterrent Effects of Arrest for Domestic Violence." *American Sociological Review* 49(2):261-272.

Skogan, W. and S. Hartnett (1997). *Community Policing, Chicago Style*. New York, NY and Oxford, UK: Free Press.

Sparrow, M. (1994). *Imposing Duties: Government's Changing Approach to Compliance*. Westport, CT: Praeger.

Taft, P. (1986). *Fighting Fear: The Baltimore County COPE Project*. Washington, DC: Police Executive Research Forum.

Tilley, N. (1999). "The Relationship Between Crime Prevention and Problem-Oriented Policing." In: C. Solé Brito and T. Allan (eds.), *Problem-*

Oriented Policing: Crime-Specific Problems, Critical Issues and Making POP Work, vol. 2. Washington, DC: Police Executive Research Forum.

—— and G. Laycock (2000). "Joining Up Research, Policy and Practice About Crime." *Policy Studies* 21(3):213-227.

Toch, H. and J.D. Grant (1991). *Police as Problem-Solvers*. New York, NY: Plenum Press.

U.S. Bureau of Justice Statistics (2000). *Sourcebook of Criminal Justice Statistics*. Washington, DC: U.S. Department of Justice.

U.S. National Institute of Justice (2001a). *Excellence in Problem-Oriented Policing: The 2001 Herman Goldstein Award Winners*. Washington, DC: U.S. Department of Justice.

—— (2001b). *Excellence in Problem-Oriented Policing: The 2000 Herman Goldstein Award Winners*. Washington, DC: Department of Justice.

—— (2000). *Excellence in Problem-Oriented Policing: The 1999 Herman Goldstein Award Winners*. Washington, DC: U.S. Department of Justice.

NOTES

1. Bittner (1990), among others, in pleading for a requirement of higher education for the police, expressed skepticism about how well this might work. He notes: "...the effort involved in problem-oriented policing requires interests, inclinations, and aptitudes that are not well represented in police personnel at this time. It is not that such persons are wholly absent. Their number is actually larger than existing recruitment and training patterns lead us to expect...The idea that the principles and procedures employed today in recruitment and training will produce people inclined toward self-directed information gathering and analysis, capable of inventive planning, and motivated to work for long-range solutions seems absurd; and farfetched is better than absurd.

2. In this same period, the community policing movement grew rapidly in policing. One element of that movement supported the police becoming less legalistically-oriented: that police should redefine their role in ways that sought to achieve broader outcomes for those, especially victims, who turned to the police for help. Beat-level "problem solving" was seen as supporting these efforts and therefore often incorporated into the community policing movement (see, e.g., Skogan and Hartnett 1997). As community policing and problem-oriented policing evolved alongside each other, the two concepts were intermingled. I contributed to some of the resulting confusion (see Brodeur, 1998). For a clarification between

the concepts, see both Brodeur (1998) and Scott (2001).

3. This is especially troubling because the reform movement in policing was, for a long time, identified as the professionalization of the police. But the exact meaning of that term has never been clear. It is most commonly associated with higher entry standards or college education. Some associate it primarily with increased integrity or efficiency. The building of a body of knowledge, on which good practice is based and with which practitioners are expected to be familiar, may be the most important element for acquiring truly professional status.

4. In the U.K., the Home Office has initiated a number of programs recently, using the Web, to support local crime prevention efforts (see www.crimereduction.gov.uk). Some of the posted material facilitates access to relevant research.

5. Referred to as the *Problem-Oriented Guides for Police* series, published in 2001 and 2002, the series is funded by the Office of Community Oriented Policing Service (COPS) of the U.S. Department of Justice. The authors of the guides on specific problems are Michael S. Scott, Rana Sampson, Ronald V. Clarke, and Deborah Lamm Weisel. There is also an introductory guide on assessing responses to problems by John E. Eck.

6. For an elaboration on these points, see Goldstein 1977, 1990.

7. Police Executive Research Forum, "Police Executive Survey — 1998." www.policeforum.org/data.htm (Question No. 45).

8. For a full discussion of this need, see Clarke, 1998.

9. While the primary focus here is on engaging more academics in research relating to the police, the importance of opening police agencies to more research should not be discounted. One of the major lessons that can be drawn from the strongest problem-oriented policing projects is that their strength grew, in large measure, from the wealth of data and insights to which the researchers involved had such easy access. Having been involved in several such studies, it is hard to contemplate how studies without such access could be as penetrating and as confidently conclusive.

10. I'm mindful, of course, that an appeal for academics to engage in research of the type proposed here requires that they face a major problem in their relationships with their peers. Such research is often labeled "applied research" — a term frequently used in a pejorative sense by academics in the social sciences. For a helpful discussion of the dichot-

omy drawn between pure and applied research, as specifically related to the police, and for some thoughts on how to get beyond the current impasse, see Bittner (1990).

11. Currently, the project underway to test the *Problem-Oriented Guides for Police* makes a part-time researcher available to each of four police agencies for the limited purpose of enabling each agency to apply the guidelines to one or two problems within the department. This is another form of collaboration that should produce additional insights on how researchers located outside a police agency might cultivate productive relationships with the police.

12. In a larger context, moving beyond just focusing on specific problems and the effectiveness of police strategies in responding to them, Geller argues for a greater commitment within police agencies to the staff and resources that would enable them to become truly "learning organizations" (Geller, 1997).

GETTING THE POLICE TO TAKE PROBLEM-ORIENTED POLICING SERIOUSLY

by

Michael S. Scott
The Center for Problem-oriented Policing, Inc.

Abstract: *Police agencies have, for the most part, not yet integrated the principles and methods of problem-oriented policing into their routine operations. This is so for several reasons. First, many police officials lack a complete understanding of the basic elements of problem-oriented policing and how problem solving fits in the context of the whole police function. Second, the police have not yet adequately developed the skill sets and knowledge bases to support problem-oriented policing. And third, the police have insufficient incentives to take problem-oriented policing seriously. This paper begins by articulating what full integration of problem-oriented policing into routine police operations might look like. It then presents one framework for integrating the principles and methods of problem-oriented policing into the whole police function. The paper then explores the particular skill sets and knowledge bases that will be essential to the practice of problem-oriented policing within police agencies and across the police profession. Finally, it explores the perspectives of those who critically evaluate police performance, and considers ways to modify those perspectives and expectations consistent with problem-oriented policing.*

Problem-oriented policing (POP), introduced to the police profession some 20 years ago, has been widely praised, and seldom seriously criticized, as a promising approach to improving police service (Brodeur, 1998; Sherman et al., 1997; Leigh et al., 1996). And yet few police agencies have fully incorporated its basic principles and methods into their structure and operations, nor has the police profession as a whole fully embraced problem-oriented policing. This paper explores why this is so and proposes steps that can be taken to get the police to take problem-oriented policing more seriously.

The Basic Elements of Problem-oriented Policing

This discussion properly begins with a review of some of the basic principles and methods of problem-oriented policing and what full incorporation of those principles and methods might look like in a police agency and across the whole police profession.

Herman Goldstein (2001:1) emphasizes 10 basic elements of problem-oriented policing.[1] He summarized them as follows:

> Problem-oriented policing is an approach to policing in which (1) discrete pieces of police business (each consisting of a cluster of similar incidents, whether crime or acts of disorder, that the police are expected to handle) are subject to (2) microscopic examination (drawing on the especially honed skills of crime analysts and the accumulated experience of operating field personnel) in hopes that what is freshly learned about each problem will lead to discovering a (3) new and more effective strategy for dealing with it. Problem-oriented policing places a high value on new responses that are (4) preventive in nature, that are (5) not dependent on the use of the criminal justice system, and that (6) engage other public agencies, the community and the private sector when their involvement has the potential for significantly contributing to the reduction of the problem. Problem-oriented policing carries a commitment to (7) implementing the new strategy, (8) rigorously evaluating its effectiveness, and, subsequently, (9) reporting the results in ways that will benefit other police agencies and that will ultimately contribute to (10) building a body of knowledge that supports the further professionalization of the police.

These basic elements, familiar to those who study and practice problem-oriented policing, are explained in detail elsewhere (Goldstein, 1990, 1979; Eck and Spelman, 1987; Scott, 2000), so here the concern is limited to considering what full incorporation of these elements might look like within police agencies and across the police profession.

Full Incorporation of Problem-oriented Policing Into Police Practice

Ideally, there would be a clearer understanding of what the term "problem" refers to: that it refers to an aggregation of smaller units of police business — incidents, complaints, crimes, calls-for-service, cases — into a larger unit of analysis known as a problem. It does not refer to any and all matters of concern to the police. It specifically does not refer to organizational, administrative and political concerns. Use of the term "problem" in the context of policing would be understood in much the same way the term "disease" is understood among health professionals.

The police would become adept at breaking down large, vague problems into smaller, more precise problems. They would cease talking in generalities about how the police are going to deal with "the drug problem" or with "crime and delinquency" or "disorder and incivility," but rather would insist upon addressing the more specific ways in which these general concerns manifest themselves in that community. They would talk more in terms of controlling problems — reducing the harm caused by them — and less in terms of totally eradicating them from the community. Their objectives would be realistic and achievable.

The police, and those who oversee their actions, would insist that the broad community interest in these problems, as well as the larger community's response to them, be explored, rather than more narrowly looking at what the police are doing to solve the problems. The police would be held more accountable for addressing problems, but less responsible for addressing them alone. The various entities that are affected by particular problems, and those who contribute to their existence, would be actively engaged in the search for an improved response. Top community leaders would help broker the ownership of community problems and resist the temptation to point fingers exclusively at the police for all crime and disorder problems.

Within police agencies we would expect to find formal and routine systems that allow one to identify problems from among the mass of the smaller units of police business handled. Police incident reports would be designed with an eye toward capturing information about incidents that would facilitate subsequent problem analysis. For example, reporting officers might be asked to record factors — social or environmental conditions — that contributed to the incident. This would make it easier for subsequent analysis to locate all incident reports with certain contributing factors.[2] Dispatch records would have more precise codes to allow analysts to distinguish among different types of problems that are often lumped together under broad dispatch codes.[3] Staff would be dedicated to identifying apparent and emerging problems that would then call for closer analysis and perhaps new responses. Again, this parallels how the public health profession has developed systems for identifying outbreaks of disease and injury that call for special interventions.

There have been tremendous advances in recent years in information technology available to police that permit them to capture, sort, display, and analyze large quantities of data (Dunworth et al., 2000). Relational databases, computerized mapping, geographic information systems (GIS) technology, and other tools are becoming standard for many police agencies. Many police agencies now routinely produce lists that identify "hot spots," chronic offenders, chronic victims, and so forth. Many police agencies are emulating the New York City Police Department's Compstat methods to present emerging trend data and hold officials accountable for developing and implementing responses to emerging crime patterns. These are generally positive developments in policing, reflecting improvements in technology and methods in comparison to what existed before. Yet these developments do not of themselves achieve the more nuanced and in-depth definition and exploration of problems that are essential to good problem-oriented policing. For example, Compstat methods tend to be limited in several important respects. They tend to emphasize Uniform Crime Report "Index" crime data over the 90% of other incident reports that are not classified as an Index crime and over data other than police crime and incident reports. They focus on short-term trends rather than longer-term trends, a focus that lends itself well to developing stop-gap crime suppression interventions, but less well to understanding persistent community problems.

If problem-oriented policing were more fully adopted, we could expect the police to improve their understanding of crime and disorder problems; to see top police administrators and mid-level managers more engaged in matters directly concerning how their agencies handle various community problems. Goldstein observed quite accurately that police administrators devote most of their time and attention to organizational, administrative, and political concerns, perhaps in the misguided belief that the standard policing strategies — embodied by preventive patrol, handling incidents, investigating crimes, and arresting offenders — are adequate means for addressing the myriad of crime and disorder problems confronting the police.

The analysis of problems in POP departments would be of sufficient depth and rigor to get beyond simplistic understandings and explanations of the causes of community problems; the search for new and alternative responses to these problems would be sufficiently broad and creative to get beyond conventional police responses; and the responses adopted would be carefully tailored to local problems. Analysis of problems would especially look to reveal the many, often conflicting, interests that various groups in the community have in each problem rather than clinging to the fiction that there is a single community with a unified interest in these problems and a consensual view as to how problems should be addressed. There would be a greater willingness to explore, challenge and change current responses.

Police agencies using POP methods would employ researchers and analysts, either as permanent staff or on a consulting basis, who are professionally trained in the principles and methods of problem analysis and action research. This staff would work closely and collaboratively with police operations officers identifying and analyzing problems, developing and implementing responses to them, and assessing the impact of those responses. Such staff would be relatively free of competing demands to perform tasks not related to substantive police concerns. Their work would extend beyond conventional crime analysis that is oriented principally toward predicting when and where future offenses will occur and guiding officers in criminal apprehension efforts. Problem analysts would be paid competitive wages and enjoy a higher level of status and influence within police organizations than they do today. They would be seen as indispensable to the routine operations of a police agency, not as peripheral support staff. There would be sufficient research and analysis staff to support routine problem-oriented activities in the agency. Even if there were only one researcher/analyst for every 100 police officers in an agency — a seemingly reasonable ratio — this would significantly enhance the current level of research and analysis support present in most police agencies today.

Measurement of success under POP would focus more directly on substantive outcomes — the degree to which problems were reduced effectively, efficiently, and equitably — and not merely on either the degree to which police involvement in problems was reduced or the extent to which responses were implemented. Police agencies would be measured in more sophisticated ways — by their relative effectiveness in addressing community problems — rather than solely by conventional measures of Index crimes, arrest rates, clearance rates, and response times.

Police agencies would prepare reports documenting problem-oriented initiatives and retain those reports and supporting documents in an organized records system. They would rely upon such reports and files to improve future problem-oriented inquiries and to share their findings with other police agencies and researchers. Problem-oriented record systems would have the same level of importance and resources as do incident records, case files, and the dozens of other records systems typically reposited in police agencies. Lessons learned from the experiences of problem-solving initiatives would be fed back into other systems in the agency: written policies and procedures would be updated and made more consistent with emerging good practice, and training programs would continually be informed by the findings and experiences that emerge from problem-oriented work.

The police profession — through government agencies and private police research organizations — would similarly collect and synthesize knowledge about how the many crime and disorder problems faced by the police should be handled. Researchers would be funded to conduct studies designed to improve the overall understanding of common crime and disorder problems and how the police can effectively address them. The knowledge gained from research studies and police problem-solving initiatives would be collected, synthesized and fed back to police practitioners. There would be journals, articles, guides, seminars, training programs, websites and so forth devoted to the police handling of substantive community problems, all of which would contain information directly relevant to police practitioners and be written and presented in styles and formats that could be readily digested by police officials.

Government officials who oversee police activities would come to expect that the police were capable of analyzing problems carefully and of devising comprehensive and customized responses to difficult problems. At the same time, and through careful analysis, government officials would better appreciate the complexity and intractability of some crime and disorder problems, and thereby become more circumspect about demanding immediate and simple solutions to some problems. They would insist upon proper analysis before investing in or authorizing new responses to problems. This is no more than is routinely expected of other government services, whether it be water and sewer service, public health, fire control, or road construction. Government officials would be more open to heeding the advice of the police about emerging community problems and the need for the community to improve its responses to them. Both the police and the local governments to whom they report would become more comfortable with the police role as the proverbial canary in the coal mine, an early warning system for emerging crime and social disorder problems.

Police officers would be trained in the principles and methods of problem solving at least as thoroughly as they are trained in other operational strategies like criminal investigation and emergency response. This would include imparting to new officers a better understanding of the range of crime and disorder problems they will confront and what is known about how these problems can be controlled. They would emerge from their training programs with a greater capacity to recognize problems and at least initiate processes to analyze and respond appropriately to them.

Police organizations would be adept at tracking the progress of problem-solving initiatives and able to mobilize the right level of resources to match the scope and seriousness of each problem being addressed. This includes providing the right level of leadership to problem-solving initiatives and combining line-level input and involvement with higher level authority and resources. Problem-solving initiatives would be brought to conclusion in a timely fashion, not left to stall for lack of attention. Greater attention would be paid to the details and challenges of implementing responses in the knowledge that many good plans fail because of poor implementation and monitoring.

The administrative and organizational systems of police agencies would be better aligned to support and enable problem-oriented activity. Officers would be expected to think and act in a problem-oriented fashion and would be evaluated, rewarded and recognized for doing so. Formal and informal communications networks within agencies would promote the sort of discussions and information exchange essential to effective problem solving.

The foregoing discussion reflects a rough ideal vision of what police agencies and the police profession might look like if the concept of problem-oriented policing were taken more seriously. We turn now to exploring why the current state of affairs remains so far from the ideal.

Why Don't the Police Take Problem-oriented Policing Seriously?

There are three main reasons why the police do not take problem-oriented policing as seriously as one might hope they would. The first reason is the police lack a complete understanding of both the basic elements of problem-oriented policing and how those basic elements ought to be integrated with conventional forms of policing. The second reason is, even where there is a good understanding of the basic elements and how they should be integrated into an agency, police agencies often lack, or lack access to, all of the skill sets and knowledge bases that are requisite for effective problem-oriented policing. The third reason is there are insufficient incentives for the police to take problem-oriented policing seriously.

Getting Police To Understand the Basic Elements of Problem-oriented Policing and How Problem Solving Fits in the Context of the Whole Police Function

That many police officers and administrators do not yet understand the basic elements of problem-oriented policing is not surprising. Although the concept has been in the public domain for over 20 years, the communication of its basic elements to the general police profession has only occurred within about the past 10 years. During that time, the concept of problem-oriented policing has been melded in some people's minds with the parallel concept of community policing. While there have been some benefits from trying to merge these two concepts into a unified whole, that effort has not always been successful and it has left some confusion and disagreement about which particular aspects of the two concepts are of highest priority (Goldstein, 1990; Scott, 2000; Brodeur, 1998). In many police agencies, for example, improving the overall relationship of the police to the community, especially to minority communities, has been a higher priority than improving analytical systems and knowledge about specific crime and disorder problems. So some police executives and researchers have devoted their time, attention and resources to opening lines of communication between the police and various community groups, and perhaps have seen this *necessary* step as also being *sufficient* toward adopting a new, more effective style of policing.

The quantity and quality of formal training in the principles and methods of problem-oriented policing has, on the whole, been inadequate (Scott, 2000). To the extent that some police officers are given any training in problem-oriented policing at all, it is often confined to a couple-day seminar, or worse, to a brief discussion in the context of a community policing seminar.[4] Few police academies devote anywhere near the amount of time to problem solving that they devote to other aspects of police work, such as patrol tactics, legal issues, weapons, emergency response, or criminal investigation. So, many police officers are left to learn problem-oriented policing principles and methods through experimentation, reading publications they come across by chance, and occasionally exchanging information and ideas with one another and with experts at conferences.

Beyond the need for teaching police officers how to identify, analyze, respond to, and assess problems, it is equally important that police administrators understand how to integrate problem-solving methods with other operational policing methods into a coherent problem-oriented framework. They need to understand how the new demands of problem solving fit with existing demands that their agencies respond to routine incidents and emergencies, investigate crimes, patrol territory, and provide other ancillary public services. With this understanding, the systems and routines essential for problem solving can better be developed and institutionalized within police organizations. Although the totality of the police function is so multidimensional and complex that it defies simple categorization, some attempt to conceptualize and contextualize police work is necessary (Goldstein, 1977; Bittner, 1970; Wilson, 1968). Police administrators need to understand the fundamental — and sometimes competing — objectives of policing, the various methods available to achieve those objectives, and how to mobilize resources at the various levels at which police agencies operate. An integrated model would help explain what the police are trying to achieve, how they are trying to achieve it, and on what scale they are operating.

Briefly, an integrated policing model recognizes that police have multiple *objectives*, summarized by Goldstein (1977) as follows:

(1) to prevent and control conduct threatening to life and property (including serious crime);

(2) to aid crime victims and protect people in danger of physical harm;

(3) to protect constitutional guarantees, such as the right to free speech and assembly;

(4) to facilitate the movement of people and vehicles;

(5) to assist those who cannot care for themselves, including the intoxicated, the addicted, the mentally ill, the physically disabled, the elderly, and the young;

(6) to resolve conflict between individuals, between groups, or between citizens and their government;

(7) to identify problems that have the potential for becoming more serious for individuals, the police or the government; and

(8) to create and maintain a feeling of security in the community.

The model further recognizes that police employ several broad *operational strategies* to achieve these objectives. These operational strategies (or modes of operation) can be conceptualized as follows:

(1) preventive patrol;

(2) routine incident response;

(3) emergency response;

(4) criminal investigation;

(5) problem solving; and,

(6) ancillary public services.

Problem solving, conceived of as an operational strategy, is, in an important respect, different from other operational strategies: the careful analysis of the police response to various crime and disorder problems that is embodied in problem solving serves to inform all other operational strategies. It helps the police to improve their patrol, routine incident response, emergency response, and criminal investigation tactics and strategies. In sum, it helps the police make better sense out of much of what they do.

Finally, an integrated model recognizes that police work occurs at various levels of aggregation, or *operating levels*, ranging from highly localized work, such as that done by a single police officer addressing a problem at a single location, to communitywide work that implicates the policies and practices of the entire police agency. Examples of how the operating levels and operational strategies of police work relate are depicted in Figure 1 below. I explained this integrated model in more detail in an earlier publication (Scott, 2000, chapter 2).

Whether through this framework or some other, police officials, particularly administrators, need to develop a clearer understanding as to how the principles and methods of problem-oriented policing fit with the whole police function and how they can be integrated into the structure and systems of police organizations. Through this model, it is easier to recognize just how inadequate are the current structures and systems of police organizations for the purpose of advancing problem-oriented policing.

In addition to educating police officials, it is increasingly important that others outside the police organization understand what problem-oriented policing is and what potential it holds for promoting safer communities. City and county administrators, local elected officials, judges, prosecutors, other criminal justice officials, community leaders, journalists, and nongovernmental organization leaders need to be exposed to the rationale for changing the present orientation of policing, the principles of problem-oriented policing, and examples of problem-oriented policing successfully practiced. Through their improved understanding they can in turn help shape the priorities of police officials and consider other changes in government and community systems that will facilitate and support problem-oriented policing.

Figure 1. Operating Levels and Operational Strategies of Police Work

Operating Level	Operational Strategy				
	Preventive Patrol	*Routine Incident Response*	*Emergency Response*	*Criminal Investigation*	*Problem Solving*
Macro	Patrol deployment plans.	Policies related to the routine handling of categories of incidents.	Policies related to categories of emergencies; e.g., responses to large scale disasters.	Policies and practices related to categories of crimes.	Policies and practices related to categories of problems affecting entire communities.
Intermediate	Directed patrols by groups of officers.	Handling of a large scale routine event; e.g., traffic control at large public event.	Response to an incident with multiple offenders or victims; e.g., a bar fight or multiple-vehicle accident.	Investigation of a pattern of crimes; e.g., a rash of burglaries in a neighborhood.	Problems affecting a neighborhood or district; e.g., prostitution on a commercial strip.
Micro	Routine preventive patrol by beat officers.	Handling of routine incidents; e.g., dispute, minor crime reporting, provision of directions, minor traffic accident investigation.	Response to a life-threatening incident; e.g., a traffic accident, with injuries; police officer in need of immediate assistance.	Investigation of a single crime; e.g, shoplifting; assault, with known suspect.	Problems concentrated at discrete locations; e.g., a single drug house.

Note: The flow of the arrows reflects the need for data from the first four operational strategies to be analyzed in the problem solving operational strategy, which in turn informs and improves the other operational strategies. For purposes of illustration, the number of operating levels is set here at three, but in reality, operating levels are on a continuum and vary depending on the size of the jurisdiction and police agency.

Developing the Skill Sets and Knowledge Bases To Support Problem-oriented Policing

Problem-oriented policing introduces a whole new analytical dimension to policing, a dimension that in some respects runs counter to more conventional dimensions of policing. Much of conventional policing is reactive, hurried, and oriented to action. Problem-oriented policing is proactive, deliberate, and oriented to analysis. Consequently, many of the skill sets and knowledge bases on which police have drawn to achieve their objectives through conventional operational strategies are ill suited to support problem-oriented policing.

To be sure, some conventional police skill sets and knowledge bases apply — indeed are essential — to effective problem solving, but not all. Conventional policing is geared for high-volume transactions under tight time constraints. There are many routine incidents to handle and emergencies to respond to, much territory to patrol, many crimes to investigate, and many citizens to serve. By contrast, problem solving contemplates carefully selecting out clusters of crimes and incidents from among this high-volume business, and carefully analyzing them as discrete problems. It calls for dedicating more time, attention and resources to studying problems than are typically devoted to handling incidents or investigating crimes. Problem-oriented policing calls for managing problem-solving projects over substantially longer time periods — months or years — than is typical for most incidents or criminal cases.

While the skills and resources necessary for effective criminal investigation most closely overlap those necessary for effective problem solving, the match is not perfect. Criminal investigators are under constant pressure to move cases along, either to drop them out of the formal system or to send them on to the next stage of the criminal justice system. They aren't typically expected to spend much time reflecting on how the investigation or prosecution of any single case, or even a class of cases, contributes to the overall safety of the community. It is nearly an article of faith that the more crimes solved, the more cases made, and the more offenders prosecuted, the safer the community will be.

Most obviously, police agencies seldom possess, or even have ready access to, the full set of research and analysis skills so critical to effective problem solving. Few have trained criminologists, methodologists, or statisticians on staff, and where there are research or crime analysts on staff, they seldom have a high degree of formal training. Where police agencies have working arrangements with outside researchers — at universities or private research organizations

— it is rare to find that those researchers share a problem-solving orientation to research. Action research of the sort envisioned by problem-oriented policing requires a different approach than conventional academic research (Kennedy, 1999; Goldstein and Susmilch, 1982). Consequently, it does not suffice just to bring in outside researchers and let them loose to evaluate police initiatives. Good action research typically involves the researcher in all phases of the initiative — defining the problem, analyzing it, developing alternative responses, choosing from among alternatives, monitoring the implementation of responses, and assessing outcomes.

Police agencies, indeed the whole police field, sorely lack a substantial, coherent, organized, and accessible body of knowledge that would serve to guide police in addressing specific crime and disorder problems. Certainly when compared to many other professional fields, police have few reference materials to advise them about what tactics and strategies do and do not work — and under what conditions they do and do not work — for the many community problems they face. The theoretical models for how police can effectively reduce and prevent crime and disorder (see Clarke and Felson, 1993; Felson and Clarke, 1998; Tilley and Laycock, 2002; Sherman et al., 1997), and the accumulated knowledge from research and practice, have only recently begun to be assembled.[5] Much more work needs to be done to allow police to advance beyond ad hoc experimentation and crude emulation as the means by which they decide how to respond to particular community problems. Once accumulated, this body of knowledge must be made available to police, and police must become familiar with it in order for it to inform their practice.

Creating Incentives for Police To Adopt a Problem-oriented Approach

In most jurisdictions the practice of problem-oriented policing is sporadic at best. It is done — sometimes well, sometimes poorly — more as an exception than as a rule. Police officials may become engaged with problem-oriented policing after attending a training program or a conference and then become motivated to put the principles into practice to address particular problems. But that enthusiasm and commitment typically wanes after a few "POP projects" are completed. Some police officials become motivated to solve community problems for various reasons: because they are personally frustrated with the persistence of a particular problem or they see doing effective problem solving as a means to recognition and career enhancement. While there is nothing wrong with these sorts of motivations — indeed, they work to get police officials to do all sorts of important things — they are insufficient to sustain the practice of problem-oriented policing over the long term. No other method of police operation depends so heavily on the personal motivations of police officials for its routine practice.

At present, there are too few incentives operating on police administrators or line officers to routinely apply problem-oriented policing methods to the community crime and disorder problems they confront. For the most part, no one outside of police agencies is pressuring or encouraging police to produce high-quality problem-oriented work. Too few mayors and city managers insist upon careful analysis of crime and disorder problems to inform policies, programs, and legislation. Many of them concern themselves primarily with the political implications of police action rather than with the policy implications. Accordingly, many police initiatives are either endorsed or criticized by elected officials on the basis of scant analytical support. With some notable exceptions, prosecutors, the defense bar, and the criminal court judiciary remain preoccupied with the processing of individual cases to the exclusion of exploring systemic responses to problems.[6] The media have thus far not shown much interest in exploring the complexities of the police and community response to particular crime and disorder problems, all too often deferring to professionals' claims that they are doing all they can to deal with the problem. To a great extent, reporters have themselves bought into the myths and unsupported assumptions about how police can and should operate. Too many community groups rely on the police for information about crime and disorder problems and defer uncritically to police explanations of the causes of problems. Few community groups seriously challenge police to analyze problems and to develop new responses, all too often accepting as the best that can be done stock police responses to various crime and disorder problems such as extra police patrols, increased arrests, or the establishment of a Neighborhood Watch.

We can learn something about what incentives might be developed to promote the practice of problem-oriented policing by considering the incentives that promote the practice of other police operational strategies: preventive patrol, criminal investigations, emergency response, handling routine incidents, and providing ancillary support services. One way this can be done is to consider the interests of those who exert significant influence on police practices, particularly on the operational strategies the police adopt to achieve their objectives. Here we consider the interests of:

- prosecutors, the defense bar, and the judiciary;
- mayors, city managers and other elected officials;

- community groups;

- media;

- academia and police research organizations;

- government funding agencies; and

- private industry.

Why do police continue to invest so heavily in patrolling their jurisdictions through highly visible uniformed police officers and vehicles, even in the face of evidence that it is limited in what it achieves in terms of deterring crime and making communities feel safe? Why do police dedicate such effort to perpetuating the illusion that all crimes are investigated thoroughly and that they are investigated for the ultimate purpose of prosecuting the offenders? Why do police continue to have such difficulty resisting requests and demands that they handle such a wide range of incidents, both criminal and noncriminal? Why do police place such a high priority on maintaining response capabilities to all manner of emergencies? And why do police dedicate so many resources to providing a range of ancillary public services that are peripheral to their core functions and objectives?

One answer to these questions is that over time constituencies have developed for particular police methods. Not only do police develop constituencies for their *objectives* (i.e., to control crime, to facilitate the movement of people and vehicles, etc.), but they develop constituencies for their methods of achieving those objectives — their *operational strategies*. Important groups in society have come to expect that police will operate in certain ways, sometimes for the larger public good and sometimes also to serve more narrow interests. Groups and individuals outside the police agency find value in certain police operational strategies; either intrinsic value because those operational strategies effectively achieve certain social objectives, or indirect value because particular police operational strategies create opportunities and benefits for particular groups.[7] Indeed, why would police continue to adopt an operational strategy if it did not produce some value for which others were willing to exert their influence to preserve?[8] Conventional police strategies such as preventive patrol and criminal investigation also have powerful intuitive appeal. People believe they work well because their underlying rationale seems so logical and correct, even if ultimately it is not. The police have cultivated some of these constituencies partly to serve some of their own interests. Constituencies both *support* the police in their efforts to employ operational strategies and *demand* that police continue to employ them. There is both a carrot and a stick quality to constituencies.

As yet, there are inadequate constituencies for the problem-solving operational strategy, and until those constituencies are well developed it is unlikely that police will take problem-oriented policing sufficiently seriously to alter their organizations, systems, routines, and practices. The capacity to effectively identify, analyze, respond to, and assess community problems is not yet seen as an essential police function. However, neither has it always been the case that preventive patrol, criminal investigation, or the handling of certain routine or critical incidents were understood to be essential to policing either: certainly not during the early eras of organized police forces, when police existed principally to serve political interests and only incidentally to control crime (Fogelson, 1977; see also Klockars, 1985 for a discussion of the evolution of the preventive patrol and detective roles). Each of the conventional police operational strategies evolved and developed over a long period of time, displacing other previously dominant operational strategies (Goldstein, 1977).

Before turning back to how a constituency might develop for problem solving as an operational strategy, let us consider the constituencies for other police operational strategies.

Criminal Investigation

Prosecutors, the criminal-defense bar, the criminal court judiciary, corrections agencies, and a host of other actors (bail bonding companies, pretrial service agencies, etc.) depend almost exclusively on police to arrest offenders for their own operations to thrive. This is not to suggest anything conspiratorial or untoward, but merely that an entire industry, of sorts, has developed that is predicated on police exercising their arrest powers sufficiently often to justify the enormous expenditures in what is commonly called the criminal justice system. An estimated $136 billion were spent in the United States in 1998 directly on police, corrections, and the judiciary (U.S. Bureau of Justice Statistics, 2001). Regardless of whether police believe that criminal investigation and subsequent arrest is an effective operational strategy toward achieving their objectives, there are strong expectations that police will continue to investigate crimes and arrest offenders. Indeed, police have come to be popularly understood as existing for this very purpose. Criminal investigative work is widely seen as the most important work police do, and detectives are perceived as the police elite. Prosecutors, correctly or incorrectly, believe they are judged by the electorate principally on their conviction rates and how aggressive they appear to be in prosecuting offenders. These and other factors place constant pressure on the police to investigate crimes well and to arrest offenders.

Preventive Patrol

Notwithstanding evidence that preventive patrol offers limited value for preventing crime and making communities feel safer, police continue to invest heavily in this operational strategy, so much so that it has become the default mode of operating for police. When they are not otherwise called to employ some other operational strategy, it is expected that police will provide a visible presence in their jurisdiction through various patrol methods. Filling beats and getting patrol cars "back in service" continue to preoccupy police supervisors. Public opinion surveys consistently reveal how strongly the public expects to see police patrolling. Neighborhoods clamor and compete with one another for extra police patrol. Police themselves perpetuate the belief that high visibility patrol is a sensible response to a wide range of crime and disorder problems. The media seldom challenge these claims, often merely content to report that police have "beefed up patrols" to respond to the latest crime concern.

Emergency Response

Police have traditionally responded to a variety of emergencies: crimes in progress, traffic crashes with injuries, suicidal persons, and so forth. Some police agencies also handle medical emergencies, training police officers as emergency medical technicians or transporting victims and patients to medical facilities. Some police agencies assume emergency response capabilities for large-scale disasters such as building or bridge collapses. In some communities, both police and fire agencies have developed sophisticated emergency response capabilities, and to some extent, they vie with one another for this important public function. Police have assumed such a large role in emergency response functions for several reasons. One reason is that the equipment, training, and legal authority that police require to perform some of their other functions are readily adapted for emergency responses. It is also the case that the emergency response function offers more immediate and tangible rewards to those who practice it. It allows police to perform a role for which the public is nearly universally grateful, something that cannot be said about many other police functions. It is an important function for establishing and maintaining public goodwill, a goodwill that helps sustain public support in the face of other more confrontational and controversial police functions. The recent experiences of the American police with respect to international terrorism reveal just how important their emergency response capabilities are to bolstering public support for the police institution. Police are quickly seeking to expand even further their capabilities to respond to new types of emergencies such as biological terrorism, that until recently seemed rather remote.

Ancillary Public Services

Most police agencies provide a variety of ancillary services to citizens, services that are only tangentially or generally related to achieving core police objectives. They run education and recreation programs for youth, conduct citizen police academies, provide copies of police reports, fingerprint citizens for official records, teach gun safety courses, store and dispose of found property, provide broad-based crime prevention programs and services, organize community cleanups, coordinate charitable programs, control animals, and so forth. Many of these programs and services are important to a community's welfare, but they are often only loosely justifiable in terms of how they contribute to core police objectives. The programs and services seldom are developed as a response to specific crime and disorder problems on the basis of a thorough analysis. The point here is not that these programs and services should be discontinued, but rather that among the purposes of these programs and services is the cultivation of a constituency of support for the police agency and the police institution. Many of these programs and services have become tremendously popular regardless of whether they are deemed effective in any specific sense.

The conventional operational strategies employed by police — routine and emergency incident response, criminal investigation, preventive patrol, and ancillary public services — continue to dominate overall police strategy and resources largely because important groups in society would miss them if they were gone, and less because they have demonstrated their value in achieving core police objectives and enhancing public safety.

This is not to say that police agencies always engage in preventive patrol, investigate crimes, or handle routine incidents and emergencies effectively. Individual police officers and the organizational systems designed to support these operational strategies fail from time to time and from place to place in implementing these operational strategies just as they fail with respect to the problem-solving operational strategy. Communities are not always faithfully patrolled, criminal cases do not always receive the investigative attention some feel they deserve, and some routine and critical incidents are mishandled. However, nearly all police agencies and police administrators aspire to be able to perform these operational strategies on a routine basis and have firmly established systems in place to see that they are at least minimally performed. One can scarcely imagine a police administrator claiming that the agency he or she runs doesn't routinely investigate crimes, patrol the jurisdiction, or respond to emergencies. It is well understood that these operational strategies are essential to running — indeed nearly the very purpose for having — a police agency. The same cannot yet be said about problem solving as an operational strategy. Few people would be as distressed to learn that their local police agency had no problem analysis function as they would be to learn that it had no criminal investigation or patrol function.

In the present state of affairs, the constituency for problem-oriented policing is weak. There are a handful of academics, researchers, and consultants who are strongly dedicated to advancing problem-oriented policing. There are similarly a handful of police executives who are committed to advancing problem-oriented policing within the situational opportunities presented to them, and a few prosecutors and local government executives who have demonstrated some commitment to the concept. The U.S. Department of Justice's COPS Office and the U.K.'s Home Office have invested resources in developing and promoting problem-oriented policing, though that objective is but a relatively small part of their organizations' overall missions. The Police Executive Research Forum's annual conference on problem-oriented policing and its Herman Goldstein Award for Excellence in Problem-Oriented Policing, along with the U.K.'s parallel annual conference and parallel Nick Tilley Award, have done much to advance problem-oriented policing and serve as incentives for some police officials and agencies to engage in this work. But awards, modest grant programs, and the personal commitment of a small number of champions will inevitably be insufficient to sustain this work over the long term.

So how might an external constituency for problem-oriented police work develop, one more powerful than that which exists today? We can consider this question for each of several major groups that might comprise such constituencies.

Prosecutors, the Defense Bar and the Judiciary

The movements toward community prosecution and problem-solving courts hold some significant potential to reinforce problem-oriented policing (Berman and Feinblatt, 2002). If judges were to adopt the habit and the mechanisms for exploring the larger context in which individual cases come into their courts, and to press prosecutors (and by extension, police) and defense counsel to consider the efficacy of current practices, policies, and programs with respect to specific crime and disorder problems, police agencies might be more inclined to undertake more sophisticated analyses of problems so that they (through prosecutors) might be better informed and prepared to respond to judges' inquiries. For example, if a criminal court judge, faced with an influx of street-level drug arrests, were in a position to inquire of the prosecutor how the prosecution of a large volume of such cases were contributing to a more effective overall response to problems created by street-level drug dealing, that prosecutor would have an incentive to have prepared a thoughtful analysis of the problem as it is experienced in the community. Defense counsel's role might expand beyond merely protecting the rights of his or her individual client to offering some additional insight into how street-level drug dealing problems might best be addressed systemically. Police officials might well find themselves testifying in court not merely about individual cases, but about whole classes of problems and their analysis of and responses to those problems. While we don't typically think of courts as public policy forums, they might in fact serve this function quite well. So-called drug courts have clearly adopted a more holistic approach to the problems associated with drug use and trafficking.

Mayors, City Managers and Other Elected and Appointed Officials

Elected and appointed government officials have been quick to embrace the concept of community policing, largely because it has such popular appeal to their constituents. Their engagement, however, with the principles and methods of problem-oriented policing, as distinct from community policing, has been less robust. But, particularly with city managers and other professionally-trained government leaders, there is little reason that must remain so. The field of city management is well positioned to embrace the analytical dimensions of problem-oriented policing. It is what the entire field is dedicated to: using analysis to inform government structure, policies and practices.[9] Rigorous analyses that inform city managers on such local governance issues as water management, environmental protection, community and economic development, public health, and disaster preparedness are standard. What is remarkable is that, to date, the city management profession has tolerated such weak analytical capacity from police or, at a minimum, have restricted their expectations to conventional crime analysis designed to predict crimes and apprehend offenders. It is to be hoped that if the professional city management field were better exposed to the principles and methods of problem-oriented policing and examples of good problem-oriented analysis, professional local government leaders would increasingly insist upon similar work in their own communities. One could imagine local governments creating a problem-oriented analysis function to inform the government executive and elected officials, or at a minimum, to support police departments in building that internal capacity.

Local government authorities in the U.K., through national legislation, appear to have gone further than their counterparts in the U.S. in promoting the idea that crime and disorder problems ought to be viewed as community problems rather than solely as police problems, which problems call for a higher degree of interagency and community partnership than has been customary in the past (Phillips et al., 2002). While this new spirit of partnership has not always translated into effective problem analysis in the U.K., it is an important start.

Academia and Police Research Organizations

Academics interested in crime and the police have generally responded favorably to the problem-oriented policing concept. But, there is now a need for interested academics to move beyond exploring the concept and the organizational implications it holds for police agencies and become more engaged working with police to practice problem-oriented policing by applying its principles and methods to actual crime and disorder problems. The relatively small field of environmental criminology has demonstrated significant interest in problem-oriented policing in recent years, and its growing body of literature in situational crime prevention has been helpful in advancing our understanding of how various crime and disorder problems can be effectively addressed. There is a need to continue developing theories of how police problems arise and how police can effectively address them. Good theories might draw more academic researchers into studying how police and others address problems.

Given that publication is the lifeblood of academia, it will be important to create and support scholarly publication opportunities related to the practice of problem-oriented policing. At present, there is no publication venue dedicated exclusively or even primarily to the practice of problem-oriented policing. Without such publication opportunities, potentially interested academics will shy away from engaging in this sort of research.

Government Funding Agencies

Providing research funding is equally important toward developing a constituency for problem-oriented work. To a certain extent, federal and state agencies that fund research into crime control and policing shape the academic and private police research agenda. In the U.K., the Home Office has a far more impressive publication record on how police can address crime and disorder problems than its U.S. equivalents.

Private organizations that conduct research on crime and policing, such as the Police Executive Research Forum (PERF), the Police Foundation, Abt Associates, the Institute for Law & Justice, and the Rand Corporation, could contribute to building the body of knowledge on which problem-oriented policing so heavily depends. Both PERF and the Police Foundation in their early years conducted important research into the effectiveness of police responses to various crime and disorder problems. The advancement of problem-oriented policing would be well served if both organizations renewed their commitment to such a research agenda.

To the extent that police officials are motivated to contribute to research knowledge, increasing the volume of funding and publication opportunities for problem-oriented research will help create a constituency within academia and the research community for problem-oriented police work. Many police executives are willing to open their agencies' doors to researchers and to participate in research projects they deem worthwhile, but all too often researchers approach them with research interests that do not speak directly to the police response to crime and disorder problems. There is little reason to think that police executives would not be open to the sort of action research envisioned by problem-oriented policing, which would actually help them better manage crime and disorder problems faced by their agencies. Several recent funding programs — the U.S. Department of Justice's Strategic Approaches to Community Safety Initiatives (SACSI), Locally Initiated Research Partnerships in Policing (LIRPP), Problem solving Partnerships Program, School-Based Partnerships Program; and the U.K. Home Office's Crime and Disorder Reduction Partnerships — are at least broadly speaking, examples of the sort of action research that can potentially add to the body of knowledge so lacking in policing today.

The Media

The media coverage of problem-oriented policing and engagement with the complex issues of crime and disorder control has been disappointing on the whole. The concept has received some important national media coverage in the U.S. — by U.S. News & World Report while the Newport News project was underway, and on a couple of occasions by the New York Times (Malcolm, 1990; Butterfield, 2000, 1999) — and, of course, more regional and local coverage. But the extent and depth of the media's treatment of complex policing issues has done little to advance problem-oriented policing. Admittedly, conveying a set of ideas about something as complex as crime control and policing to a mass audience is not easy. Some of the nation's best journalists have struggled to come to grips with the basic premises on which problem-oriented policing is built.

Police officials are seldom pressed by journalists to provide careful analyses of crime and disorder problems: a few memorable quotes will usually suffice. Occasionally, a news reporter will analyze a crime or disorder problem in an illuminating and helpful way, but then fail to explore why police agencies themselves don't routinely analyze problems thoroughly.

While it is probably too much to expect journalists to sort through and understand all the fundamental issues underlying problem-oriented policing (after all, few police executives do so), the most sensible strategy to engage the media in problem-oriented police work is to continually provide them with examples of problem-oriented policing in practice. The growing body of case studies in problem solving should be distributed to media outlets while they are fresh. Well-written case studies make for compelling reading to those interested in crime, police and local government. Media coverage of the Boston Police Department's problem-oriented policing initiative on youth gun violence is a good example of how good policy made good copy.

Private Industry

By private industry, I refer to those industries that manufacture and market products for police agencies. One need only visit the vendors' bazaar at large police conferences to appreciate how sizable this industry is. Though much of that industry manufactures and markets products that have little relevance to problem-oriented policing — weapons, vehicles, uniforms, duty equipment, and so forth — there is a growing market for information technology, some of which can be quite useful to problem analysis. We have already begun to see private companies develop software and hardware that improves the capacity of police agencies to manage data. And while the manufacturers might at first have only a vague idea, or a misguided idea, about how police might use this technology, smart vendors will be eager to exploit the opportunities that problem-oriented policing potentially presents. When problem-oriented policing experts begin to collaborate with information technology vendors in designing and marketing products that better support problem analysis, the supply of those products will generate some of its own demand as police officials shop for new products in catalogues and at conventions. Private industry has certainly capitalized on other police operational strategies — on emergency response, criminal investigation, and computer-aided dispatching products — and there can be little doubt that the police demand for, and private industry's supply of, these products feed one another. Thus, that sector of private industry that markets to police can become yet another constituency for problem-oriented policing.

Community Groups

Finally, and perhaps most importantly, the public at large represents a constituency for problem-oriented policing yet to be fully developed. The public has long been accustomed to conforming its expectations of police to what police officials have told them is reasonable. The advent of community policing has reshaped some of those expectations. Citizens and community groups have adjusted their expectations of what police can and should do to help them control crime and disorder. In jurisdictions where community policing has been adopted for a number of years, citizens have become more willing to work with police to address crime and disorder and at the same time less tolerant of police excuses for inaction. In Chicago, for example, a neighborhood umbrella group (the Chicago Alliance for Neighborhood Safety) became a forceful constituency in support of community policing, and the community problem-solving training provided to citizens by the police and the Chicago Alliance reinforced that constituency (Skogan et al., 1999). Slowly, the public is beginning to realize that the possibilities for effectively addressing and preventing crime and disorder are considerable; that the range of possible actions extends well beyond simply enforcing the criminal law. As the public gains greater access to data and information about crime and disorder and how it has been effectively addressed in other places, it is to be expected that it will put greater pressure on their local police to make use of that data to develop new response strategies.[10]

CONCLUSION

The perhaps flip, but probably true, answer to the question of what needs to be done to get police to take problem-oriented policing seriously is: everything. That is, everything that is done to align police organizations in a conventional direction must be done to align them in a problem-oriented direction. The whole of the police structure, systems, and culture must ultimately align with a problem-oriented perspective for it to take root (Goldstein, 1990; Bayley, 2001). This might be very difficult to do, but it is rather simple to understand. There isn't one thing that needs to be done, everything needs to be done. Not everything needs to be changed, but everything needs to be aligned, consistent, and coherent. The police organization cannot be made to be working against itself, at cross-purposes.

Police organizations, like most, will align themselves to suit their own interests if their external constituencies are not able to effectively communicate their needs to the organization and create sufficient pressures and incentives so that the organization meets those needs. Therein lies the challenge for the next 20 years of problem-oriented policing: to develop multiple external constituencies for problem-oriented police work such that it will become as unthinkable that police would not have the capacity to analyze problems and implement effective responses as it is that they would not have the capacity to respond to emergencies, handle routine incidents, or investigate crimes. It is perhaps the case that police officials and agencies have taken problem-oriented policing as far as they feel they need to. Without stronger external constituencies, we may have reached the limits of what internal constituencies can and will achieve.

By attending to these three elements of systemic organizational change — improving understanding of the principles and methods of problem-oriented policing and how they relate to the whole police function, enhancing necessary skills sets and knowledge bases, and creating incentives to police in a problem-oriented way through external constituencies — this theoretically-sound concept will have a better chance of achieving its promise.

Address correspondence to: Michael S. Scott, 421 Abercorn Street, Savannah, Georgia 31401. E-mail: <mscott7225@aol.com>.

REFERENCES

Bayley, D. (2001). *Democratizing the Police Abroad: What to Do and How to Do It.* Washington, DC: National Institute of Justice, U.S. Department of Justice.

Berman, G. and J. Feinblatt (2002). "Beyond Process and Precedent: The Rise of Problem Solving Courts." *The Judges' Journal* 41(1):5-6.

Bittner, E. (1970). *The Functions of the Police in Modern Society.* Chevy Chase, MD: U.S. National Institute of Mental Health.

Brodeur, J.P. (1998). "Tailor-Made Policing: A Conceptual Investigation." In: J. Brodeur (ed.), *How To Recognize Good Policing: Problems and Issues.* Washington, DC: Police Executive Research Forum and Sage Publications.

Buerger, M. (1998). "Police Training as a Pentecost: Using Tools Singularly Ill-Suited to the Purpose of Reform." *Police Quarterly* 1(1):27-63.

Butterfield, F. (2000). "Cities Reduce Crime and Conflict Without New York-Style Hardball." *New York Times*, March 4.

—— (1999). "Citizens as Allies: Rethinking the Strong Arm of the Law." *New York Times*, April 4.

Clarke, R.V. and M. Felson (eds.), (1993). *Routine Activity and Rational Choice: Advances in Criminological Theory*, vol. 5. New Brunswick, NJ: Transaction Books.

Dunworth, T., G. Cordner, J. Greene, T. Bynum, S. Decker, T. Rich, S. Ward and V. Webb (2000). *Police Department Information Systems Technology Enhancement Project (ISTEP).* Washington, DC: Office of Community Oriented Policing Services, U.S. Department of Justice.

Eck, J. and W. Spelman (1987). *Problem-Solving: Problem-Oriented Policing in Newport News.* Washington, DC: Police Executive Research Forum.

Feinblatt, J., G. Berman and D. Denckla (2000). "Judicial Innovation at the Crossroads: The Future of Problem-Solving Courts." *The Court Manager* 15(3):28-34.

Felson, M. and R. Clarke (1998). *Opportunity Makes the Thief: Practical Theory for Crime Prevention.* (Police Research Series, Paper No. 98.) London, UK: Home Office Policing and Reducing Crime Unit.

Fogelson, R. (1977). *Big-City Police.* Cambridge, MA: Harvard University Press.

Goldstein, H. (2001). "Problem-Oriented Policing in a Nutshell." Document presented at the 2001 International Problem-Oriented Policing Conference, San Diego, Dec. 7.

—— (1990). *Problem-Oriented Policing.* Philadelphia, PA: Temple University Press. (Also published in paperback by McGraw-Hill.)

—— (1979). "Improving Policing: A Problem-Oriented Approach." *Crime & Delinquency* 25(2):234-258.

—— (1977). *Policing a Free Society.* Cambridge, MA: Ballinger Publishing Company. (Reprinted in 1990 by the University of Wisconsin Law School.)

—— and C. Susmilch (1982). "Experimenting With the Problem-Oriented Approach to Improving Police Service: A Report and Some Reflections on Two Case Studies." (Volume 4 of the Project on Development of a Problem-Oriented Approach to Improving Police Service.) Madison, WI: University of Wisconsin Law School.

International City/County Management Association (2002). "ICMA Declaration of Ideals." (Accessed May 16, 2002.) Available at http://www.icma.org.

Kennedy, D. (1999). "Research for Problem-Solving and the New Collaborations." In: *Viewing Crime and Justice From a Collaborative Perspective: Plenary Papers of the 1998 Conference on Criminal Justice Research and Evaluation.* Washington, DC: National Institute of Justice, U.S. Department of Justice.

Klockars, C. (1985). *The Idea of Police.* Beverly Hills, CA: Sage Publications.

Leigh, A., T. Read and N. Tilley (1996). *Problem-Oriented Policing: Brit POP.* (Crime Detection and Prevention Series, Paper No. 75.) London, UK: Home Office Police Research Group.

Malcolm, A. (1990). "New Strategies to Fight Crime Go Far Beyond Stiffer Terms and More Cells." *New York Times,* Oct. 10.

Moore, M. and D. Stephens (1991). *Beyond Command and Control: The Strategic Management of Police Departments.* Washington, DC: Police Executive Research Forum.

Morison, E. (1966). *Men, Machines, and Modern Times.* Cambridge, MA: Massachusetts Institute of Technology Press.

Phillips, C., J. Jacobson, R. Prime, M. Carter and M. Considine (2002). *Crime and Disorder Reduction Partnerships: Round One Progress.* (Police Research Series, Paper No. 151.) London, UK: Home Office.

Scott, M. (2000). *Problem-Oriented Policing: Reflections on the First 20 Years.* Washington, DC: Office of Community Oriented Policing Services, U.S. Department of Justice.

Sherman, L., D. Gottfredson, D. MacKenzie, J. Eck, P. Reuter and S. Bushway (1997). *Preventing Crime: What Works, What Doesn't, What's Promising.* Washington, DC: Office of Justice Programs, U.S. Department of Justice.

Skogan, W., S. Hartnett, J. DuBois, J. Comey, M. Kaiser and J. Lovig (1999). *On the Beat: Police and Community Problem Solving.* Boulder, CO: Westview Press.

Tilley, N. and G. Laycock (2002). *Working Out What to Do: Evidence-based Crime Reduction.* (Crime Reduction Research Series, Paper No. 11.) London, UK: Home Office.

U.S. Bureau of Justice Statistics (2001). "Expenditure and Employment Statistics: Summary Findings." Washington, DC: Bureau of Justice Statistics, U.S. Department of Justice (www.ojp.usdoj.gov/bjs).

Walt, S. (1987). "The Search for a Science of Strategy." *International Security* 12(1):140-160.

Wilson, J.Q. (1968). *Varieties of Police Behavior.* Cambridge, MA: Harvard University Press.

NOTES

1. Goldstein and others have described the basic elements elsewhere with greater and lesser specificity, so there is nothing definitive about the number 10.

2. Examples of contributing factors to many crime and disorder problems include mental illness, alcohol and substance abuse, and drug trafficking.

3. Large numbers of calls for police service are coded as "disturbances," "suspicious persons," or "noise complaints," thereby masking many different types of problems.

4. See Buerger (1998) for a discussion of the limits of conventional police training methods in achieving significant reform.

5. A new publication series of the U.S. Department of Justice, Office of Community Oriented Policing Services, the *Problem-Oriented Guides for Police*, attempts to synthesize available research and practice related to the police response to specific crime and disorder problems. To date, the series includes guides on the following problems: assaults in and around bars, street prostitution, speeding in residential areas, drug dealing in privately-owned apartment complexes, false burglar alarms, disorderly youth in public places, loud car stereos, robbery at automated teller machines, graffiti, thefts of and from cars in parking facilities, shoplifting, bullying in schools, burglary of retail establishments, burglary of single-family houses, acquaintance rape of college students, panhandling, rave parties, clandestine drug labs, and misuse and abuse of 911.

6. A small, but growing number of jurisdictions are experimenting with practices that are referred to as community prosecution and problem-solving courts: courts that specialize in drug, gun, domestic violence,

mental illness, or public disorder cases and which emphasize alternative sanctions to incarceration (Feinblatt et al., 2000).

7. The police, like the military, do not decide upon strategy in a purely scientific realm; they operate in a political realm in which they see advantages to controlling access to important information that might be used to criticize or compromise their strategic decisions. See Walt (1987) and Morison (1966) for parallel discussions of how military strategy is powerfully shaped by organizational interests, often times in the face of scientific evidence.

8. Moore and Stephens (1991) consider how police administrators might apply a corporate strategy to shape their police agencies' mission and methods of achieving that mission. They describe how organizations naturally seek to provide value to external constituencies in order to maintain or enhance their share of a market, including the market for providing public services.

9. One of the declared ideals of the International City/County Management Association is to: "Develop responsive, dynamic local government organizations that continuously assess their purpose and seek the most effective techniques and technologies for serving the community" (ICMA, 2002).

10. A notable effort is being made by police in St. Louis, MO. to develop a website that makes it easier for the public to access detailed information on crimes and calls for police service such that anyone can begin to analyze that information and perhaps press the police to analyze it and develop more effective responses.*

POLICE PROBLEMS: THE COMPLEXITY OF PROBLEM THEORY, RESEARCH AND EVALUATION

by

John Eck
University of Cincinnati

Abstract: *Advancement of problem-oriented policing has been stymied by over-attention to police organizations and under-attention to police problems. This paper develops a research agenda for understanding police problems by addressing four fundamental questions: What are problems? What causes problems? How can we find effective solutions to problems? And how can we learn from problem solving? For each question a possible direction for theory, research, or evaluation is suggested. The variety of police problems, their non-linear feedback systems, the diversity of responses that can be applied to problems, and the difficulty of learning from problem-solving experiences highlight the complexity of police problems. The paper closes with a list of research questions designed to improve the science and practice of problem analysis and solution.*

WHAT IS THE PROBLEM WITH POLICE RESEARCH?

Problem-oriented policing has become the victim of the disease it was meant to cure, the "means over ends syndrome." Symptoms of this disease include studies examining the internal workings of police organizations implementing problem-oriented policing, confusing problem-oriented policing with community policing, and generally failing to recognize that a new approach to policing requires a different approach to research. Though the number of police agencies applying problem solving has grown rapidly, particularly since 1987, the theory and practice of problem-oriented policing has grown slowly and fitfully. In the absence of leadership and goading from full-time researchers, it is understandable that practitioners did not explore unknown territories and push the boundaries of problem solving (Eck, 2003).

Most police, and community members, when confronted with a problem immediately turn to notions of deterrence and incapacitation. Only when these fail to adequately address the problem, often failing repeatedly, do the police and the public explore something new. An important reason for the development of problem-oriented policing was the overreliance on the criminal law. Yet, to most police, and their publics, it is not immediately clear what the alternative is. In the United States, when alternatives are presented they often take the form of some method for reforming prospective or existing offenders — reaching out to disaffected youth, providing anti-drug education, managing sport and recreation opportunities for teens, and similar programs designed to thwart the development of criminal propensities.

Using the law to sanction offenders or using social programs to forestall criminogenic tendencies is not always ineffective, though many such approaches are ineffective (Sherman et al., 2002). The difficulty is that both approaches are far too limited to have much impact. Further, overreliance on coercive authority has major negative effects on police legitimacy, and the police are singularly ill-equipped to provide effective assistance to potential offenders.

The deficiencies of these approaches have been described elsewhere (Felson and Clarke, 1998). Other work describes why problem-oriented policing has made limited progress and clarifies some of the confusions that have crept into writing and practice (Eck, 2003).

This paper describes how research and evaluation can improve the theory and practice of problem-oriented policing. This paper does not discuss community involvement, multiagency collaborations, and related topics. These are important topics in their own right, they are quite valuable in practice, and they need to be examined. But a paper on the technical nature of problems is not the best place to address these issues. Indeed, most of what this paper describes could be applied by community organizations addressing problems or other governmental agencies, with or without the police. All concerned — not just the police — require a deeper understanding of problems. But a deeper understanding of problems will not come from studies of how police and communities work together (or fail to), or how local government administration can be organized to create partnerships among government agencies.

It is also important to understand that problems are real and have a "life" that is only loosely coupled with people's perceptions of them. Observations that beat cops are concerned with hard crimes, like robberies, but the public is concerned with incivilities, like litter, do not imply that there are not robbery problems, or that robbery problems are really litter problems (nor does it imply the opposite). This paper examines the diversity and causes of problems, not how priorities are set. How priorities are made and who makes them is not the subject of this paper. Ultimately, it will not matter how priorities are set, or who is involved in addressing problems, if we do not understand them and have useful ways of solving them.

Basic Questions

This paper is organized around four basic questions that parallel the SARA problem-solving process. The first section examines how to answer the question, "What are problems?" Until recently, this question has been answered rather simplistically. But recent developments in problem classification reveal an extraordinarily complex world of police problems.

The second section examines the question, "What causes problems?" Until we can provide the police and the public with coherent and useful alternatives to common notions of deterrence and incapacitation, we cannot expect them to routinely solve problems. The thesis in this section is that problems are created by the breakdown of feedback processes that help people regulate potential offenders and potential problem situations.

The third section asks the question, "How can we find effective solutions to problems?" This section introduces a question-based protocol for taking a problem solver through the steps from a description of a problem to applicable solutions. Even a rudimentary prototype problem-solving protocol suggests levels of complexity that neither police nor research have come to grips with.

The fourth section examines the question, "How can we learn from problem solving?" Increasing systematic information exchange among police agencies is part of the answer. Another part of the answer is developing techniques for synthesizing low quality evaluations to provide real time "best" advice to problem solvers. This will be an ambitious undertaking, but there are some clues how we could proceed.

The final section summarizes the implications from these sugges-tions and outlines a research agenda for problem-oriented policing.

WHAT ARE PROBLEMS?

Police problems are typically described as groups of related inci-dents of concern to the community. There are three elements here. First, problems are groups of incidents, not singular events. Second, the incidents in this group are connected in some meaningful way, not random or arbitrary. These two elements suggest that the events that make up a problem stem from the same underlying cause. The third element requires that the incidents be disturbing or harmful to members of the public, not just to the police (Goldstein, 1990; Office of Community Oriented Policing Services, 1998). This definition in-cludes an extensive range of concerns and it provides limited guid-ance to the police or the public. The principal use of this definition is to define the outer boundaries of the problem territory — individual crimes are outside this territory, for example, as are police policies and procedures.

Just as a problem is made up of similar events, so a problem type is made up of closely related problems (Figure 1). If we are confronted with a problem, and we have information from other problems, then we can apply this experience to the new problem. Currently police and researchers do this on an ad hoc basis. But to make greater pro-gress more quickly, we need a problem classification scheme. A problem classification scheme building on Routine Activity Theory has been proposed (Eck and Clarke, in press).

The Eck-Clarke problem classification scheme begins with a dis-tinction between common problems and system problems. Common problems involve offenders coming into contact with their targets (human, animal, or thing). These make up the bulk of problems con-fronted by local police agencies. Two elements are particularly critical for understanding common problems: the behaviors of the people in-volved and the environment (or place) in which these behaviors occur. When offenders do not have to come into contact with their targets, we are dealing with a system problem. System problems are more typically the province of national police agencies and private organi-zations. Though the behaviors are similar, a system substitutes for the environment. A common example of a system problem is a de-structive computer virus. The offender uses a worldwide system to vandalize targets at great distances. A series of mail bombings is an-other example of a system problem.[1]

Figure 1: Events, Problems, and Problem Types

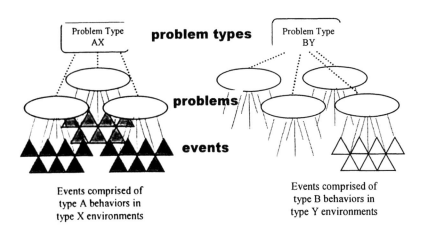

Events comprised of
type A behaviors in
type X environments

Events comprised of
type B behaviors in
type Y environments

To classify common police problems,[2] Eck and Clarke identified six behaviors and eleven environments. The behavioral dimension is important because it draws attention to the way people act, the interaction among participants in a problem, and their motivations. The environmental dimension points to who owns the locations and has control over behaviors of people using the environment. The 66 problem types are shown by the cells formed by the intersection of the two dimensions in Table 1.

This classification scheme requires a revision in the definition of common problems. Not only must a problem involve repetitive related events of concern to the public, but a definition of a particular problem must also include a description of a behavior and an environment. This eliminates from consideration such concerns as neighborhoods (they may contain problems but are not problems in themselves), status characteristics (like loitering or truancy), and other things that cannot be located in this grid. Removing vague concerns and requiring specificity enhances problem analysis and solution identification.

Table 1: The Eck-Clarke Common Problem-Classification Scheme
(Eck and Clarke, in press)

Environments	Behaviors					
	Predatory	Consensual	Conflicts	Incivilities	Endangerment	Misuse of Police
Residential						
Recreational						
Offices						
Retail						
Industrial						
Agricultural						
Educational						
Human service						
Public ways						
Transport						
Open/Transitional						

In the long run, we would expect to be able to link solution types to particular classes of problems with statements like, "If the problem is of type XY then solutions of forms A, B, and C are most likely to be helpful, but solutions of the forms D and E will be ineffective, and solutions of the form F will be counterproductive."

This classification scheme was deliberately kept as simple as possible to make it useful (and it probably cannot be made much simpler and retain its utility). More importantly, it is maybe too simple. Here are some reasons why. First, consideration of system problems could easily double the count of problem types. We propose that the classification of system problems use the same behavioral dimension, but substitute a system dimension for the environments dimension (Eck and Clarke, in press). If there are more than 11 important systems, then the total number of problems will more than double.

Second, there may be other dimensions not considered in this scheme. For example, elsewhere it has been suggested that all problems are of one of four types: repeat offender, repeat victim, repeat place, or a combination of these three repeats (Eck, 2001). It might be useful to add this or some other dimension.

Third, within each of the two existing dimensions, the categories are rather large. These need to be subdivided further. Public ways, for example, consist of highways, roads, paths, and parking lots. And Eck and Clarke (in press) propose three subcategories for incivilities. So 66 problems is small compared to the number of problems we are likely to uncover if this classification scheme is developed further.

As a thought experiment, consider only common problems. Begin with the current classification scheme, but imagine some simple modifications. First, assume that, on average, the column and row headings are divided into three subcategories each, and there is a new third dimension with only four categories. Now the number of possible common problems has grown to 2,376 (=33 x 18 x 4). This number sounds absurdly large.

To see if this number is really absurd, let's look at one cell of Table 1 and see what happens if we probe deeper along each of its dimensions. Predatory-residential problems are reasonably common, so this is a useful example. First, let's subdivide predatory behaviors into:

- Breaking in and taking things;
- Breaking in and attacking people;
- Entering unsecured structures and taking things;
- Entering unsecured structures and attacking people;

- Deceptive entry and taking things;
- Deceptive entry and attacking people;
- Burning structures for profit;
- Burning structures for retaliation;
- Burning structures for intimidation;
- Vandalism for retaliation;
- Vandalism for intimidation;
- and others.

These 11 types of predatory behavior are only some of the forms of the predatory behaviors we might find associated with residential environments. But 11 is enough to make the point that there are many.

Next, let's look at possible types of residential environments. Again, we will only list some of the most obvious types and keep in mind that the list is probably much longer:

- Nursing homes;
- High-rise hotels in cities;
- Motels on highways;
- Single-family residential homes;
- Duplex family residential homes;
- Garden apartment complexes;
- High-rise condominiums;
- Single-room occupancy hotels;
- Mobile home parks;
- Rental vacation cottages;
- Summer homes;
- College dorms;
- and others.

If we combine these two lists, we have 11 x 12 = 132 forms of residential-predatory problems. Some of these 132 problems may be rare "boutique" problems (deceptive entry into rental vacation cottages and attacking people, for example, is probably a rare incident and unlikely to be a frequent problem). Nevertheless, even if many police departments have few encounters with most of these problems, some police department is likely to encounter some of them, and even the rare problems will be familiar to some agencies.

Now, consider expanding each of the column and row elements in Table 1. Finding 10 or more discrete forms of each behavior, and 10 or more distinct forms of each environment is not unlikely. This suggests that each cell of Table 1 could contain, on average, over 100 problems. And this implies that there may be over 6,600 problems. And this number was calculated without consideration of systems problems and without adding any new dimensions.

So rather than being absurd, 2,376 might be a low estimate of the number of problems. But the point of this exercise was not to come up with even a gross estimate of the number of problems. Rather, it was to provide an idea of the level of magnitude of the number of problems. And the reason for trying to get a level of magnitude is to demonstrate how little we know about problems.

But even if there are only 66, it also is clear that we know very little about any of the problem types in the Eck-Clarke classification system, and for most problem types we have virtually no systematic knowledge. Any reasonable modification to the scheme shows that our ignorance is vast.

This exercise demonstrates several important facts. First, there are many problems. Second, we know little about the vast majority of them. And third, taken as a whole, problem solving is extremely complex.

So the first topic in a problem-oriented research agenda is the documentation and cataloging of different problem types. This includes identification of specific problems, their defining characteristics, and methods for usefully classifying them.

WHAT CAUSES PROBLEMS?

We get another hint of how little we know about problems when we examine the causes of problems. Not surprisingly, our ignorance of causes is even greater than our knowledge of the types of problems. This section summarizes and expands the current set of problem theories, once again by drawing heavily on Routine Activity Theory and related theories.

By itself, Routine Activity Theory cannot explain problems; neither can theories that address fewer elements than Routine Activity Theory. Nevertheless, it can help use develop a framework for understanding problems.

Routine Activity Theory is an explanation of crime events. Though it was developed originally to explain macro-level crime trends through the interaction of targets, offenders, and guardians (Cohen and Felson, 1979), it has been expanded over the years to include handlers of offenders (Felson 1986), places (Felson, 1987), and place managers (Eck, 1994, 1995). We can summarize a recent version of Routine Activity Theory (Felson, 1995) with the statement that: a crime is highly likely when an offender and a target come together at the same place at the same time, and there is no one nearby to control the offender, protect the target, or regulate conduct at the place. This is diagramed in Figure 2, where the inner triangle contains the elements necessary for a crime and the outer triangles contain the controllers sufficient for prevention.[3] How can we move from this explanation of events to an explanation of problems?

One possibility is to explain problems by way of offenders. Another is to explain problems by way of targets. So problems could be locations with many offenders or with many targets. Separately, neither of these explanations is adequate, however. First, we need targets and offenders together, at the same time, at the same place. So looking at either targets or offenders alone is inadequate. We need both. Second, we have to explain the absence of controllers — people who can intervene with the offender, target or place and keep the crime from occurring.

Though we cannot explain problems solely on the basis of offenders or targets, examining offenders, targets, and places gives us a starting point in our search for an explanation. The empirical literature illustrates that offenders, targets, and places show highly skewed crime distributions. A few targets, places, or offenders are involved in a large proportion of the problem events, and all problems involve repeat offending, repeat victimization, repeat places, or some mixture of these repeats (Eck, 2001). A pure repeat-offending problem involves an offender attacking different targets at different places. A pure repeat-victimization problem involves a victim repeatedly attacked by different offenders at different places. A pure repeat-place problem involves different offenders and different targets interacting at the same place. This is not a complete explanation (because it does not deal with the controllers) though it does address the first criticism above.

Figure 2: Routine Activity Theory's Crime Triangles

Controllers are at the heart of any useful theory of problems. Or to put it more precisely, problems are created when offenders and targets repeatedly come together and controllers fail to act. It is the breakdown of controllers that is the most important feature of this explanation, as offenders and targets often come together without any problem being created. To see how this breakdown occurs, let's look at Figure 3.

Here we have the same elements as shown in the Routine Activity Triangles along with their lines of influence. Starting on the periphery and working inward we see that the controllers (manager, handler, and guardian) have influence over places, offenders, and targets. These elements together, in turn, directly influence whether a problem event will occur. Going in the other direction we see that the presence (or absence) of a problem event has a direct influence on places, offenders and targets. Problem events have direct, and indirect influence on controllers, depending on the nature of the element being controlled.

Figure 3: Primary Lines of Influence and Feedback

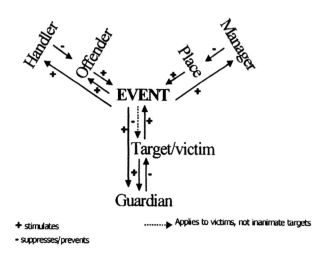

+ stimulates

- suppresses/prevents

........▶ Applies to victims, not inanimate targets

These influences create a number of feedback loops. When a problem event occurs it influences how the offender behaves, which, in turn, affects the chance of another event. The positive signs on the arrows between the offender and event indicate a reinforcement process when the offender is successful and a suppressing effect when the offender is unsuccessful. But we also have to take into account the handler, if present. The offender's involvement in a problem stimulates the handler (positive sign) to suppress the offender's activity (negative sign). The handler might learn directly about the problem events, or from contact with the offender. But in either case, an effective handler will attempt to suppress the offender's problem behavior. Similar processes engage managers, guardians, and victims.

With one exception, all of the loops act like thermostatic controls by dampening crime potential. The exception is the offender-crime loop, which aggravates crime potential when the offender is successful and dampens it when the offender is unsuccessful. So when the complete system of relationship is fully functioning, two things occur.

The offender is reinforced, but the countervailing forces from the controllers (and victim, if we are dealing with a human target) make the place and target less vulnerable. This decreases the chances of the next attack being successful and thereby reduces the number of repeat attacks.

What happens when this system is not fully functioning? Let's begin with the offender. If the offender does not get positive rewards from offending, then the offender will cease to offend. But let's assume that the offender continues to get positive rewards. If any of the negative lines of influence diminish or disappear, then the system will be slower to respond to offender attacks, thereby increasing the chances of subsequent attacks, and increasing the number of repeats. An extreme breakdown is shown in Figure 4, where all of the negative feedback has disappeared so that the target is likely to be continually attacked at the same place. The offender is reinforced. The handler, in this example, is stimulated, but cannot influence the offender. The manager is unconnected with the place, and the place is unaffected by the crime. The absence of a negative influence on the target suggests that the target cannot take effective precautions. And, in this example, though there is a guardian, the guardian cannot influence the target. This might be a diagram of a serious domestic violence problem.

The system just described is far simpler than exists in the real world. One obvious oversimplification is that it does not include learning from the experiences of others. This and other features could be added and would help our understanding. For now it's important to draw attention to the idea that problems occur because offenders continue to get some kind of reinforcement, but those who can do something to stop their troublesome behaviors: a) do not learn about the events, b) choose not to act, or c) cannot act effectively. Such feedback malfunctions are characteristic of all problems.

Pure repeat-offender problems occur when offenders get reinforcement and are able to locate temporarily vulnerable targets and places. The controllers for these targets and places may act to prevent future attacks, but the offenders move on to other targets and places. It is the offender-handler breakdown that facilitates pure repeat-offender problems.

Figure 4: Controller Collapse Due To Feedback Malfunction

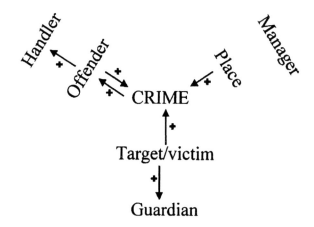

Pure repeat-victim problems occur when victims continually interact with potential offenders at different places, but the victims do not increase their precautionary measures based on past encounters and their guardians are either absent or continually ineffective. The handlers may prevent the offenders from engaging in more of these events, and the managers may improve how they regulate conduct at their places, but the victim moves to other encounters with other offenders at other places.

Pure repeat-place problems occur when new potential offenders and new potential targets encounter each other in a place where management does not change conditions. The setting continues to facilitate the problem events, even though handlers suppress offending and guardians suppress victimization.

It seems highly unlikely that pure repeat problems are extremely common. Instead, there is likely to be some overlap, particularly for serious problems (Farrell and Sousa, 2001). The extent of this overlap is extremely difficult to measure because each repeat is best detected through a different type of data. Repeat offending is best detected through offender interviews and arrest records that do not document the places or victims well. Repeat victims are best detected through victimization surveys, but these will have scant information on places and even less on offenders. Repeat places are best detected through police call-for-service and reported crime data. Even when these sources have information on victims, they seldom capture offender information, unless someone has been caught (Eck, 2001). For this reason, we should not expect precise measures of overlap for all three repeats, though pairs of repeats might be feasible in some circumstances (see, Everson and Pease, 2001).

We should expect offenders, victims, and controllers to generalize from their personal experiences and to learn from the experiences of others. An offender, after successfully attacking a particular target, might seek out other targets that have similar characteristics. Pease (1998) identified the phenomenon of "virtual repeats," which occurs when offenders learn from successful attacks on one target and go on to attack nearby targets. Townsley (2000) has documented this phenomenon in an Australian community. This is similar to the process that gives rise to "hot products" (Clarke, 2000). But generalization may also operate to suppress crime. After unsuccessfully attacking a target an offender might avoid targets with similar characteristics. Offender generalization from their negative experiences helps explain diffusion of crime prevention benefits (Clarke and Weisburd, 1994).

Generalization is probably not peculiar to offenders. Handlers can generalize from one experience to more closely monitor other similar situations in which the offender might get into trouble. Similarly, after being attacked in a particular place, a victim might avoid similar places and his guardian might be more vigilant in these places. A manager might more carefully monitor the behaviors of individuals who bear similar characteristics to prior offenders or victims.

It is not difficult to see how these generalizations on the part of victims and controllers might prevent future problem events. But it is also easy to see how this very same behavior can lead to discriminatory practices aimed at individuals who are not likely to get into trouble. The less precise the information used to make the generalization, the more likely discrimination will arise.[4]

We might imagine each of these actors imbedded in a network of relationships that keeps them informed about the experiences of others. Offenders communicate with other offenders and with others who communicate with offenders. Gang membership is one form of such a network, and this might explain why gang members are more criminally active than offenders not in gangs (Thornberry, 1998). Among college males, social support for aggressive sexual encounters is associated with high rates of forced sex with women (Schwartz et al., 2001). Information about successful and unsuccessful attacks of others changes offender expectations about potential targets and places. Handler networks can help forestall the acts of potential offenders. Potential human targets and guardians might also be part of network that provides information about the attacks on others. Finally, managers can exchange information that helps update them on their places' vulnerability to future attacks. Professional associates often provide such information, and some, like local banking associations, may have institutionalized relationships with the police and other security professionals.

The implication of generalization and networks is that the most successful offenders will have heightened abilities to generalize and learn from the experiences of others. Handlers, victims, guardians, and managers who have limited abilities to generalize and are least connected to networks will be the least successful in preventing problem events. The stability in repeat offending, places and victimization found by Spelman (1994a, 1994b, 1995) is due to the effect of these feedback loops breaking down around victims and places, but being reinforced for offenders.

This discussion of generalization and networks requires us to expand the concept of feedback. The lines of influence shown in Figure 3 are only some of many possible connections that help the participants learn and adapt. For any participant, the less connected they are the less information they will receive, and the less successful they will be.

The breakdown in controllers along with the stimulation of offenders can be readily appreciated in a number of business contexts. Large-scale merchants who do little to prevent theft because they can absorb the costs become repeat victims as offenders learn they are easy marks. Clarke and Goldstein (2002) provide another illustration of this phenomenon. New housing developers in the Charlotte area of North Carolina experienced a large number of thefts of appliances. The appliances were delivered to new housing developments prior to the houses being sold and as a consequence were unprotected after work hours, on weekends, and on holidays. To address this problem, the police tried to persuade the builders to alter the appliance installation schedule so that they would be delivered and connected just before or just after an owner occupied a residence. This approach was somewhat successful. The important point for this discussion is that it was the failure of the builders to change their behavior in the face of offending that allowed the problem to develop. The solution, like the solution to most problems, was to get one of the controllers to change their behavior in response to the offending behavior.

In summary:

- The existence of a problem suggests that some offenders learn how to take advantage of particular situations.

- All problems require the breakdown of one of one or more control systems.

- The systems that break down lead to specific types of repeats — offenders, targets, places.

- And how control systems break down and what can be done to repair the feedback system depend on the problem type and associated behaviors and environments.

This group of propositions presents framework for research and action. It draws attention to problem features that are common across all problems. Still, it is not detailed enough to provide an in-depth understanding of specific types of problems. When one combines this framework with the problem types it is apparent that the propositions are likely to manifest themselves differently in each type of problem. Even if this rudimentary theory of problems is helpful, considerable work is required to adapt it to various problem types.

This system of relationships not only contains a set of feedback mechanisms, but also is nonlinear. The nonlinearity comes from Routine Activity Theory (Eck, 1995). Feedback and nonlinearity suggest that problems are highly complex and maybe chaotic. It is hard to predict the behavior of chaotic systems, though short-term predictions are sometimes possible. The reason for this is that small changes in the system get magnified in unexpected ways (Williams, 1997). The combination of feedback and non-linearity also suggests that the systems may be highly stable under some conditions (Mainzer, 1997). The possibility that some problems may be stable while others are chaotic presents another line of enquiry. But it is a line of enquiry that is very difficult to study in real world settings. Under these conditions, experimentation with simulated artificial problems can be extremely productive (Casti, 1997). For example, Liang (2001) has built a simulation of commercial robbery that can be experimentally manipulated based on the concepts of feedback elaborated above.

This section describes problems as outgrowths of complex adaptive systems resulting from breakdowns in some feedback systems and reinforcement of offender feedback. Adaptation by all of the parties involved should be one of the most important topics of research. The goal should be a unified understanding of the four Ds:

- Desistance — problem reduction;
- Defiance — problem amplification;
- Diffusion — problem contraction; and,
- Displacement — problem spread.

Since these are not mutually exclusive outcomes of problems with multiple actors, research in this area will be difficult and will require us to expand the variety of analytical tools we use.

HOW CAN WE FIND EFFECTIVE SOLUTIONS?

One of the greatest difficulties for problem-oriented policing becomes apparent when one moves from analyzing a problem to responding to the problem. There is no obvious link between these two stages of the problem-solving process. In fact, there is a very large gap and we expect police problem solvers to leap easily across it. One bridge across this gap is the recent series of problem-specific guides developed by the Office of Community Oriented Policing Services of the U.S. Department of Justice (see, for example, Sampson, 2001). How do we know that the data collected point to a specific set of solutions? Or given a particular solution, how do we know that the data support its use? What features of a problem suggest that any one of the 16 types of interventions suggested by Situational Crime Prevention (Clarke and Homel, 1997) has a high likelihood of success, for example?

Currently, we expect beat-level problem solvers (see Goldstein, in this volume) to identify a problem, collect information about it, and develop some insights leading to a solution. We call this professional judgment. As important as professional judgment is to developing a solution, no profession relies on it exclusively. Case studies of problem-solving efforts can improve professional problem-solving judgment. But in most professions more than case studies support professional judgment. It is also supported by theories and sets of protocols that link symptoms, diagnosis and action. With regard to problem solving, a protocol should have four characteristics.

First, the average beat-level problem solver should be able to use it in a variety of settings after some training. Second, the protocol should provide reasonably useful guidance to a broad range of problems. Third, the protocol should be theoretically-based. The previous section described a framework for examining problems. This framework can be used to direct problem solvers' attention to potential responses. Additional theoretical support comes from Offender Search Theory (Brantingham and Brantingham, 1981) and Situational Crime Prevention (Clarke and Homel, 1997). Fourth, the protocol should be question-based, rather than information-based (see also Townsley, in this volume). That is, the problem solver should be asked a series of questions, the answers to which point to possible solutions. A guide that is a compendium of data sources or analytical techniques is far less useful to practitioners, given the variability of data access across police agencies. Finally, the protocol should reveal multiple possible responses, rather than a single response.

Figure 5 provides an example of what such a protocol might look like. It is an extract from a draft protocol (the questions and responses shown here deal with only place managers).[5] To use this protocol requires some basic understanding of the theoretical perspectives noted above. Following a set of instructions, this prototype is divided into two parts. The first part (upper part of Figure 5) is a set of 155 questions about the problem, offenders, handlers, targets, guardians, places and managers. Additionally, it contains questions about tools that offenders, handlers, victims, guardians, and managers use. And it contains questions about movement patterns. A problem solver can attempt to answer some or all of the questions, depending on what she knows about the problem. Most of the questions point to a type of solution (when a "yes" answer is followed by a alpha-numeric code linked to a response). The solutions are listed in the second part of this prototype in 58 broad categories (bottom part of Figure 5). Importantly, these solutions are not detailed plans, but are instead pointers to classes of interventions. It is also possible to begin with a potential solution and work backward to determine if there is sufficient information to support its application.

Here again we see a hint at the hidden complexity of problems, and the corresponding depth of our ignorance. This initial attempt at a general purpose beat-level problem-solving protocol suggests that there is a very broad array of potential solutions, each of which is potentially appropriate in some specific contexts, but few of which are generally applicable to most problems, regardless of context. It is also quite likely that for any particular problem in a specific context, there may be several alternative solutions.

A protocol like this could be used by an individual or by a group, by police officers, community members, or by others involved in beat-level problem solving. If encoded in software with the problem classification scheme described earlier, it could provide links to earlier problem-solving experience that could provide additional guidance. If connected to a problem-solving information system that tracks problem-solving efforts, the guide could facilitate management oversight and training improvements.

This example protocol is based almost totally on theory. As greater empirical knowledge of the types of solutions that are effective (and ineffective) for particular problem types is acquired, the questions and responses can be updated, or even completely replaced. This requires that the police profession improve the way it learns from experience.

HOW CAN WE LEARN FROM PROBLEM SOLVING?

A problem-solving protocol like that described in the previous section is designed to suggest possible actions. Though it is theoretically based, the theoretical foundations applied here are far too general to provide more than a pointer to possible solutions. Two things are lacking. First, we have little empirically-based information about what responses are appropriate for particular problems. Second, there are few empirical tests of responses applied to specific problems. For these reasons, any problem-solving protocol must be supported by systematic evaluations of problem-solving responses. And these evaluations must be synthesized to improve our understanding of what solutions are most appropriate for each type of problem.

Learning what types of solutions work for what problem is a daunting task. We can see how daunting if we make some unrealistically simple assumptions. First, based on the problem classification scheme, let's assume that there are exactly 66 types of problems. Second, based on the draft protocol described above, let's assume that there are only 58 solutions. Nevertheless, 58 solutions applied to 66 types of problem yields 3,828 possible applications of solutions to problems for testing. We have good reason to believe these figures for problems and solutions are low. But because we are multiplying, even small increases in either the number of problems or the number of solutions will dramatically increase the number of combinations.

Figure 5: Example of a Question-based Problem-solving Protocol for Beat Level Problem Solving

A GROUP OF ANALYSIS QUESTIONS...

<u>MANAGERS (M)</u>

131.	Who owns and manages the place?			
132.	Is a manager available who can regulate the behavior of place users?	☐ No ☐ Yes	☐ No	☐ Yes-M1
133.	If NO, can a manager be put into the place?	☐ No ☐ Yes	☐ No	☐ Yes-M2
134.	Do place managers watch activities at the site?			
135.	If NO, can employee surveillance be enhanced?			
136.	What information do managers need?			
137.	Do managers have this information?	☐ No ☐ Yes	☐ No	☐ Yes-M3
138.	If NO, can this information be provided?	☐ No ☐ Yes	☐ No	☐ Yes-M4
139.	Do managers know how to regulate conduct at the place?	☐ No ☐ Yes	☐ No	☐ Yes-M5
140.	If NO, can they be trained or educated to do this?			
141.	Do managers have the authority to regulate conduct?	☐ No ☐ Yes	☐ No	☐ Yes-M6
142.	If NO, can they be provided the needed authorization?			
143.	Are managers around when problem behaviors take place?			
144.	If NO, can management presence be rescheduled?			
145.	Are managers carrying out their obligations and duties?	☐ No ☐ Yes	☐ No	☐ Yes-M7
146.	If NO, can they be compelled to perform them?			
147.	Are rules of conduct established, communicated and enforced?	☐ No ☐ Yes		
148.	If NO, can rules be established, made known, and enforced?		☐ No	☐ Yes-M8

-99-

MANAGEMENT TOOLS (MT)

149. What tools do managers need and use? _____

150. Are these tools available?   ☐ No ☐ Yes

151. If NO, can these tools be provided?   ☐ No ☐ Yes   ☐ No ☐ Yes-MT1

152. Do managers know how to use these tools?   ☐ No ☐ Yes

153. If NO, can they be trained or educated to use these tools?   ☐ No ☐ Yes   ☐ No ☐ Yes-MT2

154. Are the tools functional and effective?   ☐ No ☐ Yes

155. If NO, can the tools be repaired or improved?   ☐ No ☐ Yes-MT3

AND THEIR CORRESPONDING RESPONSE PROMPTS

MANAGERS—tactics that augment the capacity to control crime by people who own and regulate conduct at places.

M1   Identify, select and nominate (e.g., hiring resident managers for rental property) [133]

M2   Surveillance by employees (e.g., putting conductors on busses) [135]

M3   Provide information (e.g., telling landlords about drug dealing on their property) [138]

M4   Educate or train (e.g., teaching park employees how to recognize prostitution activity) [140]

M5   Empower (e.g., providing power of attorney to a third party to handle property) [142]

M6   Schedule (e.g., develop an maintenance schedule that facilitates observations of place) [144]

M7   Compel (e.g., use of nuisance abatement threats to compel landlords to evict drug dealers) [146]

M8   Rule setting (e.g., posting signs on beaches regulating behavior) [148]

MANAGEMENT TOOLS—tactics to help place managers regulate their location.

MT1   Provide or subsidize (e.g., supply paint for graffiti removal) [151]

MT2   Train or educate in use (e.g., showing public housing residents how to use power tools to repair buildings) [153]

MT3   Repair or improve existing tools (e.g., fixing intercom system for residents' visitors) [155]

Three things are readily apparent. First, gaining systematic knowledge about what types of solutions work best for which types of problems, and what types of solutions make things worse for which types of problems, is a task that is beyond the capabilities of any single police agency. However we approach this we know this must be a group effort involving many police agencies and many researchers.

Second, given our experience with randomized experiments, it is clear that we cannot rely on them to make substantial progress at even a modest pace. Randomized trials cannot be applied to problems with small numbers of cases, unless one is willing to wait a very long time or involve large numbers of police agencies in a single experiment. Randomized trials require separable units of analysis — individual people or places that do not communicate with each other. Many problems do not have this characteristic. Randomized trials are often difficult to implement without organizational disruption. When the problem is common and serious and the tested solution is controversial, expensive, or has serious negative side effects, such disruption may be worthwhile. But few organizations will have the stomach to participate in such experiments on a regular basis. A single randomized experiment is insufficient; replication is required. But as the Spouse Abuse Replication Program demonstrated, multiple experiments in the absence of detailed theory may lead to interesting questions, but not necessarily to definitive conclusions (Maxwell et. al., 2001).

Randomized experiments may be the gold standard of drug and medical procedure testing, but can it be the gold standard of crime science? The needs of crime science and the limits on randomized experiments[5] might mean that we have to go off the gold standard.[6] People still use gold as an investment tool, though most of us conduct most of our commercial transactions without it. Similarly we should continue to use randomized experiments in special cases, such as when large claims are made for expensive programs or when interventions may have strong negative side effects, or when a program is otherwise controversial. When program claims are sweeping, randomized experiments perform a very useful pruning function: deflating these claims by pointing out that the intervention does not work well for everyone or everywhere. This is the negative function of experiments (Eck, 2002b).

Randomized experiments also have great utility when the following conditions can be met:

(1) The problem is specific and well defined;

(2) The problem is serious and widespread;

(3) There is a well-defined and tested theory of the problem;

(4) That theory clearly implies a coherent intervention;

(5) The intervention is expensive, has strong side effects, or is controversial;

(6) The theory clearly implies the context in which the intervention will work, and contexts in which it will not work;

(7) Discrete isolated intervention units (people or places) exist in sufficient quantity that an experiment of reasonable power can be applied;

(8) The base rate of the events for these units is high enough that a drop in the number of events can be detected; and,

(9) The experimental intervention closely mimics the form the intervention would take when it is operationalized in everyday practice.

When these conditions are met, a randomized experiment simultaneously tests the intervention and the theory. Conditions one and two limit experiments to clearly defined problems that are common and serious enough that experimentation is worthwhile. When conditions three and four are not met, then randomized experiments can provide a useful method for eliminating ineffective, expensive programs that have become entrenched. Nevertheless, we learn more from experiments if there is a sound theory behind the intervention. Condition five requires that there are real stakes in the outcome. A cheap intervention, with no side effects, that everyone likes is not worth the time and expense of a randomized experiment. Conditions six through eight assure that the experiment can provide meaningful results. The last condition assures us that the experimental conditions are not so artificial that they have no application to real world settings.

This leads us to the third thing we know. We know that police agencies have trouble mounting complex evaluations on a routine basis. Some improvements can be realized, but we cannot expect the same level of rigor we would from a fully funded academic evaluation. In fact, there is a very sound reason for applying weak evaluation designs to problem-solving efforts. If the problem solver is more interested in whether the problem declined than in taking credit for the decline, and has little interest in promoting his particular solution, the problem solver is justified in using a simple evaluation design. Only when the problem solver expects to use the solution again, in a similar context, is a rigorous design, which eliminates most threats to validity, justified (Eck, 2002b). But even in these cases, there are quasi-experimental designs that yield highly valid conclusions (Campbell and Stanley, 1963).

We need to distinguish between two types of response assessments. A basic assessment tries to answer the question, "Did the problem go down?" These assessments do not attempt to determine what caused a drop in the problem. Simple pre-post designs are very practical for answering this question (Eck, 2002a). Extending the length of time for the post-intervention measures can help determine if the problem bounced back or stayed down.

Advanced assessments address the question, "Did this treatment cause the problem to go down?" Interrupted time series and multiple time series designs are the most practical way to address this question.

We need replications to answer the question, "Is the response generally effective or ineffective against this problem type in this context?" Replication requires that we have to compare multiple interventions to the same problem, all in a similar context. In principle, we could apply randomized experiments. But for the reasons listed above, this is not likely to be a practical solution in many situations. Generalization to other settings requires multiple interventions in multiple contexts. Meta-analysis also might be promising, but the instability of the results of such syntheses, due to unmeasured sources of variation, limit their utility (Lipsey and Wilson, 2001).

It is as important to discover *what does not work* against a specific problem in a specific circumstance, as it is to discover what works. In general, many opportunity-blocking tactics appear to be very effective (Eck, 2002c), but we know much less about the specific contexts in which they are ineffective. It is far more useful to know that lighting, for example, is effective under conditions A, B and C but is ineffective in conditions D through G, than it is to come to some global assessment of lighting's effects on crime.

We might be able to obtain positive and negative results from many simple evaluations of interventions, along with some contextual information about the problems and the responses. Unfortunately, most attempts to synthesize findings from multiple evaluations have focused on those evaluations with few methodological weaknesses and have difficulty making sense out of the many weak evaluations. From a methodological perspective, this makes a great deal of sense. But from a practical standpoint, it disposes of a great deal of information. To continue with the gold analogy: it is like only keeping the large nuggets from a gold mine and throwing the small ones and dust out with the tailings. If the gold seam is rich, this makes some sense. But we are working in a mine with few nuggets and a great deal of dust and there is little prospect of this changing. Consequently, we need to be able to glean bits of information from large numbers of weak studies.

The task before us is to devise a method for sharing weak evaluation information among hundreds of police agencies, synthesizing this information, and coming up with robust results that can improve daily police practice. This will not be easy, but there does not seem to be an alternative.

The minimal requirements are as follows.

(1) A system linking hundreds of police agencies in North America, the United Kingdom, Scandinavia, Australia, and other countries where problem-oriented policing is being applied. The World Wide Web is probably the best platform for this system.

(2) A centralized or distributed database of problem-solving efforts conducted by participating agencies. This requires a sponsoring agency or consortium of agencies to provide the staff to maintain the system. The system would have to be subsidized initially, but might be able to charge fees for services once it has demonstrated its utility.

(3) Descriptions of problem-solving projects in two parts: a narrative and a set of quantitative descriptors. A narrative format based on the SARA process, or any similar process, would simplify submissions, collation, and dissemination. A problem-classification scheme would be the basis for indexing.

(4) A standard reporting form for quantitative descriptors of problems, their contexts, how they were identified, analyzed, and responded to, along with descriptions of evaluation methods, measures of effectiveness, and results. A computer-based problem-solving protocol could automatically create such reports.

(5) A process analyzing the database to create rank-ordered lists of possible responses to problems in particular contexts. It would also show what types of responses are unlikely to be effective, or even counterproductive, for particular contexts. Currently, multivariate models are used in meta-analysis, but these might not be suitable for this application. Other approaches may be possible, such as the use of artificial neural networks.

(6) A process for disseminating information about specific problem-solving efforts. This could be automated within a website and using e-mail.

(7) A procedure for commissioning special reports from the database.

None of these requirements appear to be beyond current capabilities. Development of an analytical process (item 5) to synthesize the findings may be difficult. But even here, it might be feasible to start with a crude process and upgrade it overtime as the analytical technology improves.

The greatest challenge will be to assure that negative evaluation results are reported along with positive findings. Despite our interest in successful cases, they are of limited use without counterexamples to which they can be compared. This is true in biology (Dawkins, 1996; Mayer, 2001), engineering (Petroski, 1992), and in science in general (Popper, 1992). It is the unsuccessful cases that allow us see the limits of interventions, reveal where we are ignorant, stimulate us to look further, and provoke our creativity.

WHERE SHOULD WE GO?

This paper outlines a rudimentary theory of problems that draws substantially from Routine Activity Theory. This problem theory involves a hierarchy of events, problems, and problem types which is codified in a problem-classification scheme (Table 1). Events that occur in similar environments, involve similar behaviors, and are linked by the place, target, or offender, belong to the same problem. Problems comprised of behaviorally and environmentally similar events form problem types (Figure 1). Events cluster to form problems and problems cluster to form problem types. Events are of very short duration and usually occur in distinct locations. Problems are longer lasting, sometimes spanning years. Common problems are geographically-bounded. These boundaries include blocks, neighborhoods, cities, and, on occasion, regions. System problems are constrained only by the system's geography. Problem types of any sort have no temporal or geographic bounds. That is, any conclusion one draws about a particular problem type should be applicable to any problem of this type, wherever or whenever they are found.

Linking problem types is a theory of problems. A theory of problems is applicable across all problem types. Problems arise from the repeated coming together of places, offenders, and targets when there are no capable controllers (Figure 2). The repetition stems from positive feedback to offenders and ineffective feedback to one or more of the controllers (Figure 3).

Figure 6: A Hierarchy of Interventions

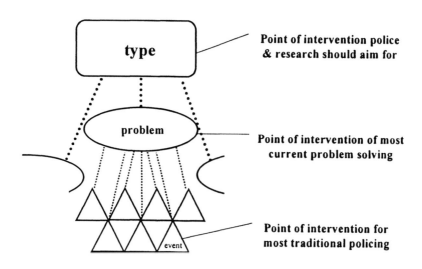

The form of policing that problem-oriented policing seeks to replace — incident-driven policing — focuses most of its attention on events. To the extent that any problem solving is undertaken in incident-driven policing it is erratic and outside the day-to-day functioning of the police agency. Some agencies take on problems as they are identified (and as resources allow), but there is little consideration of the systemic processes that give rise to these problems and how problems are clustered by type. The overall goal of problem-oriented policing has always been to build a knowledge base about types of problems that guides police action at the problem and event levels (Goldstein, 1979). This relationship among events, problems, problem types and the nature of police work is illustrated in Figure 6.

A truly problem-oriented police agency does not just do problem solving. It has systemic processes to learn from problem solving.

This paper attempts to give a sense of how little we currently know, how difficult this undertaking is likely to be, and how many years must pass before we can legitimately claim we have made substantial progress. Police research should focus on the four questions examined here: What are problems? What causes problems? How can we find effective solutions? And, how can we learn from problem solving? A research agenda formed around these questions is rich with possibilities. Some of the questions that such a research agenda might address are:

What Are Problems?

(1) What are the appropriate dimensions?

(2) What problem types are possible?

(3) Are the types useful?

(4) What is the prevalence of problems by type?

(5) What are the symptoms of problems for each type?

(6) What causes problems?

(7) Do different problem types have different relationships among problem elements?

(8) How do these relationships influence feedback?

(9) How does environment influence feedback?

(10) When does victim or controller feedback break down and why?

(11) What preserves effective victim or controller feedback?

(12) What promotes offender feedback?

(13) When does offender feedback break down?

(14) How do offenders adapt to victims and controllers and under what circumstances do desistance, defiance, diffusion, and displacement occur?

(15) What problems are stable, and under what circumstances?

(16) What problems are unstable, and under what circumstances?

(17) What problems are chaotic, and under what circumstances?

How Can We Find Effective Solutions?

(1) Do generic problem analysis protocols lead to effective solutions?

(2) What questions should problem solvers ask to reach effective solutions for specific problems?

(3) How do these questions vary by problem type?

(4) What responses appear to be particularly suitable for specific problem types?

How Can We Learn From Problem Solving?

(1) How can a system to exchange problem-solving information be developed?

(2) What form of database should this system use?

(3) What is an effective way of describing problem-solving efforts that facilitates information exchange and learning?

(4) Can we develop analytical process to synthesize basic assessment results and provide useful information to practitioners and researchers?

(5) What would such an analytical process look like?

Address correspondence to: John Eck, University of Cincinnati, Division of Criminal Justice, P.O. Box 210389, 600 Dyer Hall, Cincinnati, OH 45221-0389 USA. E-mail: <john.eck@uc.edu>.

Acknowledgments: Special thanks to my colleagues Bonnie Fisher and Graham Farrell for their stimulating conversations on many of the topics discussed here. I also owe debts to Johannes Knutsson and Ronald V. Clarke for their very useful comments, and to the other participants at the Kleivstua meeting for their help in thinking through these issues. All errors in this paper are my responsibility.

REFERENCES

Brantingham, P.L. and P.J. Brantingham (1981). "Notes on the Geometry of Crime." In: P.J. Brantingham and P.L. Brantingham (eds.), *Environmental Criminology.* Beverly Hills, CA: Sage.

Campbell, D.T. and J.C. Stanley (1963). *Experimental and Quasi-Experimental Designs for Research.* New York, NY: Houghton Mifflin.

Casti, J.L. (ed.) (1997). *Would-Be-Worlds: How Simulation is Changing the Frontiers of Science.* New York, NY: Wiley.

Clarke, R.V. (2000). "Hot Products: A New Focus for Crime Prevention." In: S. Ballintyne, K. Pease and V. McClaren (eds.), *Secure Foundations: Key Issues in Crime Prevention, Crime Reduction and Community Safety.* London, UK: Institute for Public Policy Research.

—— and H. Goldstein (2002). "Reducing Theft at Construction Sites: Lessons from a Problem-Oriented Project." In: N. Tilley (ed.), *Analysis for Crime Prevention.* (Crime Prevention Studies, vol. 13.) Monsey, NY: Criminal Justice Press.

—— and R. Homel (1997). "A Revised Classification of Situational Crime Prevention Techniques." In: S.P. Lab (ed.), *Crime Prevention at the Crossroads.* Cincinnati, OH: Anderson.

—— and D. Weisburd (1994). "Diffusion of Crime Control Benefits: Observations on the Reverse of Displacement." In: R.V. Clarke (ed.), *Crime Prevention Studies.* (Crime Prevention Studies, vol. 2.) Monsey, NY: Criminal Justice Press.

Cohen, L.E. and M. Felson (1979). "Social Change and Crime Rate Trends: A Routine Activity Approach." *American Sociological Review* 44(3):588-605.

Dawkins, R. (1996). *Climbing Mount Improbable.* New York, NY: Norton.

Eck, J.E. (2003). "Problem-Oriented Policing and Its Problems." In: W. Skogan (ed.), *Community Policing: Can It Work?* Belmont, CA: Wadsworth.

—— (2002a). *Assessing Responses to Problems: An Introductory Guide for Police Problem-Solvers.* Washington, DC: Office of Community Oriented Policing Services, U.S. Department of Justice.

—— (2002b). "Learning From Experience in Problem-Oriented Policing and Situational Prevention: The Positive Functions of Weak Evaluations and the Negative Functions of Strong Ones." In: N. Tilley (ed.), *Evaluation in Crime Prevention.* (Crime Prevention Studies, vol. 14.) Monsey, NY: Criminal Justice Press.

—— (2002c). "Preventing Crime at Places." In: L.W. Sherman, D. Farrington, B. Welsh and D.L. MacKenzie (eds.), *Evidence-Based Crime Prevention*. New York, NY: Routledge.

—— (2001). "Policing and Crime Event Concentration." In: R. Meier, L. Kennedy and V. Sacco (eds.), *The Process and Structure of Crime: Criminal Events and Crime Analysis*. New Brunswick, NJ: Transactions.

—— (1995). "Examining Routine Activity Theory: A Review of Two Books." *Justice Quarterly* 12(4):783-797.

—— (1994). "Drug Markets and Drug Places: A Case-Control Study of the Spatial Structure of Illicit Drug Dealing." Ph.D. Dissertation, Department of Criminology and Criminal Justice, University of Maryland, College Park.

—— and R.V. Clarke (in press). "Classifying Common Police Problems: A Routine Activity Approach." In: M. Smith and D. Cornish (eds.), *Theory for Practice in Situational Crime Prevention*. (Crime Prevention Studies, vol. 16.) Monsey, NY: Criminal Justice Press.

—— and W. Spelman (1987). *Problem Solving: Problem-Oriented Policing In Newport News*. Washington, DC: Police Executive Research Forum.

Everson, S. and K. Pease (2001). "Crime Against the Same Person and Place: Detection Opportunity and Offender Targeting." In: G. Farrell and K. Pease (eds.), *Repeat Victimization*. (Crime Prevention Studies, vol. 12.) Monsey, NY: Criminal Justice Press.

Farrell, G. and W. Sousa (2001). "Repeat Victimization and Hot Spots: The Overlap and Its Implications for Crime Control and Problem-Oriented Policing." In: G. Farrell and K. Pease (eds.), *Repeat Victimization*. (Crime Prevention Studies, vol. 12.) Monsey, NY: Criminal Justice Press.

Felson, M. (1995). "Those Who Discourage Crime." In: J.E. Eck and D. Weisburd (eds.), *Crime and Place*. (Crime Prevention Studies, vol. 4). Monsey, NY: Criminal Justice Press.

—— (1987). "Routine Activities and Crime Prevention in the Developing Metropolis." *Criminology* 25(4):911-931.

—— (1986). "Linking Criminal Choices, Routine Activities, Informal Control, and Criminal Outcomes." In: D. Cornish and R.V. Clarke (eds.), *The Reasoning Criminal: Rational Choice Perspectives on Offending*. New York, NY: Springer-Verlag.

—— and R.V. Clarke (1998). *Opportunity Makes the Thief: Practical Theory for Crime Prevention*. London, UK: Research Development and Statistics Directorate, Home Office.

Goldstein, H. (1979). "Improving Policing: A Problem-Oriented Approach." *Crime & Delinquency* 25(2):236-258.

—— (1990). *Problem-Oriented Policing.* New York, NY: McGraw-Hill.

Leigh, A., T. Read and N. Tilley (1996). *Problem-Oriented Policing: Brit Pop.* London, UK: Home Office, Police Policy Directorate.

Liang, J. (2001). "Simulating Crimes and Crime Patterns Using Cellular Automata and GIS." Ph.D. Dissertation, Department of Geography, University of Cincinnati.

Lipsey, M.W. and D.B. Wilson. (2001). "The Way in Which Intervention Studies Have 'Personalities' and Why it is Important to Meta-Analysis." *Evaluation and the Health Profession* 24(3):236-254.

Mainzer, K. (1997). *Thinking In Complexity: The Complex Dynamics of Matter, Mind, and Mankind.* New York, NY: Springer.

Maxwell, C.D., J.D. Garner and J.A. Fagan (2001). *The Effects of Arrest on Intimate Partner Violence: New Evidence from the Spouse Assault Replication Program.* Washington, DC: U.S. National Institute of Justice.

Mayer, E. (2001). *What Evolution Is.* New York, NY: Basic Books.

Office of Community Oriented Policing Services (1998). *Problem-solving Tips: A Guide to Reducing Crime and Disorder Through Problem-Solving Partnerships.* Washington, DC: U.S. Department of Justice.

Pease, K. (1998). *Repeat Victimisation: Taking Stock.* London, UK: Research Development and Statistics Directorate, Home Office.

Petroski, H. (1992). *To Engineer is Human: The Role of Failure in Successful Design.* New York, NY: Vintage.

Popper, K.R. (1992). *Conjectures and Refutations: The Growth of Scientific Knowledge.* New York, NY: Routledge.

Sampson, R. (2001). *Drug Dealing in Privately Owned Apartment Complexes.* (Problem-Oriented Guides for Police Series, vol. 4.) Washington, DC: Office of Community Oriented Policing Services.

Schwartz, M.D., W.S. DeKeseredy, D. Tait and S. Avi (2001). "Male Peer Support and a Feminist Routine Activities Theory: Understanding Sexual Assault on the College Campus." *Justice Quarterly* 18(3):623-650.

Sherman, L., D. Farrington, B. Welsh, and D.L. MacKenzie (eds.), (2002). *Evidence-Based Crime Prevention.* New York, NY: Routledge.

Spelman, W. (1995). "Once Bitten, Then What? Cross-sectional and Time-course Explanations of Repeat Victimization." *British Journal of Criminology* 35(3):366-383.

—— (1994a). "Criminal Careers of Public Places." In: J.E. Eck and D. Weisburd (eds.), *Crime and Place.* (Crime Prevention Studies, vol. 4.) Monsey, NY: Criminal Justice Press.

—— (1994b). *Criminal Incapacitation.* New York, NY: Plenum.

—— and J.E. Eck (1989). "The Police and the Delivery of Local Government Services: A Problem-Oriented Approach." In: J.J. Fyfe (ed.), *Police Practice in the '90s: Key Management Issues.* Washington, DC: International City Management Association.

Thornberry, T.P. (1998). "Membership in Youth Gangs and Involvement in Serious and Violent Offending." In: R. Loeber and D. Farrington (eds.), *Serious and Violent Juvenile Offenders: Risk Factors and Successful Interventions.* Thousand Oaks, CA: Sage Publications.

Townsley, M.K. (2000). "Spatial and Temporal Patterns of Burglary: Hot Spots and Repeat Victimization in an Australian Police Division." Ph.D. Dissertation, School of Criminology and Criminal Justice, Griffith University, Adelaide, Australia.

Weisburd, D., C.M. Lum and A. Petrosino (2001). "Does Research Design Affect Study Outcomes in Criminal Justice?" *The Annals of the American Academy of Political and Social Science* 578 (November):50-70.

Williams, G.P. (1997). *Chaos Theory Tamed.* Washington, DC: Joseph Henry Press.

NOTES

1. As the events of September 11, 2001 show, the boundary between system and common problems is not clearly marked. In this series of incidents, an international crime organization was able to seize control of a system — commercial aviation — though to do so, some its members had to come into direct contact with their targets.

2. Eck and Clarke (2002) did not attempt to develop a comprehensive classification for system problems. Instead, they show how one can be developed.

3. There has been some speculation on the origins of the inner triangle (Leigh et al., 1996:18, footnote 1). It comes from the collaboration among William Spelman, Rana Sampson, and myself at the Police Executive Research Forum in the early 1990s. Sampson developed the triangle to teach police problem analysis based on earlier work (Eck and Spelman, 1989; Spelman and Eck, 1989).

4. This suggests that one form of discrimination can be characterized as prediction errors — false positives — that fall disproportionately on one group of people.

5. For more information on the draft protocol, contact the author at john.eck@uc.edu.

6. Comparisons of randomized experiments and non-randomized evaluations appear to show a systematic difference in results. Randomized experiments often show smaller treatment effects than their non-random cousins (Lipsey and Wilson, 2001; Weisburd et al., 2001). The one common explanation for this is that non-randomized studies are biased because they cannot control for all possible confounding variables. This leads to the "methods paradox."

Premise 1.	Randomized trials are the most valid method of drawing conclusions about interventions (from experimental theory).
Premise 2.	Systematic reviews of evaluations show meaningful differences between randomized experiments and non-randomized studies, with the randomized results showing weaker performance for the interventions (from results of systematic analyses).
Conclusion A.	Non-randomized studies are biased toward finding stronger effects than randomized studies.
Premise 3.	Systematic reviews are non-randomized studies (from examination of these studies).
Conclusion B.	Differences between the randomized trials and the non-randomized studies are exaggerated by non-randomized systematic reviews.

Conclusion B challenges the truth of premises 1 and 2 or the validity of conclusion A. Regardless of the source of the contradiction, the implication is that randomized experiments may not offer substantial improvements over non-randomized studies. The methods paradox is a variant of the ancient Greek "liar's paradox," so it can be summarized as "A non-experimental study shows all non-experimental findings overestimate their results." Or, in the language of a recent large-scale systematic summary of evaluation research (Sherman et al., 2002), "A level 1 study shows that all studies below level 5 overestimate their results."

THE SEQUENCE OF ANALYSIS IN SOLVING PROBLEMS

by

Deborah Lamm Weisel
North Carolina State University

Abstract: *Traditional crime analysis has limited utility for police problem solving. Such analysis usually involves summary reports and aggregated statistics, primarily of Part 1 crimes, providing little insight into most crime problems. Although technology and techniques such as Geographic Information Systems are increasingly used to address crime and disorder and identify trends and patterns, such methods, which focus exclusively on temporal and spatial relationships, typically lack the rich contextual variables that offer us the potential for understanding problems. These methods are useful for enumerating, establishing prevalence and identifying subsets of problems to be examined. Analysis for problem solving requires an iterative process of developing and testing provisional hypotheses, often through the collection of primary data about community problems.*

Meaningful analysis in problem solving requires a fundamentally different approach than the secondary analyses that dominate crime analysis functions in American police agencies. Indeed, effective analysis of crime and disorder is a major impediment for many police agencies attempting to address community problems.

Traditional crime analysis has limited utility for problem solving. Traditional analysis usually involves summary reports and aggregated statistics, primarily of Uniform Crime Reports Part 1 crimes, providing little insight into most crime problems. Although technology and techniques such as Geographic Information Systems (GIS) are increasingly used to address crime and disorder and identify trends and patterns, such methods, which focus exclusively on temporal and spatial relationships, typically lack the rich contextual variables that offer us the potential for understanding problems. In terms of problem solving, much of what passes as analysis might well be considered as equivalent to scanning — the preliminary selection and confirmation of the existence of a problem (Eck and Spelman, 1987). This paper explores analysis-related functions and practices that can extend and enhance the contribution of crime analysis to solving problems, including the expansion of primary data-collection methods. Regardless of what organizational unit is responsible for analysis of problems, more attention should be given to the *process* of analysis.

For many, the use of the term "analysis" in addressing community problems is misleading. In practical terms, analysis is the systematic collection of knowledge about a particular problem *and* the drawing of inferences from that information. Analysis of problems is often confused with the largely descriptive summary functions resident in many police crime analysis units.

To improve analysis of problems, there does need to be some substantial improvement of structure and access in data collection: police records are not collected for purposes of research and hence suffer from major research limitations. It is widely acknowledged that further expansion of problem solving as a practice would "require a substantial upgrading of the information production and processing capacity of the police" (Mastrofski, 1998:175). That task necessitates devoting resources to research and development (Goldstein, 1990; Reiss, 1992; Mastrofski, 1998).

Within current resources, however, effective analysis requires more thinking and wider participation in primary data collection by crime analysts and others in police agencies. This paper sets forth an analytic approach for systematically examining problems, a process that will enhance our ability to draw inferences from data and inform the development of appropriate responses to problems of crime, disorder and public safety.

GUIDANCE ON ANALYSIS

In principle, analyzing problems is simple and common-sensical (Read and Tilley, 2000; Bynum, 2001).[1] In practice, key analytical tasks necessary for problem solving have not been clearly articulated and sequenced, making analysis an ambiguous process in which objectives are unclear, data are often weak and incomplete, and the process is often compressed and artificially truncated. While there are established practices for social science research, which inform analysis for problem solving, these processes do not closely fit the *practical* requirements for police in examining problems.

To date, insufficient attention has been given to analysis in problem-oriented policing, and it is a process that police often overlook or address superficially (Sampson and Scott, 2000; Scott, 2000; Bynum, 2001; Clarke, 1998). Indeed, Scott (2000) points out that additional guidance on analysis is necessary. For such guidance, one can turn to the extensive analysis guide in Eck and Spelman (1987); the crime triangle (described in Bynum, 2001 and Scott, 2000) which focuses researchers on offenders, victims and locations; or, a recent contribution, Bynum's (2001) guidebook on analysis.

But what exactly do we mean by the term "analysis" in the context of solving problems? Goldstein (1990) says analysis is an in-depth probe about the factors that contribute to a problem. Moore (1992) calls this "thoughtfulness" about problems; Sampson and Scott (2000) also describe analysis as a "thoughtful, in-depth" process. Sherman et al. (1998) says problem-oriented policing is "essentially about insight, imagination and creativity." Bynum (2001) says analysis requires creativity and innovation. Goldstein (1990:36-37) elaborates that analysis is:

> An in-depth probe of all the characteristics of a problem and the factors that contribute to it — acquiring detailed information about, for example, offenders, victims, and others who may be involved; the time of occurrence, locations and other particulars about the physical environment; the history of the problem; the motivations, gains and losses of all involved parties; the apparent (and not so apparent) causes and competing interests; and the result of current responses.

These descriptions of analysis for problem solving are suggestive of a process that may be extremely intimidating for many police practitioners.

Based on published descriptions of problem-solving efforts, we know little about how problem solvers go about analyzing problems. We are, however, keenly aware of the limited contribution of problem analysis in many cases. Part of this absence is attributable to the rational reconstruction of problem-solving efforts. Descriptions of most problem-solving efforts focus on the responses implemented — and results achieved — rather than a retrospective retelling of how they got there. Even more rare are descriptions from practitioners of failed attempts at analysis. Rosenthal (1979) calls this the "file drawer problem," popularizing a term for our tendency to record efforts that show a substantial impact and relegating those without impact to the filing cabinet. Whether we discuss the absence of practical significance or statistical significance related to "failed" analysis, the effect is the same: to reduce by some level the number of problem-solving efforts, hence analytical processes, available for examination. (Read and Tilley [2000], examined problem-solving failures; however their descriptions of the efforts were rudimentary and did not illuminate analytical processes undertaken.) Thus, positive outlooks on problem solving may be due to a process of selective reporting, in which failures are rarely included (Moore, 1992). It is not so much that failures are included or excluded from the problem-solving literature; much of the narrative about analysis in problem solving presents data that do not appear to further our understanding of problems. Not all analyses in problem solving are constructive; however, their blanket inclusion in descriptions becomes a red herring to those who might read problem-solving descriptions for instruction.

Our knowledge of problem solving in written descriptions is also limited by the narrative construction of authors, who exercise selectivity in presenting details of problem-solving practices. It is human nature to report behavior based on positive decision outcomes, which distorts our perspective on the problem-solving process. What are the missteps and wrong turns that successful problem solvers took in analysis?[2] Was the process linear, or as creative and thoughtful, as has been suggested is necessary? The presentation of key facts and information about problem analysis is a rational reconstruction of an inherently untidy process. But the steps of problem analysis can be sorted out somewhat and logically sequenced to provide a model for problem solving. The remainder of this paper makes a preliminary attempt to do just that.

KEY STEPS FOR PROBLEM ANALYSIS

There are three major stages of problem analysis through which most problems will proceed in a somewhat sequential nature. The first phase involves documentation of the problem — justification for undertaking a detailed analysis of the specific problem and determining the appropriate scale or scope of the problem and its investigation. This phase is virtually synonymous with the scanning function described by Eck and Spelman (1987). Police, however, have often been troubled by the distinction between scanning and analysis, including the point at which one ends and the other commences; indeed, the distinctions between the two stages of problem solving may be virtually indistinguishable, one fading into the other by matter of degree. Nonetheless, the tasks of scanning are distinctive and critical to moving forward with analysis. The major steps include parsing, enumeration and establishing prevalence.

The second phase of problem analysis is data collection — typically primary data collection, as it will be quite rare to find that existing data are sufficient to develop an effective response to a problem of substantial size or duration. The last phase involves analysis and interpretation of findings. The stages of analysis are subsequently described and visually displayed in Figure 1.

Parsing of Problems

Clarke and Goldstein (2002) suggest that the "classic pattern" of problem-oriented policing is to address a subset of an original problem: to reduce the problem from its first conception to a manageable subset. This task of data reduction or parsing may involve selecting the largest subset of an identified problem. In their paper, the chosen subset consisted of the theft of appliances from construction sites — an identifiable subset of the larger problem of theft from construction sites, which also included the theft of tools, heavy equipment, supplies and so forth. Each was a subset of the more generalized crime-recorded problem of commercial burglary. The type of property stolen was the key variable upon which existing police data were sorted, and thus it was used as a criterion for parsing.

In many cases, spatial — or temporal — parsing has been established as a primary method of data reduction. The need for parsing varies, often depending on the size of or presumed heterogeneity within the problem. Large scale problems — as reflected by a large volume of calls, incidents or complaints — typically contain variations which can be disentangled. (Although smaller scale problems may also contain variations, the small volume may not permit meaningful disaggregation.) Parsing may precede or follow enumeration. Parsing of problems from existing data is often a practical necessity, and should not be tedious given the widespread prevalence of automated data systems. But, parsing will not always be possible and may in fact suggest difficulty with problem selection if problems are inherently "too small." Clarke (1998) notes that police frequently undertake problems that are too small, and thus are inconsistent with the definition of problem-oriented policing. In this case, police should aggregate up — reverse parsing — to determine if isolated incidents fit some larger pattern of problems. Is the case under investigation an isolated example, or does it reflect a larger pattern?

Figure 1: The Sequence of Analysis

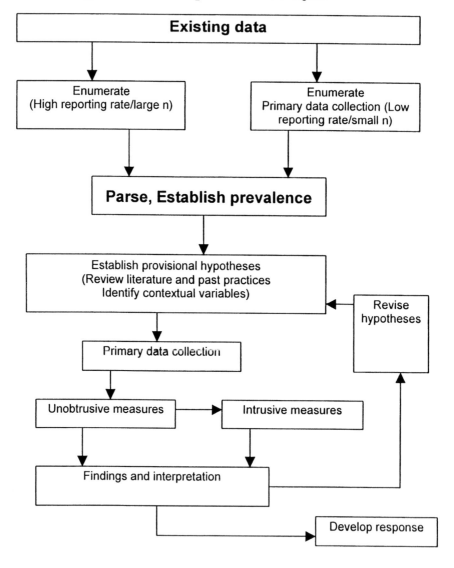

In contrast to small problems, analysis of large problems is complicated by complexities associated with heterogeneity. For example, analysis of a residential burglary problem — among the most numerous of crimes reported to police — may include a range of housing types: apartments, condominiums, public housing, duplexes and single-family housing. Determining, for example, the type of property stolen or the point of entry may bias the analysis toward the housing type that dominates burglaries. If break-ins occur mostly at apartments, sliding glass doors will appear as the most common entry point; if break-ins occur mostly at single-family houses, front doors may be kicked through in a residential version of smash-and-grab. Or contrarily, property stolen from apartments may consist primarily of highly portable goods, such as jewelry and cash, while property taken from houses may include larger electronic equipment, the former being accomplished quite easily on foot with the latter — typically — requiring private transportation.

Parsing the problem into different housing types — or different types of property stolen — permits an independent analysis of the characteristics of burglaries in quite different dwelling types. Since housing types may not be easily extracted in many police data sets, justifying the extra effort of collecting additional data for parsing may take some convincing of practitioners. As Tilley (2002) notes: "Patterns identified at a higher level will be checked out for their relevance at a lower level." The opposite, of course, will apply as we can aggregate — or replicate and validate — lower levels of analysis to build an accurate picture of larger-scale problems in jurisdictions.

Determining where and how to parse a problem is part art, part science. Sometimes natural break points will occur in data, suggesting natural subtypes. Parsing should be sensible. While one can typically easily combine problems at later stages in analysis if the level of parsing is too fine, delaying the desegregation of problems may mask important distinctions within data.

Enumeration

The use of recorded police data is the starting point for analysis for many problems. The routine collection of data by police about problems — recorded crime problems — provides valuable and historic baseline information often over multi-year periods. Based on existing data, we can rather reliably determine how many reported offenses of a single type occurred during any given time period. When engaging in problem solving, police tend to examine crime problems rather than problems related to disorder or public safety (Rojek, 2001). Indeed, the availability of recorded and automated crime data has likely contributed to a predilection of police to undertake problem-solving initiatives about recorded crime problems. It is easiest to examine that which is at hand.[3] For most police agencies, these data on hand include incidents, calls-for-service and arrests. In some agencies, such data may also include field interviews and citizen complaints.

Police data, of course, suffer from many problems, including underreporting, generic classifications, and data entry errors or backlogs. For example, in Charlotte-Mecklenburg Police Department, an agency with a reputation for professionalism, more than half the annual incidents of appliance theft from construction sites were not recorded as such in the agency's records management system, necessitating a manual review of incident reports to compute the correct incidence of the problem (Clarke and Goldstein, 2002). Similarly, reports of graffiti to police in San Diego were recorded as vandalism, requiring an extensive effort to compute the reported incidence of graffiti (Police Executive Research Forum, 2001). In Memphis, TN, a project funded to examine the correlation between crime and crash locations was predicated upon the availability of automated crash data. After an extensive search for the data, the crash records were found — a two-foot pile of paper reports. Miscoding, missing or otherwise limited data are characteristic of police data, rather than being exceptions. For the most part, these limitations can be overcome through manual sorting, reading narrative reports, and supplementing with other data sources such as criss-cross directories and so forth; these steps are extraordinarily time consuming but quite necessary in analysis. Analysts in problem solving must learn to anticipate such data problems and be willing to invest the time and effort necessary to overcome data limitations.

Of course, many problems of concern to police are not sufficiently counted to provide a baseline measure of incidence. While it may be widely recognized that there are problems with speeding, graffiti, loitering, homelessness, bullying, underage drinking, gang-related problems and the like, there is typically no reliable data source about the incidence of these problems. Thus, methods must be established and data collected to enumerate many problems. Enumeration is typically a greater challenge for problems not routinely reported to and recorded by the police.

Analysis of official data about problems often distorts findings in ways we cannot usually detect. Most types of reported crime are substantially underreported: only about 36% of felony crimes are reported in the United States (Walker, 2001), and about half of all crime is reported in Great Britain (Laycock, 2001). For example, residential burglaries are typically reported in about half of all offenses, and underreporting is most common where the offense is attempted but not completed. In what other ways is underreporting distorted?

Burglary victims are less likely to report subsequent offenses if they are revictimized than they are to report the first or initial offense. Thus, examining only data for offenses that are reported may clearly skew our thinking about specific problems; unfortunately, it distorts our thinking in ways that we cannot clearly determine. Similarly with arrest data, because few offenses are cleared up through arrest. For example, 17% of arsons and 19% of larceny-thefts are cleared through arrest in the United States (U.S. Federal Bureau of Investigation, 2000). Are these offenders representative of all offenders for that crime type?

What is the importance — and the contribution to analysis — of offenses that are unreported to the police?[4] Is it possible to enumerate unreported problems? Of course, some enumeration can be achieved through simple counts. In Newport News (VA), officers documented the number of prostitutes in a two-mile area through field interviews, noting that prostitutes were easy to identify through suggestive clothing, congregation in specific areas at certain times, and excessive friendliness (Eck and Spelman, 1987). The investigating officer used field interviews to identify the prostitutes by name and monitored their presence over several months. Other problems require more effort to enumerate. Surveys are routinely used to enumerate the incidence of crime problems. Occasionally, proxies may be used when data are not available for enumeration. For example, motor vehicle crashes may be a proxy for speeding.

The contribution of enumeration in the problem-solving process is easily ascertained; documentation of baseline levels of problems provides a convenient pre-post design — the type missing in many problem-solving efforts.[5] For example, in Newport News, the number of prostitutes working a four-block area dropped from 28 to 6. (Of course, the remaining prostitutes may have been especially prolific; Eck and Spelman failed to estimate the amount of business generated by the prostitutes, the number of hours on the street or other empirical measures of their activity.) However, the decline in the number of prostitutes on the street provided a useful measure of police effectiveness in addressing problems in the area. And there are many other examples in which enumeration provides both baseline and impact measures for problem solving.

Despite the presumptive nature of enumeration, counting of a problem is an inherently critical first step in problem solving: it reveals the scope or scale of the problem. Thus, it may reveal that there are too few instances of a problem to invest a substantial effort, or such a large-scale problem that additional resources should be identified, or that the problem boundaries should be recast and scaled down to be consistent with available resources.

Establishing Prevalence

A recent newspaper article decried underage drinking in bars in Montgomery County (MD). Nearly 100 incidents of underage drinking had been detected in undercover stings in the preceding three years (Becker, 2002). Was that a lot or was it a little? How did that amount compare to prior years, surrounding jurisdictions, or to anything comparable? Simple counts of problems in specific locations often do not provide a sufficient basis for examination of a problem, particularly in drawing comparisons between similar problems in different locations. (Of course, this example is also inadequate because it is a police activity measure not an incidence measure.)

The work of Clarke and Goldstein (2002) suggests that enumerations are not of great value unless an accurate denominator can be determined. (For example, the number of tricks by the prostitutes described previously.) In that article, Clarke and Goldstein needed to know the number of dwellings under construction to use as a denominator for number of thefts. That number could be obtained relatively easily through a review of certificates of occupancy, a government-issued permit. Similarly, for thefts of and from cars in commercial parking lots, the number of parking spaces is useful (see Clarke and Goldstein in this book) — information that may be obtained from parking companies or undertaken through visual assessments. For speeding problems, one must determine the volume of traffic in an area to determine the proportion of speeders.

For some crime and disorder problems, determining a denominator is a challenging task. For example, in examining stops-and-searches — or racial profiling — researchers and policy makers have extensively debated the selection of an appropriate denominator. There is consensus on the numerator — the ethnicity of drivers stopped and/or searched by police. For the denominator, however, should one use the ethnic composition of the resident population of an area, of licensed drivers, of the license-eligible population of an area, of persons engaged in motor vehicle crashes, or the driving population (that is, the persons who actually use the roadways under question)? Of course, each denominator has drawbacks. The ethnic composition of residential populations is relatively easy to determine, even for relatively small areas, using census data. Licensed drivers can be determined spatially; however, the holding of a license may have no relationship to presence on the roadways. Even driving populations — those persons available to be stopped — vary substantially by time of day, and even on roadways quite close to one another. Determining racial characteristics of drivers through observations is very difficult. In other words, determining an appropriate denominator — and collecting data about it — may be a cumbersome task. How necessary is this step? In many cases, it provides critical information about the proportions of the problem. For example, the detection of repeat victimization has little meaning without comparison to those victimized once only and those never victimized. Determining an accurate denominator has the potential to greatly illuminate a problem and point to directions for intervention.

COLLECTION OF DATA

Once the major tasks of documenting, delimiting and verifying a problem have occurred, the analysis process will typically turn to collection of data. This is not a task that should be undertaken without direction. I recall interviewing officers from the Baltimore County (MD) Citizen Oriented Police Enforcement (COPE) unit in the late 1980s (Taft, 1986), who described how they would immediately conduct a standard community survey once a problem was identified. In general, rote data collection tasks will not provide the most precise information about problems. Instead, data collection protocols must be designed for each problem-solving effort; while such efforts should make use of prior data collection efforts, each should flow from the problem being examined.

Testable Hypotheses

The practice of social science research relies on specifying hypotheses and collecting data to test them. Laycock (2000) says we need practitioners to help develop testable hypotheses. In police parlance, these hypotheses may be considered "hunches" about what factors contribute to a problem. Once articulated, a series of working or provisional hypotheses can be examined and empirical data collected to either confirm or falsify the hunches. This process is consistent with social science methods, although in analyzing problems great effort should be made to identify multiple hypotheses, and to revise and re-articulate hypotheses during collection of empirical data.[6] This search for explanation thus consists of the raising and discarding of ideas about the problem.

In this way, problem-solving research is more complex — or adaptive — than much social science research and more consistent with the "grounded theory" described by Glaser and Straus (1967). Grounded theory employs a process of progressive elaboration in which a design "builds up" from substantive facts to a set of theories, which can be subject to testing and verification with empirical methods. Thus, the articulation of testable hypotheses in problem solving will typically follow the processes of parsing, enumeration, establishing prevalence, and preliminary trend or pattern analysis — the exploratory and descriptive methods of research. Once we have established the parameters of the problem under consideration, we can undertake the next phase of analysis, the search for explanation.

A testable hypothesis should be explanatory in nature and conjecture primarily about the "why" of a problem. It should be well understood that testable hypotheses are preliminary in nature. Through primary data collection, the hypotheses will be tested and refined, elaborated or discarded. Only when the preliminary hypotheses are articulated can one identify the appropriate tools for data collection.

Provisional or working hypotheses are not about establishing causality beyond any doubt; instead, the hypothesis should illuminate or add insight to the process of causation. And it is of critical importance that the hypotheses examined are those that are amenable to intervention. Occasionally, the construction of such hypotheses may be quite obvious, but criminal justice researchers have been soundly criticized in the past for ignoring the obvious, and identifying intervention points which cannot be realistically addressed — such as racism, poverty and other deeply rooted social dynamics. This objective of analysis — finding an appropriate intervention — has been called the "pinch point" by Read and Tilley (2000), the "points of intervention" in Bynum (2001), and the "entry point" (Toch and Grant, 1991). Toch and Grant (1991) note that a complex problem may have multiple entry points, while the number of entry points for a simple problem may be singular. Indeed, the search for interventions will likely prioritize possible pinch points based on responses or interventions that are the least expensive and the least coercive.

In this way, analysis for problem solving inherently involves both applied *and* basic research; the first seeks to identify an opportunity for intervention in order to reduce a problem, the latter seeks to measure and understand the problem. Thus, problem-solving research is an "empirical investigation that describes and explains how things behave and how that behavior can be changed" (Reiss, 1992:86).

Identifying Contextual Variables

The articulation of testable hypotheses relies on generating a range of variables that are presumed to be associated with the problem. These contextual variables are factors that have the potential to shed new light on the causal sequencing of the problem being examined. The identification of key contextual variables is not necessarily intuitive, although prior research, expert knowledge of settings, and other factors may point one to important variables that may suggest intervention points.

A review of some recent problem-solving efforts demonstrates the value of identifying key contextual variables:

- *Security practices.* In Charlotte-Mecklenburg, key variables about appliance theft from construction sites included identifying the stage of construction, builder, and security practices employed (Clarke and Goldstein, 2002). In San Diego, a review of management and leasing practices in a self-storage warehouse were the key to a response (Sampson and Scott, 2000).

- *Apartment building size.* In a study of drug dealing locations in San Diego, smaller apartment buildings were used more often by drug dealers than the larger buildings, because the former typically had fewer resources to control behaviors (Eck, 1995).

- *Placement of cash registers.* In the Gainesville, FL convenience store study, stores which had interiors not clearly visible from outside and those with fewer employees had a higher risk of robbery. Robbery risks were also higher when a store's cash register — often by virtue of its placement — was obscured from exterior view (Clifton, 1987).

- *Coin-operated gas meters.* Coin-operated gas meters in public housing in Kirkholt, England, were the frequent targets of residential burglaries. The pay-as-you-go meters provided a pre-set amount of gas for heating and cooking. Although emptied periodically, the meters could hold a large amount of money. Removing them contributed to a 40% decline in burglaries in the first year and a sustained decline over the next three years (Forrester et al., 1988, 1990).

- *Width of aisles in stores.* In a study in England, narrow aisles in shopping markets were found to facilitate purse snatching, as offenders bumped patrons. Consequently, the aisles of the markets were widened and reported thefts declined 44% (Poyner and Webb, 1992).

- *Traffic volume and flow.* Street closings and rerouting of traffic have had a major effect on a wide variety of crimes, according to the review in Sherman et al. (1997). Such changes in traffic patterns have reduced prostitution, drive-by shootings, homicides, violent crime and burglary.

- *Duration of visibility.* Studies of graffiti have shown that decreasing its duration reduces its prevalence. Left to fester, graffiti acts like a magnet for other graffiti. Quick removal of graffiti denies vandals the pleasure of having the graffiti seen. Of course, one can't easily measure the duration of graffiti unless it has been carefully enumerated (Sloan-Howitt and Kelling, 1990).

- *Placement of gas islands.* In Kansas City, MO, the placement of gas station islands influenced the ability of employees to monitor drive-offs and employee theft (Police Executive Research Forum, 2001).

Of course, one wants to identify these key variables as early as possible in the analysis process. To do so early saves time, money and energy. In some cases, the routine examination of recorded crime data may point to key variables. For example, such a routine examination will include point of break in, type of property stolen, proximity to schools, bars or other crime generators, time of day of offense and so forth.

In most cases, a review of the literature is a necessary step for identifying possible variables of interest. Such an examination, for example, for residential burglary would unearth variables such as the presence of an alley, corner location, typical occupancy patterns, traffic ingress and egress, proximity to pedestrian paths, proximity to neighbors, and a host of other variables that have been associated with burglary (Weisel, 2002).

Sequencing Research Steps

The ordering of data collection matters, for both practical reasons and for shedding light on problems. It matters how one proceeds with research. The idea is not to throw out a huge net and reel in whatever gets caught up in the net. Instead, a strategic analytic process will involve sequencing research steps. The general process is to move from the broad to the specific, and do so in a way that information collected and examined in one stage, informs the questions in the next. (The research steps and sequencing are laid out in Figure 1.)

Both Bynum (2001) and Clarke (1998) suggest that analysis be organized to answer the questions of who, what, where, why, when and how? In practical terms, the sequence should consist of what (problem) occurs when (time of day or other temporal dimension) and where (geographic location) and affects whom (victims or offenders)? This examination should also illuminate exactly *how* the problem occurs, but the ultimate objective of analysis is to understand *why* a problem recurs at a particular time and place in the way that it does. In general, we can expect what, when, where and who to be identified through existing databases, and to be examined in preliminary analyses.

Systematic analyses should begin with an examination of existing data: the incident reports, arrests and call data mentioned previously. There are practical reasons for this: the data are available and, since they are largely automated, they are available quickly and can be downloaded to personal computers for examination. For problems that are numerous and are well represented in police data — burglaries, robberies, homicides and the like — this data source is sufficient for enumeration. The data are used to confirm the presence of the problem and begin a preliminary examination for trends within the data. By sorting and classifying the data, we can examine and detect initial patterns of space, time, premises, property taken, offenders' addresses and a host of other variables identified in the data set.

Successful problem solving suggests that analytic tasks cannot occur all at once. A complete examination of secondary data — records of calls, incidents, arrests and other data — should be the first step of analysis. This examination of existing data should be a fairly rigorous examination, in which trends, classifications and explanatory patterns are sought — while recognizing the limitations of the data source. These existing data sources reflect a single perspective (law enforcement), and historic patterns of information-gathering (calls) and police activity (arrests). Thus, these data omit offenses that are unreported, and other key points of view from interest groups such as citizens or businesses, and they reflect the biases associated with arrest patterns. In other words, existing data represents a sample of some unknown population. Despite these limitations, existing data may point problem solvers in the direction to ask key questions about the problem, and will likely suggest ways of prioritizing primary data collection.

For problems which are few in number or otherwise not well-represented in the police data base — domestic violence, graffiti, prostitution, problems with the homeless or mentally ill, and the like — efforts must be made to document or approximate the extent of the problem. This task of enumeration will likely involve primary data collection. The primary method of enumeration includes observation (e.g., of speeders, loiterers, prostitutes or customers in drug markets) or close substitutes such as surveillance, video surveillance, traffic counters and the like. The goal is to approximate what existing data — if available — would demonstrate about the problem: what, where, when, who and how questions. While some problem-solving efforts may be inclined to conduct surveys at this point or engage other high-resource tasks, these are better deferred until more is known about the parameters of the problem.[7]

Upon completion of trend analyses, before much effort has been expended in analysis, problem solvers should parse the problem, usually scaling back the problem under investigation. This parsing will often involve geography — e.g., alcohol consumption in a park (or group of parks), speeding through school zones, gas drive-offs at convenience stores, and the like. But parsing may reflect other sub-categories of existing problems: e.g., homosexual prostitution, motor vehicle theft for parts, or burglary by juveniles. Once the parameters of the problem are established, every effort should be made to establish the prevalence of the problem by determining an accurate denominator.

A review of literature on the problem should occur at this point, as well as a review of past practices to address the problem. The reviews should carefully identify contextual variables that were key elements in other work, in research or prior experience. Clear identification of these variables allows the analysis to determine if the local problem is consistent with other studies or whether variations exist.

And now comes the creative part of analysis: primary data collection. Primary data collection tends to be overlooked and is likely disregarded for a variety of reasons. First, as Caulkins (2000) notes: "We tend to measure what is easy to measure, not just what is important." Primary data collection requires the most resources of any analytic process employed thus far. It can be quite time consuming, and requires careful construction of data collection instruments — sometimes employing outside experts; establishment of sample procedures to be followed; and administration or actual collection of the data. If not well-designed, primary data collection is subject to much criticism.

The creative dimension of primary data collection involves determining the research questions about the problem that remain unanswered through other data, and determining the best way to get answers to these questions. Perhaps a single tool can be used to answer the remaining questions. If multiple tools will be used, it is best to plan these to follow sequentially. For example, interviews with police officers could precede interviews with building managers; interviews with building managers should precede environmental surveys; and environmental surveys should precede a community survey. In this way, resources and interim findings can inform each successive data collection effort. The police surveys may reveal the role of non-residents in a drug problem in an apartment complex. The building owner-manager may reveal management practices that control ingress to properties. An environmental survey may reveal the contribution of lighting or traffic patterns to a contained neighborhood. Thus, the data collected in each wave of data collection are evaluated to determine, and offer questions of greater specificity to be included in, the subsequent data collection tool. This sequencing of data collection and analysis — collect, analyze, revise hypothesis; collect, analyze, revise hypothesis — is intuitive for experienced researchers. However, it needs to be made explicit to offer guidance for problem solvers with less experience.

There are two major types of primary data collection: unobtrusive and intrusive measures. Unobtrusive measures primarily include observation and surveillance; these methods are somewhat broader, however, and may include traffic counters, CCTV, environmental surveys and other devices. Intrusive data collection measures include surveys, interviews, and focus groups — measures that involve face-to-face interaction. If more than one primary data collection instrument is to be used, it is often best to employ non-intrusive measures first, and obtrusive measures last. The practical reason for this is that it is difficult to revise a survey after it has been completed, and it is difficult to reschedule and carry out focus groups and the like. Typically, non-intrusive measures are less expensive and can be replicated, and even expanded; surveys, more complex and much more expensive, are typically a one-shot deal. Just as we favor the least intrusive and least expensive responses, so to do we prioritize analysis tasks, avoiding large investments of time and resources when quicker and cheaper options will answer the same questions.

These latter analysis measures are sometimes more complex and more labor intensive than the preceding tasks and every effort should be made to craft instruments and data collection processes that will answer any remaining questions about a problems. This is sort of the last gig, so it needs to be good. The most technical part of this type of data collection may involve the use of sampling, and this is an element that requires a modest level of expertise. (Of course, if the complete population will be surveyed — all burglary victims, all motel owner-managers, all the residents or businesses around a prostitution problem — then there is no sampling involved.)

Lastly, of course, we examine the overall picture provided by data and draw inferences from it. The goal should be to develop a coherent story about the problem, identifying the key constructions that contribute to its existence as a problem. This should determine the most viable pinch point or point of intervention. All of the data collected will not fit into or contribute to the story about the problem.

Increasing Use of Qualitative Methods

We have described how analysis of problems involves articulating working hypotheses, the search for alternative explanations, ruling out rival hypotheses, and recasting hypotheses. As a result of this iterative process of elucidation and explanation, research on problems is inherently multi-method. Thus, the progression towards "identification of proximal cause" is developmental. Such an approach is consistent with qualitative research designs, which can be employed for primary data collection.

When police think of data, they tend to think of quantitative data. But important qualitative data can be collected about problems, using empirical methods to operationalize and enumerate key constructs. As Schmerler and Velasco (2002) note, police or crime analysts must collect primary data, including qualitative data, to shed light on problems. Such data can illuminate the inherently flawed official records about crime and crime-related problems.

Although data gained through these qualitative methods may be viewed as unscientific, there are established practices that sufficiently increase the validity of collected data. In particular, primary data collection can and should be conducted systematically; for example, observations should be conducted at specific times, and interviews should use established questionnaires. Qualitative research methods can overcome limitations of data availability and resolve some issues related to bias since existing or quantitative data about problems are based primarily on official sources and records such as recorded calls-for-service, reported crime, arrest reports, field interviews and citizen complaints.

Qualitative research has often been viewed as subjective, non-scientific research that is laden with the researcher's own values. Its historical beginnings may have contributed to the stereotype that "anything goes" in qualitative research, stereotyping the social science method as inferior and unscientific. This view of qualitative research continues today. The primary criticisms of qualitative methods include its subjectivity or inherent bias, the absence of sufficient rigor (contributing to weak validity), the inability of the method to establish causality, its inherent unsuitability for answering empirical questions, and limited generalizability. Increasingly, however, most qualitative researchers emphasize the importance of objectivity. Of course, all research methods are vulnerable to bias because there are judgment calls inherent in selecting issues to study, questions to include and subjects to study (Kuhn, 1962; Cook and Campbell, 1979.)

Quantitative studies, especially experimental or quasi-experimental designs, were developed for their capacity to reduce the uncertainty associated with making causal claims. In general, quantitative researchers use Popper's (1959) concept of falsification, "proceed[ing] less by seeking to confirm theoretical predictions about causal connections than by seeking to falsify them." In contrast, qualitative studies aim to develop "the very theoretical constructs which the quantitative research seeks to falsify" (Cook and Campbell, 1979). In other words, one method develops, one method disproves; the former by finding examples, the latter by finding the exceptions. The former involves continuous revisions of classification schemes as additional data are collected, and thus the use of "provisional hypotheses" to suggest lines of investigation. This approach is essential for the conduct of analysis for problem solving.

It is widely accepted that qualitative methods cannot be used to establish causality — but they can inform causal sequencing. Qualitative studies also can be rigorous and rule out numerous threats to validity through a series of verification tactics. Internal validity can be increased by insuring data reliability through a triangulation process of: repeated verification using different kinds of measures of the same phenomenon; corroborating or seeking contradiction of findings from informants; making comparisons between data sets; examining the meaning of outliers, searching for rival explanations and negative evidence; ruling out spurious relationships; and replicating findings.

The rigor of qualitative studies can also be enhanced through the use of systematic processes for data collection, recording and coding of data – generating categories, themes and patterns; data reduction and interpretation; testing the emerging hypotheses against the data; and searching for alternative explanations. Techniques such as pattern matching, comparative studies and cross-site case studies can be structured to collect quantitative data, and thus answer many empirical questions (Glaser and Straus, 1967; Marshall and Rossman, 1995; Miles and Huberman, 1984; Hedrick, 1994; Kirk and Miller, 1986).

Much qualitative data can be converted into quantitative information through coding and counting, permitting the statistical testing of data gathered through qualitative methods. This analysis produces greater explanatory power and greater generalizability. Glaser and Straus claim random sampling is not necessary to discover relationships and is important only if the researcher wishes to describe "magnitude of relationship within a particular group." Indeed, random sampling is not always possible because of our inability to determine the parameters of many populations of interest. Sampling limitations limit statistical validity, but Glaser and Straus (1967:228) point out that data can be verified through the "aggregation and comparison of evidence of different kinds and from different sources."

ANALYTIC TECHNIQUES

In most social science research, we are concerned with the validity of our data: Do the data accurately reflect the phenomenon we intended to measure? Design sensitivity, data measurement and quality are important issues, which are beyond the scope of this paper. But these issues have important implications for analysis — hence evaluation — of problem-solving efforts. For example, the scale of the problem-solving effort has major implications for the type of analyses that may be undertaken. To detect results, problems of sufficient size are necessary to detect effects (see Weisburd, 1993, for a detailed description of this issue) and quantitative data are inherently necessary to measure the magnitude of problem reduction.

The preceding section of this paper describes systematically collecting data about problems. The process of analysis in problem solving, however, is about more than collection of data. To be useful, the data must be interpreted or evaluated in some way to make sense of them. In a 52-page guide for law enforcement published by the U.S. Department of Justice about the analysis of problems, Bynum (2001) dedicates a single paragraph — actually a single sentence — to the actual analysis of data. He suggests that data be analyzed with descriptive univariate statistics (frequency distributions), and two-by-two cross-tabulations of multivariate statistics. Other studies compare prevalence between locations and consist of correlational studies. These are not complex procedures.

Is this an adequate analytical rigor given the extensive efforts in which we have engaged to enumerate and examine the problem? It is true that we can't make statistical inferences from most data collected for problem solving. In many cases, convenience or purposive samples are drawn from populations that do not have established parameters (Maltz, 1994).

The analytic methods employed in recorded problem-solving efforts have varied. In descriptions of the six Herman Goldstein award winners in 2000 at the annual Problem-Oriented Policing conference, no sophisticated statistical analyses were used (Police Executive Research Forum, 2001). The primary method of analysis consisted of reporting frequency distributions. Perhaps the most complex analysis was an examination of gas thefts in Kansas City, MO that compared frequency distributions of offenses between police patrol divisions, and detected the concentration of offenses at three addresses within the patrol division of interest. This analytic task — searching for patterns of temporal and spatial clustering — is a recurring phenomenon in analysis; indeed, classification and sorting of data are the major analytic processes used in problem solving.

To increase reliability and validity of data, most analytic procedures for problem solving — however rudimentary — should include triangulation, to verify and confirm findings, and rule out rival hypotheses or contradictory findings. But how much analysis is necessary? This will depend upon the scope and severity of the problem, but in general analysis should be sufficient to tell a coherent story about a problem.

The level of analytical skills necessary need not be daunting. For example, in Clarke and Goldstein (2002), several analytic processes were undertaken to examine a problem for which there were 109 incidents in the baseline year. The scale of the problem was not huge, and in fact it may be a fairly typical-sized problem-solving effort. The major analytic tasks included the following:

- Collection of reported crime data on theft from construction sites; determination of number involving appliances.

- Identification of low clearance rate for crimes.

- Review of property stolen: type and brand of appliance, plug-in versus hard-wire installation.

- Identification of builders.

- Determination of median loss per break-in.

- Calculation of break-in risks by builder, based on number of occupancy certificates.

- Review of builder security practices.

The list of analytic tasks proceeds more or less chronologically, demonstrating how successful analysis moves systematically in three key ways:

- From an examination of existing data (reported crime) to primary data collection;

- From the broad to the narrow; and

- Building analytic tasks one upon another, suggesting that thought follows each major analytic task.

Thus, although the analytical techniques employed are not statistically sophisticated, the process of concatenation — the coupled sequencing of the analytical process — provided insight into the problem being examined. This sequencing — moving down a cone of resolution — is a key element of analyzing problems.

One of the biggest problems with primary data collection appears to be the absence of a coherent plan for data collection tasks. Based on case studies, there is some evidence that primary data collection efforts of police are highly unfocused.[8] Consider for example, the winner of the 2000 Herman Goldstein award (Police Executive Research Forum, 2001). The case study of addressing a graffiti problem identified a list of major analytic tasks undertaken, included the following in what appears to be the temporal sequencing employed:

- A community meeting in which the graffiti problem was voiced.

- A mapping survey of graffiti, determining the type, location, and offenders (gangs, crews of individuals responsible for tags).

- Research of expenditures on graffiti removal.

- A focus group of 10 convicted taggers, exploring motives.

- Calls-for-service, arrests, type, suspect age, proximity of tagging to suspects' residences.

- A survey of 25 taggers in custody, exploring motives.

- Examination of prior responses, including police response and dispositions.

- Examination of responses by other jurisdictions.

While their data collection efforts were extensive, there is no indication that any analytic task — and its findings — led to any other analytic task. Reading the case study leaves the reader — at least this one! — confused as to the sequencing of the tasks, their thoroughness, and even their purpose.[9] For example, the officers undertook a mapping survey of a two-square mile area, counting more than 300 incidents of graffiti. (This task would be consistent with the practice of enumeration recommended earlier in this paper.) The case study reported that the officers stopped counting at 300, suggesting that the enumeration was not complete and there were more than 300 instances of graffiti. Did this number represent most of the graffiti in the four-square mile police division being examined or a small portion? There is no indication of how the survey was carried out: were major streets, or "hot" graffiti locations sampled or any systematic method of data collection followed? The absence of information about this critical analytic step is suggestive that the data collection occurred haphazardly.

Despite weaknesses in the method of data collection, the data were used as if they were reliable. For example, police examined the relationship between tagging locations, and the routes to and from school of the homes of taggers (presumably homes of the 10 convicted taggers who were part of a focus group). Elsewhere in the case study, police stated "70% of graffiti tags were reported," presumably relating 218 calls-for-service in 1998 to the 300 counted incidents of graffiti, concluding that graffiti is underreported.[10]

Similarly, the report states that 265 of the graffiti incidents appeared at rental housing, while 35 occurred at single-family houses. The counted graffiti on these two building types totals the claimed 300 incidents, but the narrative goes on to describe the prevalence of graffiti at business corridors, in alleys, on dumpsters, poles and boxes, and school walls. It is unclear whether the graffiti on these surfaces and buildings went uncounted and, if so, why?

Importantly, the case study claimed a 90% in reduction of graffiti after a series of responses were implemented. Although not stated, the presumption is that the 300 incidents were used as a baseline measure; the post-intervention measure was described as "an inspection of the neighborhood." The reader might presume that this inspection followed the same data collection path as was used in the original mapping survey, but I suspect such a presumption gives credit where it is not due.

This case study of graffiti efforts was noteworthy: the officers carried out a great deal of investigative work, were wide-ranging in their efforts to collect information, and involved some other agencies in development of their response. They were well-intentioned, committed and showed a sustained commitment to the project over time. They were innovative, and did not leap immediately to an enforcement-based response as often occurs. The judges who selected the project as the Goldstein award winner stated that the "project was exemplary," citing the "dramatically positive" effect of the response (presumably that 90% reduction in graffiti).

Perhaps the most noteworthy aspect of this case study is that it had the *potential* to be an exemplar of problem solving. There was a large problem, high levels of concern, and a high level of commitment from the officers who worked hard on the project. If this is true, what went wrong with this project? The biggest weakness in the case seems to be analysis and the unsystematic manner in which a series of analyses were undertaken. Based on the written narrative, the police undertook the mapping survey fairly soon after a community meeting in which graffiti was voiced as a concern. The mapping survey was used to "quantify the extent of the problem," or validate the concerns expressed by citizens. In hindsight, the officers may have been better served to first review existing data (arrests, calls-for-service and such) about graffiti, and put more development effort into the design of the mapping survey (actually an environmental survey), even tapping the expertise of experts such as crime analysts. The "pinch point" of the analysis was this mapping survey, and its development and administration should probably have shared the rigor often associated with development and administration of a community survey.

The study may also have suffered from a predisposition to focus on active and potential taggers. For example, an analytical task that appeared to have occurred early in the project involved a focus group of 10 taggers, in which a psychologist "counseled" taggers for three months to uncover their motivations and reasons for tagging.

Perhaps the most sophisticated statistical methods to be commonly employed in analysis for problem solving involve community surveys or other data collection methods, which usually involve sampling, and thus inferential statistics. The development of sophisticated data collection instruments also requires a level of expertise in developing neutral questions, determining an appropriate sample, and administering the survey. If the survey is to be administered to a sample, sample selection and size determination is a task in which most practitioners would have little experience.

FUTURE OF ANALYSIS

The future of analysis in solving persistent community problems will involve the dramatic expansion of data collection methods and a rising interest in data-driven decisions. Accountability of police and their relative effectiveness — including cost-effectiveness — are likely to have a strong influence on policy making and police practice in the future. Since problem-oriented policing is dependent on good quality information, knowledge and expertise, the future of problem solving in policing will be dependent upon the "collection, processing, analysis and dissemination of information" (Brodeur, 1998:50). Indeed, the increased availability of computerized data has already transformed decision making in police agencies (Reiss, 1992). Increasingly in the 2000s, new technologies can expand data collection and analysis methods and contribute to our understanding of problems.

A wide variety of technologies are changing the ability of police to collect information about crime and public safety problems. For example, tools such as CCTV, used to monitor traffic conditions and misbehaviors, can also be used as baseline measuring devices of volume, demographics, and road use behaviors. Other technologies may be used to gather information:

- With its Fast Fax program, the Fairfax County Police Department (Virginia) can send important information to hundreds of local businesses in a matter of minutes. A fax might detail a recent robbery and describe the suspect or notify business owners of the next scheduled crime prevention meeting (Waggoner, 1997). This communication may also work for notification of police.

- In some Chicago neighborhoods, community policing officers carry beepers to help them respond to the concerns of local business owners. To divert nonemergency calls from an overburdened 911 system, shopkeepers report such incidents as loitering, shoplifting, panhandling, parking problems, and suspicious activity (Waggoner, 1997). Such data — if recorded and analyzed — provide valuable information to police.

- In Baltimore, nearly 60% of the calls received by the 911 emergency system during 1995 were not emergency calls. During the first year of operation of a 311 non-emergency number, 911 calls for police service declined 24.7%, and the number of calls dispatched declined by 6.6%. Citizen satisfaction rate for request-for-service calls to the 311 center was 98.4%. Although early evaluation data suggested the 311 concept could enhance the police department's community policing goals (Baltimore Police Department, 1997), later studies unfortunately showed that referral data were not tracked (Mazzerole et al., 2002). Data available from 311 systems provide a wealth of information about neighborhood problems that are often difficult to discern from emergency calls.

- Police patrol vehicles are increasingly equipped with cameras. Cameras provide a rich source of information for addressing underlying questions of minority trust and confidence in the police. Thousands of traffic stops are videotaped — and held for up to a year. The tapes provide a rich data source for examining the ways in which law enforcement and those stopped respond to these stressful encounters.

- Video surveillance of drug or other illegal markets can document the way markets operate. In Charlotte-Mecklenburg, center city cameras were able to zoom in and identify a previously unidentified drug market. One of the main sellers would open the hood of his car and fake working on it, to alert buyers that the business was open. This is inherently a qualitative measure. Video surveillance as an unobtrusive measure has potential to further enrich our limited understanding of drug markets and other illegal markets.

- Community surveys have become a routine method for police to gather information from citizens. According to the U.S. Justice Department, 62% of law enforcement agencies conduct citizen surveys to inform police regarding problems of crime and disorder (Reaves and Holt, 2000). Such surveys can be tailored to elaborate citizen perceptions about specific problems, providing a valuable source of information to police and a basis of comparison in different areas.

- Mapping of crime and public safety information is a useful way to sort and represent data, and present information in a way that is easily understood. The increased availability of PC-based mapping software enables most police agencies to engage in mapping crime and disorder, facilitating an examination of problems by time and geography. According to the Justice Department, 68% of law enforcement agencies in the U.S. use computerized geocoded and mapping data (Reaves and Holt, 2000). This includes mapping of arrests, incidents and calls-for-service — with arrest data mapped the least often and incidents the most often.

- The National Incident Based Reporting System (NIBRS) — a system designed to collect more information about crime incidents than UCR — provides a wealth of additional information about crime-related problems, especially victims. According to the Justice Department, 56% of law enforcement agencies in the U.S. are NIBRS-compliant (Reaves and Holt, 2000).

Not since the Uniform Crime Reports were established in the 1930s in the United States have we had such a windfall of information about crime. The locus for much of the increased availability of information will not be crime analysis units as currently configured. Although such units exist in two-thirds of police agencies in the United States (Reaves and Goldberg, 1999), crime analysis units are inherently organizationally decoupled from the police agency. Indeed, 15 years ago Eck and Spelman (1987) criticized the dependence on crime analysis units for problem solving because of the analysts' reliance on existing police records. A core component of problem-oriented policing is research, yet few police departments, if any, have research and development units; instead, the loci for information about crime — crime analysis units — choose to focus on descriptive, aggregate statistics.

In practical terms, analysis should not be relegated to crime analysis units, which may suffer from rudimentary dependence on existing data, are often decoupled from the police agency and its officers, and detached from communities. Nor should analysis be resident among patrol officers, with their penchant for enforcement responses and reluctance to invest the necessary time for careful research. Nor should analysis be entrusted to the hands of academics, who may try to impose excessive rigor, be overly time-consuming (Bynum, 2001), miss the obvious and otherwise provide research that is not relevant for practitioners (Duffee et al., 2000; Laycock, 2000). A former chief of the San Diego Police Department suggested that analysis is best left to the "homework squad" — people who both care and have the capacity to do research. But this too has weaknesses — those who could contribute most and benefit most from the research, are left out of the process (Toch and Grant, 1991). In practice, effective problem solving will invariably involve some combination of these actors, interacting in ways such that each may substantially contribute to developing both an understanding of a particular problem and developing the solution that will be most effective.

Address correspondence to: Deborah Lamm Weisel, North Carolina State University, Department of Political Science and Public Administration, 1307 Glenwood Avenue, Suite 157, Raleigh, North Carolina 27605. E-mail: <dlweisel@social.chass.ncsu.edu>.

REFERENCES

Baltimore Police Department (1997). "Baltimore Police Department Communications Division 3-1-1 Non-emergency Telephone Number First Annual Program Evaluation (October 1996/September 1997)." Baltimore, MD: author.

Becker, J. (2002). "Montgomery Called Lax on Alcohol." *Washington Post,* p.B1 (Feb. 12).

Brodeur, J.P. (1998). *How to Recognize Good Policing.* Thousand Oaks, CA: Sage Publications.

Bynum, T.S. (2001). *Using Analysis for Problem Solving: A Guide for Law Enforcement.* Washington, DC: U.S. Office of Community Oriented Policing Services, Department of Justice.

Caulkins, J.P. (2000). "Measurement and Analysis of Drug Problems and Drug Control Efforts." In: *Measurement and Analysis of Crime and Justice.* (Criminal Justice 2000 series, vol. 4.) Washington, DC: Office of Justice Programs, National Institute of Justice.

Clarke, R.V. (1998). "Defining Police Strategies: Problem-Solving, Problem-Oriented Policing and Community Oriented Policing." In: T.O. Shelley and A.C. Grant (eds.), *Problem-Oriented Policing: Crime Spe-*

cific Problems, Critical Issues and Making POP Work. Washington, DC: Police Executive Research Forum.

——— and H. Goldstein (2002). "Reducing Theft at Construction Sites: Lessons From a Problem-Oriented Project." In: N. Tilley (ed.), *Analysis for Crime Prevention.* (Crime Prevention Studies, vol. 13.) Monsey, NY: Criminal Justice Press.

Clifton, W. (1987). "Convenience Store Robberies in Gainesville, FL: An Intervention Strategy by the Gainesville Police Department." Gainesville, FL: Gainesville Police Department (photocopy).

Cook, T.D. and D.T. Campbell (1979). *Quasi-Experimentation: Design and Analysis Issues for Field Settings.* Boston, MA: Houghton Mifflin.

Duffee, D., D. McDowall, L.G. Mazerolle and S.D. Mastroski (2000). "Measurement and Analysis of Crime and Justice: An Introductory Essay." (Criminal Justice 2000 series, vol. 4.) Washington DC: National Institute of Justice, U.S. Department of Justice.

Eck, J.E. (1995). "A General Model of the Geography of Illicit Retail Marketplaces." In: J.E. Eck and D. Weisburd (eds.), *Crime and Place.* (Crime Prevention Studies vol. 4.) Monsey, NY: Criminal Justice Press.

——— and W. Spelman (1987). "Who Ya' Gonna Call? The Police as Problem Busters." *Crime & Delinquency* 33(1):31-52.

——— and W. Spelman (1987). *Problem-Solving; Problem-Oriented Policing in Newport News.* Washington, DC: Police Executive Research Forum.

Forrester, D.I., S. Frenz, M. O'Connell and K. Pease (1990). *The Kirkholt Burglary Prevention Project: Phase II.* (Crime Prevention Unit Paper no. 23.) London, UK: Home Office.

——— M.R. Chatterton and K. Pease (1988). *The Kirkholt Burglary Prevention Demonstration Project, Rochdale.* (Crime Prevention Unit Paper no. 13.) London, UK: Home Office.

Glaser, B. and A.L. Straus (1967). *The Discovery of Grounded Theory: Strategies for Qualitative Research.* Chicago, IL: Aldine.

Goldstein, H. (1990). *Problem-Oriented Policing.* New York: McGraw Hill.

Hedrick, T. (1994). "Possibilities for Integration." In: C.S. Reichardt and S.F. Rallis (eds.), *The Qualitative-Quantitative Debate: New Perspectives.* San Francisco, CA: Jossey-Bass Publishers.

Hunter, R.D. (1999). "Convenience Store Robbery Revisited: A Review of Prevention Results." *Journal of Security Administration* 22(1):1-14.

Kirk, J. and M.L. Miller (1986). *Reliability and Validity in Qualitative Research.* Beverly Hills, CA: Sage Publications.

Kuhn, T.S. (1962). *The Structure of Scientific Revolutions.* Chicago, IL: University of Chicago Press.

Laycock, G. (2001). "Scientists or Politicians: Who Has the Answer to Crime." Lecture, Jill Dando Institute of Crime Science, University College, London, April 26.

—— (2000). "Becoming More Assertive About Good Research: What Police Practitioners Should Ask of the Academic Community." *Subject to Debate* 14(7):1-4.

Maltz, M.D. (1994). "Deviating From the Mean: The Declining Significance of Significance." *Journal of Research in Crime and Delinquency* 31(4):434-463.

Marshall, C. and G.B. Rossman (1995). *Designing Qualitative Research.* Newbury Park, CA: Sage Publications.

Mastrofski, S.D. (1998). "Community Policing and Organization Structure." In: J.P. Brodeur (ed.), *How to Recognize Good Policing: Problems and Issues*, Washington, DC: Police Executive Research Forum, and Sage Publications.

Mazzerole, L., D. Rogan, J. Frank, C. Famega and J.E. Eck (2002). "Managing Citizen Calls to Police: An Assessment of Non-Emergency Call Systems." *Criminology and Public Policy* 2(1):97-123.

Miles, M.B. and A.M. Huberman (1984). *Qualitative Data Analysis: A Sourcebook of New Methods.* Newbury Park, CA: Sage Publications.

Moore, M.H. (1992). "Problem-solving and Community Policing." In: M. Tonry and N. Morris (eds.), *Modern Policing.* (Crime and Justice series, vol. 15.) Chicago, IL: University of Chicago Press.

Police Executive Research Forum (2001). *Excellence in Problem-Oriented Policing: Winners of the 2000 Herman Goldstein Award for Excellence in Policing.* Washington, DC: PERF and the Office of Community Oriented Policing Services, U.S. Department of Justice.

Popper, K.R. (1959). *The Logic of Scientific Discovery.* New York, NY: Basic Books.

Poyner, B. and B. Webb (1992). "Reducing Theft from Shopping Bags in City Center Markets." In: R.V. Clarke (ed.), *Situational Crime Prevention: Successful Case Studies.* New York, NY: Harrow and Heston.

Read, T. and N. Tilley (2000). *Not Rocket Science? Problem-Solving and Crime Reduction.* (Crime Reduction Research Series, Paper No. 6.) London, UK: Police Research Group, Home Office.

Reaves, B.A. and A.L. Goldberg (1999). *Law Enforcement Management and Administrative Statistics.* Washington, DC: U.S. Bureau of Justice Statistics.

—— and T.C. Holt (2000). *Law Enforcement Management and Administrative Statistics, 1999: Data for Individual State and Local Agencies with 100 or More Officers.* Washington, DC: Bureau of Justice Statistics, U.S. Department of Justice.

Reiss, A.J. (1992). "Police Organization in the 20th Century." In M. Tonry and N. Morris (eds.), *Modern Policing.* (Crime and Justice series, vol. 15.) Chicago, IL: University of Chicago Press.

Rojek, J. (2001). "A Decade of Excellence in Problem-Oriented Policing: Characteristics of the Goldstein Award Winners." Presentation at the Academy of Criminal Justice Sciences annual meeting, Washington, DC (April 6).

Rosenthal, R. (1979). "The 'File Drawer Problem' and Tolerance for Null Results." *Psychological Bulletin* 86(3):638-641.

Sampson, R. and M.S. Scott (2000). *Tackling Crime and Other Public Safety Problems: Case Studies in Problem Solving.* Washington, DC: Office of Community Oriented Policing Services, U.S. Department of Justice.

Schmerler, K. and M. Velasco (2002). "Primary Data Collection: A Problem-Solving Necessity." *Crime Mapping News* 4(2):4-8.

Scott, M.S. (2000). *Problem-Oriented Policing: Reflections on the First 20 Years.* Washington, DC: Office of Community Oriented Policing Services, U.S. Department of Justice.

Sherman, L.W., D. Gottfredson, D. MacKenzie, J. Eck, P. Reuter and S. Bushway (1998). *Preventing Crime: What Works, What Doesn't, What's Promising: A Report to the U.S. Congress.* Washington, DC: U.S. National Institute of Justice.

Sloan-Howitt, M. and G. Kelling (1990). "Subway Graffiti in New York City: 'Getting' Up vs. 'Meaning It and Cleaning It.'" *Security Journal* 1:131-136.

Taft, P.B. (1986). *Fighting Fear: The Baltimore County COPE Project.* Washington, DC: Police Executive Research Forum.

Tilley, N. (2002). "Introduction: Analysis for Crime Prevention." In: N. Tilley (ed.), *Analysis for Crime Prevention.* (Crime Prevention Studies, vol. 13.) Monsey, NY: Criminal Justice Press.

Toch, H. and J.D. Grant (1991). *Police as Problem Solvers.* New York, NY: Plenum Press.

U.S. Federal Bureau of Investigation (2000). *Crime in the United States.* Washington, DC: U.S. Department of Justice.

Waggoner, K. (1997). "Creative Solutions to Traditional Problems." *FBI Law Enforcement Bulletin* 66(8):8-12.

Walker, S. (2001). *Sense and Nonsense About Drugs and Crime* (5th ed.). Belmont, CA: Wadsworth.

Weatheritt, M. (1986). *Innovations in Policing.* London, UK: Croom Helm.

Weisel, D.L. (2002). *Burglary of Single-Family Houses.* (Problem-Oriented Guides for Police Series.) Washington, DC: Office of Community Oriented Policing Services, U.S. Department of Justice.

Weisburd, D. (1993). "Design Sensitivity in Criminal Justice Experiments." In: M. Tonry (ed.), *Crime and Justice: A Review of Research*, vol. 17. Chicago, IL: University of Chicago Press.

NOTES

1. Some authors, such as Weatheritt (1986), suggest that even simple problems may require complex analyses.

2. Clarke and Goldstein (2002) describe two missteps in their analysis of thefts from construction sites: the use of building permits rather than the more precise certificates of occupancy, and problems with a survey of security practices among builders that needed to be revised mid-way in the survey process. Both missteps were corrected.

3. This issue is further characterized by the ongoing debate regarding the proactive versus reactive orientation of police. The availability of recorded crime data rests, of course, on the willingness or ability of people to call the police (Goldstein, 1990); hence police responses to these problems are considered reactive. The extent to which police organizations are proactive has relied primarily on units such as traffic, narcotics, vice, and organized crime because recorded data about the problems addressed by such units is not reliable or representative: it represents convenience samples, changing interests, visibility and other factors.

4. In many ways, the matter of our interest in unreported crime is a practical and an ethical issue. To what extent is unreported crime a concern to police? One concern is that increased efforts result in increased crime, as reported crime tends to increase. Both the British Crime Survey and U.S. National Crime Victims Survey suggest that the proportion of crime reported to police has increased in recent years in the U.S. and Great Britain. Despite protestations to the contrary, we measure much of police effectiveness (or ineffectiveness) by declines (or increases) in reported crime.

5. Sherman et al. (1998) note that the inclusion of a pre- and post-test would strengthen many research designs. The inclusion of a matched comparison group is also made possible through enumeration, and would further strengthen research designs.

6. Much social science research focuses on the testing of a single hypothesis or two, and may exclude alternative or rival hypotheses.

7. Bynum (2001) suggests surveys should be conducted very early in the analysis process since they tend to be time consuming; however, given limited resources and the difficulty in repeating a survey once more is

known about a problem, I advise waiting until secondary analyses have been completed, and non-intrusive and/or inexpensive data collection has occurred, and findings established. One can easily repeat these steps if necessary, but surveys are difficult to revise or repeat.

8. This appearance may in fact be an artifact of police writing about their problem-solving efforts.

9. The review of this case study of graffiti is not intended to criticize the officers who engaged in an extensive amount of work. It is used as an example because it was the *winner* of the Goldstein award, presumably an exemplary effort, yet suffers from major analytic weaknesses.

10. In most places, 70% reporting would not be considered to be a large amount of underreporting.

THE ROLE OF RESEARCH AND ANALYSIS: LESSONS FROM THE CRIME REDUCTION PROGRAMME

by

Karen Bullock
Research Development and Statistics Directorate,
U.K. Home Office

and

Nick Tilley
Jill Dando Institute of Crime Science
University College, London

Abstract: *The British Crime Reduction Programme ran from 1999 to 2002. One of its streams, the Targeted Policing Initiative, was specifically concerned with fostering problem-oriented policing. Fifty-nine projects were funded at a cost of some £30 million, over two rounds. This paper outlines the ways in which projects were agreed and reviews the analyses contained in the bids for funding. As with previous British and American accounts of analysis in problem-oriented policing, the extent and quality of the work undertaken was found to be rather limited. Several possible implications of this pattern of findings are outlined and discussed. First, despite the difficulties uncovered, it does not follow that problem-oriented policing is fundamentally flawed and should be abandoned. Second, problem-oriented policing may require substantial increases in agencies' capacities for the required forms of analysis. Third, the Crime Reduction Programme may have provided inadequate and inappropriate support for problem-oriented policing, and thus comprises a flawed test of police analytic potential. Fourth, differing types of problem addressed by a problem-focused police agency may require varying types of analytic skill, not all of which could realistically be expected within a police agency.*

Crime Prevention Studies, vol. 15 (2003), pp. 147-181.

Introduction

This paper focuses on the British police service's capacity for problem specification and analysis in the context of a national crime reduction program, one stream of which was intended in particular to encourage and enable problem-oriented policing. The paper provides an overview of relevant bids for funding prepared under the auspices of the program, and looks in more detail at what was considered the best-evidenced bid. The findings are set in the context of British and American reviews of problem-oriented policing projects and of the implementation of problem-oriented policing more generally. The conclusions are not encouraging. The bids continued to show rather limited analysis in attempting to deal with the substantial and recurrent problems that were targeted. Some potential implications are outlined and discussed.

THE CRIME REDUCTION PROGRAMME

The British Government's Crime Reduction Programme was a three-year initiative that ran between 1999 and 2002. The program spent around £400 million over this period (including over £150 million on closed-circuit television [CCTV]) on crime reduction projects and their evaluation.

The decision to fund the program was informed by a review of existing research (Goldblatt and Lewis, 1998), which identified crime reduction lessons learned to date and knowledge gaps that the program might usefully fill. The Crime Reduction Programme aimed to improve the evidence base about:

- what works in reducing crime;

- rolling out and mainstreaming crime reduction projects; and

- the cost-effectiveness of crime reduction projects.

To this end a variety of funding streams were established, within each of which a series of projects ran. Table 1 shows a breakdown of the main funding streams, allocated funding and the areas that the stream covered.

In addition, just under £20 million was spent in a variety of other areas, including partnership development, vehicle crime awareness-raising, a series of web-based crime reduction tool kits, and grants to Rape Crisis and the Suzy Lamplugh Trust.[1] The rest of the £400 million in funding was spent on research and development.

Table 1: Streams of the Crime Reduction Programme

Initiatives	Projects	Total Allocated	Use of Funding
CCTV	683	£169,000,000	For funding schemes nationally.
Targeted Policing	59	£30,000,000	For helping the police to develop and implement a problem-oriented approach.
Reducing Domestic Burglary	246	£24,000,000	For targeting neighborhoods in England and Wales with high burglary rates.
Drug Arrest Referrals	1	£20,000,000	For the development of face-to-face arrest referral schemes that aim to impact upon drug-related offending in England and Wales.
Treatment of Offenders	1	£14,362,000	For a range of initiatives to develop effective practice in working with offenders.
Effective School Management	38	£10,330,000	To integrate approaches to improving schools' management of pupils' behavior and reducing truancy and exclusion.
Violence Against Women	58	£9,655,000	To fund projects on domestic violence, rape and sexual assault.
Youth Inclusion	70	£8,620,000	For Youth Inclusion schemes.

continued

Table 1 (continued)

Initiatives	Projects	Total Allocated	Use of Funding
Locks For Pensioners	1	£8,000,000	For improvements to home security for pensioners living in low income households in neighborhoods suffering high domestic burglary rates.
Neighbourhood Wardens	85	£6,000,000	To develop a strategy for neighborhood renewal.
Vehicle Crime	13	£5,218,000	For improvements to vehicle licensing and registration systems.
On Track	26	£4,390,000	To identify and assist children and families at risk of getting involved in crime.
Sentencing	3	£3,900,000	To develop the evidence base for sentencing and enforcement practices.
Summer Schemes	147	£3,600,000	For diversion schemes during school holidays in low income areas.
Design Against Crime	4	£1,570,000	To encourage crime-resistance in the planning and design of goods services and buildings.
Distraction Burglary Projects	3	£1,010,000	For projects aimed at reducing distraction burglary amongst the elderly.
Distraction Burglary Taskforce	1	£1,000,000	For staffing of dedicated policy team to reduce distraction burglary.
Tackling Prostitution	11	£871,000	For local agencies working within a multi-agency context to implement local strategies for reducing prostitution-related crime and disorder.

THE TARGETED POLICING INITIATIVE AND PROBLEM-ORIENTED POLICING

The Targeted Policing Initiative was one of the larger funding streams within the Crime Reduction Programme. Thirty million pounds was allocated to 59 projects. These aimed to reduce a variety of crimes not specifically addressed in other funding streams, using a problem-solving and problem-oriented methodology, drawing on the tenets first set out by Herman Goldstein (Goldstein, 1979, 1990). The intention was to build on the problem-oriented and problem-solving policing styles currently being espoused by many British police forces (Read and Tilley, 2000; Her Majesty's Inspectorate of Constabulary [HMIC], 2000).

The first experiments in problem-oriented policing (POP) in Britain occurred in the Metropolitan Police in the mid-1980s. Sporadic efforts took place in the following years to introduce it in various places, but it failed fully to take root anywhere. A demonstration project in Leicestershire in the mid-1990s was, however, associated with renewed interest (Leigh et al., 1996, 1998). Since that time there have been growing numbers of police services committed to operating along problem-oriented principles. Problem-oriented policing has also been officially advocated in Britain as an effective and efficient way of reducing crime (HMIC, 1998, 2000). At the time of writing few, if any, British forces would repudiate it as a form of policing to which they aspire.

Despite a relatively long history of efforts to introduce problem-oriented policing in the U.K. (and some successes in specific initiatives), a range of implementation problems have been consistently encountered (Leigh et al., 1996, 1998; Read and Tilley, 2000; Irving and Dixon, forthcoming). A recent national overview found that though there was almost universal support for problem solving in the police force, high quality problem solving was still exceptional (Read and Tilley, 2000). Common problems have included:

- weaknesses in data analysis, limited data sharing and shortages of analysts;

- inadequate time set aside for problem solving;

- a focus only on local low level problems;

- crudely operated performancc indicators;

- inattention to and weakness of evaluation; and

- inadequate partnership involvement.

Through the special funding being made available, the Targeted Policing Initiative was designed to provide the incentives and wherewithal to show what could be achieved by adopting a systematic problem-oriented approach in relation to substantial issues.

Applying for Funding under the Targeted Policing Initiative

Applying for funding from the Targeted Policing Initiative posed a test for the police and their partners. In order to receive funding, bidders were expected to show that they were able to apply problem-solving principles. It was hoped that the resources available would encourage, enable and motivate police forces to spend time identifying and analyzing significant problems and developing responses to them based on the analysis. In addition, funding was partly dependent on partnership involvement in the proposed scheme.

Police forces, in conjunction with local crime and disorder reduction partnerships (CDRPs), were invited to submit proposals for funds through two rounds of competitive bidding. They had roughly a month to prepare their initial bids, though there was scope for later elaboration.

Round One began in 1999. Police forces and their partners completed a basic application form. This asked the project:

- to provide a description of the problem that they sought money to tackle;

- to indicate how the problem related to the findings from local crime and disorder audits and strategies;

- to show how the problem related to the local policing plan;

- to spell out how the problem would be tackled, specifying in particular whether the project would make use of:
  - structured crime/incident data,
  - new structures/arrangements, and
  - innovative tactics;

- to show what crime reduction targets could be achieved;

- to note related initiatives;

- to list other factors affecting the area; and

- to indicate what resources would be required.

A group of Home Office researchers and policy officials reviewed proposals and made recommendations to ministers about which projects to fund.

Ten projects received funding in the first instance, though an eleventh was supported later following extensive revisions to the proposal. Researchers, including external academic consultants, paid a one to two day visit to the personnel involved in each of the projects funded, to discuss the proposal and view the site where the project was to be implemented. The team of researchers then prepared a report on the proposals with recommendations for revisions, which normally included calls for clarification and explanation for the proposed action. The project staff then revised their original proposals and it was these revised proposals which were put to ministers to obtain funding. In most instances the changes made were minor, though in a couple of cases they were substantial, including the one case where the funding decision was carried forward to the following year.

The second round of competitive bidding for funded projects began in 2000. Of 170 proposals that were received, 27 were recommended for funding. There were differences in the way that proposals were selected between Round One and Round Two. In Round Two, projects were asked to submit an "expression of interest" rather than fully developed proposals. Projects filled in a form including the following:

- an outline of the size and the nature of the problem;

- a description of why the problem was worth tackling;

- an explanation of why the problem was amenable to a problem-oriented approach;

- objectives/targets for dealing with the problem;

- possible interventions to tackle the problem;

- an outline of funding required;

- details of planned or ongoing initiatives;

- a timetable.

After a preliminary assessment by Crime Reduction Team staff in Regional Government Offices, Home Office researchers and officials scored the expressions of interest. The following factors were considered:

- innovation: i.e., were novel interventions or adaptations of established interventions to a different type of problem proposed? And was anything new added compared to projects funded under Round One?;

- potential applicability of findings to other areas and forces;

- sustainability of the proposed solution;

- value for money (in terms of the seriousness of the target crime and the likely impact on that crime, and the lessons that might be learnt from the project);

- suitability for evaluation; and

- whether the project was eligible for funding under a different Crime Reduction Programme stream.

The top-scoring 51 expressions of interest were discussed by an assessment panel which consisted of Home Office researchers and policy teams, staff from Her Majesty's Inspectorate of Constabulary, and a representative from the Association of Chief Police Officers. The Local Government Association was invited, but was unable to take part. In addition to the criteria set out above, the panel aimed to select at least one project dealing with each of following:

- property crime

- vehicle crime

- drug related crime

- violent and/or racially motivated crime

- and fear of crime and anti-social behaviour.

As a secondary consideration, if possible it was hoped also to achieve a geographical spread of funded projects across England and Wales.

Home Office staff and external academics again made a series of visits to the 27 projects recommended for funding, following these sifting processes. The aim of these visits was to work through the proposals with those making them to ensure that the projects were targeted and that the police and partners had the support and capacity to implement them properly. The visits were rather more pro-active than those that had been conducted in Round One. Evaluation teams looking at first round projects were already identifying problems in project implementation. The idea of the Round Two visits was to provide supplementary advice about the proposal, especially in relation to problem analysis and targeting the interventions, in order that future implementation difficulties were anticipated and minimized. The proposals were then re-drafted and submitted for ministerial approval. All in all, this process took about six months.

It should by now be clear that a number of criteria were used in determining whether to fund the proposed initiatives. These reflected the dual — research and service delivery — purpose of the Crime Reduction Programme. The projects were expected to be consistent with past research (hence research-aware), to be innovative (hence capable of yielding fresh findings), and to be focused on substantial problems (hence making a significant impact on an important problem). They were also expected to address a given range of issues and to provide funds across the country. The criteria for selection were thus only partially concerned with the quality of the initial problem-analysis.

Table 2: Targeted Policing Projects Not Selected by Competitive Bidding

Project	Initiative	Reason for Funding
Rural crime	Tackling cross-border crime and repeat victimization in three rural forces.	Fear of crime following the shooting of a burglar in Norfolk.
Knowsley Basic Command Unit (BCU) project	Suspension of "ordinary" performance indicators. Academic and technical support to highlight and tackle local trends in crime.	To assess the impact of problem-oriented policing.
Manchester gun project	Problem-solving project aimed at tackling serious gang-related violence in South Manchester.	Interest from Manchester police following successful project in Boston, USA.
National problem-solving training	Dedicated problem-solving team to develop and deliver training to officers at middle-management level on deploying a problem-solving approach. Research and maintenance of a good practice database.	To disseminate good practice. To provide support for forces seeking to implement POP.
The Pathfinder Project	Application of enhanced DNA techniques and other evidence gathering to volume crime.	To investigate the potential benefits from extending the collection and analysis of DNA trace evidence.

A number of other projects supported by the Targeted Policing Initiative did not have to compete for funding in the same way. For example, police forces or related agencies could actually apply for funding at any time, though few did so outside the two rounds of competitive bidding described so far. Moreover, some work was funded under the Targeted Policing Initiative that did not originate from local areas. A selection of projects that were supported financially outside the two rounds of competitive bidding, is shown in Table 2.

The Evaluation of the Targeted Policing Initiative

In keeping with the aims of improving understanding of what works and what is cost effective in reducing crime, 10% of the Targeted Policing Initiative budget was originally allocated for evaluation. All of the Round One projects were evaluated by teams of external academics and consultants, who were selected by competitive tender in late 1999.

It had originally been intended that all the funded projects would be subject to independent evaluation. There were changes, however, in the amount of money available for the evaluation of Round Two projects. At the end of 2000 it was decided that a higher proportion of the money should be spent on implementing projects and correspondingly less on evaluation. Thus provision for independent evaluation was made for only nine of the 27 Round Two projects. Home Office researchers evaluated a number of the projects and the rest went out for competitive tender, as with the evaluation of Round One projects. The decision to evaluate a project or not was based on answers to the following questions:

- Did political imperatives suggest that evaluation was unavoidable?
- Was the initiative targeting a key knowledge gap?
- Was it a good quality proposal, with
  - decent problem analysis
  - a proposed solution that was linked to problem analysis, and
  - a realistic planned timetable and resource use?
- Was implementation failure likely?
- Was evaluation failure likely because:
  - insufficient data were available or collectable, and/or
  - other initiatives were likely to interfere with outcomes in intervention area?

Though initially there was some disappointment that funding was insufficient for evaluation of all 27 funded Round Two projects, in the event it was felt that provision to evaluate all that might yield useful findings had been made.

Data Analysis in Round One and Round Two of Competitive Bidding for Funding

The Experience of Round One

Ten projects were funded initially under Round One. These ten proposals were examined for the data sources used, and the extent and forms of initial analysis undertaken. As successful proposals, the 10 were amongst the better ones that were received in the first round. Table 3 shows all of the data sources used in the successful Round One proposals.

The table shows the very limited use made of differing data sources to develop the interventions for Round One proposals. Of these ten successful proposals, two included no data or analysis of any sort. Of the eight that did contain data, three of them did not include any information on recorded crime or disorder. Of the five that contained crime or disorder data, four made use of recorded crime data and two of incident data.

Whilst the table demonstrates the limited sources of data presented in the proposals, it does not show that even where data were available, there were often very limited analyses of them. For example, only one of the proposals managed to identify patterns of repeat victimization using crime data. This was in relation to crime against businesses. Most of the recorded crime or incident data identified nothing more than the total number of recorded crimes of a particular type. Four of the five that included crime or incident data identified changes in numbers of recorded incidents over more than one year. Two gave the specified crime types as a percentage of all crime.

The story is similar for the few proposals that used police data sources other than recorded crime. The one proposal that made use of arrest data merely presented the total number of arrests for the crime type of interest. Similarly, in the one proposal that used information on detections, only the total number of detections for the relevant crime type was included. There was not even, for example, a calculation of the number of detections or arrests as a proportion of the total number of recorded crimes of that type.

Table 3: Data and Analysis Included in Successful Round One Proposals

Problem/proposed project focus	Recorded crime data	Incident data	Fear of crime survey	Repeat victimi- sation	Arrest data	Detection rates	BCS	Audit	Complaints	Demo- graphics
Reduction in market for stolen goods (2 projects)	✓									
Fear of crime in rural areas			✓							
Crack Cocaine dealing			✓	✓	✓			✓		
Vehicle crime	✓					✓				
Alcohol-related crime	✓						✓			✓
Car crime	✓	✓					✓			✓
Race crime in four boroughs										
(a)			✓					✓		✓
(b)										
(c)			✓							✓
(d)			✓							✓
Disorder		✓							✓	
Disorder in children's homes										

The use made of the non-police data sets was even more limited. One proposal referred to complaints to the local authority as a measure of a disorder problem, but did not say how many there were, just that there were a lot of them. Three referred to fear of crime surveys, but merely to state that there were "high" levels of fear of crime. None had survey data that corresponded exactly to the area where the project was to be based. Three provided some form of demographic data, but not one used the information to work out rates.

The analyses included in the successful proposals for Round One funding, which were on the whole the better ones, were, thus, very limited.

The Experience of Round Two

Ninety-seven Round Two bids were looked at systematically by an external consultant (see Bullock et al., 2002). The proposals were scored on various dimensions including, among others, numbers of sources of evidence used, quality of analysis, and relevance of analysis to targeting of interventions. No evidence was presented in 13% of bids, and only police data in a further 55%. In 31% of the bids there was no analysis of the data to define the nature of the problem, and in a further 46% the analysis was deemed only very basic. In only 2% of the bids were the interventions considered well-targeted in the light of the analysis. Thus, across the board the Round Two bids were found to have made relatively little use of data, to have included only limited analyses, and to have proposed interventions that were rarely well-targeted in the light of analysis.

Twenty of the unsuccessful proposals received for Round Two funding were also randomly selected and reviewed individually. In addition, 10 of 27 successful proposals were also selected randomly and examined for data sources used in them.

Table 4 shows the crime data used in the 20 unsuccessful proposals that were selected.

Of these 20 unsuccessful proposals, 13 contained crime data (12 recorded crime data and one incident data). As in Round One, most of the proposals did little more than present the total number of a specific crime type. Eight of the 12 that included recorded crime data showed the changes in specific categories over time. Six proposals looked at counts of recorded crimes in comparison to counts elsewhere. Five used percentages — normally the specified crime problem as a proportion of all crime. Only two of the 12 contained rates of crime and two identified patterns of repeat victimization. Of those proposals that included recorded crime data, on average they went back 2.3 years.

Table 4: Crime Data and Analysis Included in a Sample of Unsuccessful Round Two Proposals

ID	Totals	Percentages	Rates	Change	Seasonal/ temporal changes	Repeat victims	Comparisons	Years of data
1	√							1
2								0
3	√					√	√	1
4								0
5	√			√			√	1
6	√			√				0
7	√	√						2
8	√	√						3
9	√	√		√		√	√	3
10	√				√		√	1
11								0
12								0
13			√	√	√		√	3
14	√	√					√	1
15	√			√				2
16								0
17	√	√		√				4
18	√		√	√				4
19								0
20	√			√				3

As with Round One, little use was made of data other than those for recorded crimes. One proposal used incident data. Yet this related to only one year, and what was presented was simply the total number of calls-for-service. Of the other forms of police data used, one proposal made use of arrest data, one of information on detection and one other used police intelligence. Four proposals used other information from police sources, including property recovery rates and numbers of known sex offenders.

Six proposals used data from non-police sources. Most commonly this comprised a fear of crime survey (three of the six). Other sources of information came from the probation service and drugs teams, and a couple estimated the costs of crime. Nine of the proposals used some kind of context data, most commonly measures of population or deprivation. But as in Round One, not one used this information to calculate rates.

Table 5 shows the crime data presented in the 10 sampled successful Round Two proposals.

Though Table 5 shows that as many as half did not make use of recorded crime data at all, this partly reflects the type of problem being addressed. In fact, over all slightly better use was made of data. The crime data listed here were not really relevant, for example, for the financial investigation project, which was primarily aiming to increase the assets seized by the courts. Similarly the repeat offenders project focused on identifying prolific offenders through intelligence, evidence for which was provided. The violence in hospitals proposal used health authority data relating to the number of assaults against staff in the hospitals over four years. This was partly because these data were more easily accessible, though it was also because hospitals often do not report incidents to the police. The antisocial behavior project that did not make use of recorded crime data did make use of complaints to social landlords.

Where recorded crime data were provided, all the proposals went further than merely providing total counts of relevant crime types. Three of the five identified the percentage of that crime type as a proportion of all crime. The alcohol related violence project in particular provided quite detailed analysis of the problem at a local level. It identified "hotspots" and compared local levels of crime with recorded national levels. None of the proposals made any use of incident (calls-for-service) data, despite the fact that three were addressing antisocial behavior.

Table 5: Crime Data and Analysis Included in Successful Round Two Proposals

Project	Totals	Percentages	Rates	Change	Seasonal/ temporal changes	Repeat victims	Comparisons	Number of years
Violence in hospitals								
Antisocial behavior 1								
Repeat offenders								
Financial investigations								
Antisocial behavior 2	✓	✓						1
Hate crime	✓			✓				1
Antisocial behavior 3	✓	✓						1
Alcohol-related violence	✓		✓		✓		✓	1
Drugs 1	✓	✓						1
Drugs 2								

All 10 of the sampled successful Round Two projects made some use of non-police data sets and other information, but probably no more so than the Round Two unsuccessful projects. Three proposals included data on the target problems from other sources. One used assault data from hospitals, as already indicated. Both of the antisocial behavior projects included complaints to social landlords as a measure of the size of the problem. Five of the projects included demographic and other context information about local deprivation.

However, as in Round One and in the unsuccessful Round Two projects, with the exception of the alcohol-related violence project, proposals did not tend to make use of data, crime or otherwise, for purposes beyond that of estimating the size of the target problem. None of the sampled proposals made any effort to examine repeat victimization. Only one identified rates or hot spots.

Over all, Round Two bids performed slightly better than those in Round One in terms of the scope of data sources used and the detail of the analysis undertaken, but the improvement was not great.

The Best Bid

One TPI bid stood out from the rest for the breadth and depth of its analysis. It seems unlikely that any British force could have done much better at the time without external help. The analysis the bid contains thus shows the limits of what was likely to be achieved at the time.

The problem to be addressed related to drugs and prostitution in one local authority with a population of roughly 200,000. The targeted drug problem concerned crack cocaine across the local authority. The prostitution problem was located in one specific area, comprising some 10,000 residents in about 4,500 dwellings.

A wide range of crime data was provided, comparing the 23 wards that made up the local authority. The data covered:

- monthly domestic burglary counts, rates (by dwelling) and ranks for 1997-98, 1998-99, and 1999-2000;
- annual domestic burglary counts and percentage changes over three years;
- monthly robbery counts, rates (by population) and ranks for 1999-2000;
- annual robbery and personal theft counts and percentage changes over three years;
- monthly theft from person counts, rates (by population) and ranks for 1999-2000;

- annual theft from motor vehicle counts and percentage changes over three years; and

- monthly theft from motor vehicle counts, rates (by population) and ranks for 1999-2000.

Non-crime background data were also provided, again comparing wards. Tables here related to:

- unemployment (for all and by age group and by period of unemployment);

- education and skills (semi and unskilled heads of household, residents aged over 18 with qualifications, pupil profiles);

- health (mortality, birth weight, health deprivation index etc.);

- housing (flats/apartments, rooms, bedsits, social services referrals, benefits claimants, etc.);

- poverty (income support claimants, job seekers allowance recipients, family credit claimants, free school meal recipients etc.); and,

- indices of local deprivation.

These data, alongside some qualitative evidence, showed the target area for the prostitution-related project to be relatively disorderly and deprived by the standards of the local authority.

As well as this information, there was more detailed analysis of the presenting problems and their relationships to one another.

Drugs

In relation to the drugs issue, health authority and police data were interrogated. Data were provided on numbers of callers on drug advisory services with crack as their main drug, numbers of needle kits issued, and the breakdown of clients by age, sex and gender. Further health diagnosis team data were provided estimating numbers of referrals where crack was of primary concern. Police data were presented on drugs seizures, drugs offences, and drug-related crime by time and type, and by the age, sex, ethnicity, address and previous crimes of offenders. Police intelligence was drawn on to clarify the travel patterns of those coming to the local authority to buy illicit drugs.

Attributes of the 72 crack houses identified by the local police intelligence unit were looked at in some detail. Their geographic concentration, customer profile, apparent proximity to transport nodes, forms of tenure, types of accommodation, and occupant prostitution and drug-taking behaviours were described. The frequent discovery of stolen goods during raids, the role of prostitutes as drug runners, and reports of intimidation of nearby residents were also emphasised.

Prostitution

The current location for the problem of prostitution was explained in part as a function of displacement from a nearby area, where efforts to design out prostitution had been implemented some years previously.

Community concerns over prostitution that had been raised with police officers were noted. These included:

- men discomfited by walking past/being approached by prostitutes;
- women discomfited by kerb-crawlers;
- caretakers, parents and teachers concerned at children finding condoms and needles in playgrounds;
- community concern at "sex litter" in parks;
- adverse effects on property values;
- noise, including hooting, car door slamming and highly audible price negotiation between prostitutes and clients;
- sights of overt sexual activity;
- associated problems of crime and disorder; and,
- signs of prostitution leading to perceived danger to residents and neighborhood decline.

Police data on prostitution and kerb-crawling were presented, including:

- incidents of prostitution by time — month, day of week and time of day;
- incidents of prostitution by place — street, part of street, nearness to station, and impressions of proximity to street drinking and needle find locations;
- prostitute attributes, including age and repeat offending patterns; and,
- kerb-crawler ethnicity, age, and (lack of) repeat offending.

A strong link was drawn between prostitution and the crack houses. This was not just because prostitutes acted as drug runners.

They were also found to be customers for drugs, and they accepted payment in drugs for sexual services.

In the course of the analysis various references were made to ways in which the data might mislead, for example because patterns could reflect police activity rather than the distribution of problem behaviors. Some variations in ways of interpreting the material were highlighted. For example, the association of transport nodes, crack houses and robbery might, it was suggested, reflect either the flow of potential victims from stations or the movements of the many customers of crack houses. Appropriate comparisons were made with the findings of relevant, previously published research studies.

The major conclusions drawn from this analysis, notwithstanding the acknowledged data problems and uncertainties over their interpretation, were that:

- the borough had a significant and increasing drugs problem;
- crack houses comprised a "closed" market for crack; and,
- there was a link between prostitution and crack.

The proposed strategy was:

- to disrupt the drugs market and prevent its re-establishment, targeting crack houses in particular;
- to disrupt the relationship between prostitution and crack;
- to remove the association between prostitution and the area in which it flourishes; and,
- to prevent any further area in the local authority developing the same set of problems.

This was to be achieved by:

- periodic intensive policing efforts, including "sustained high visibility patrol";
- provision of exit strategies for prostitutes wishing to change and leverage on those not wishing to do so in the form of Anti-Social Behavior Orders (ASBOs);
- environmental improvements to make prostitution more difficult;
- enforcement activity against crack houses; and,
- support for the community and environmental improvement to prevent the re-establishment of crack houses.

This analysis stood out from others in several respects. There was more use of available recorded crime data. Both quantitative and qualitative materials were used. Several complementary data sources were drawn on. The patterns described went over several years. The account of the results refers to other published research to put local findings in context. The data are treated with proper caution — their reliability and validity are not taken for granted — but nor are they summarily dismissed. There are efforts to interpret the data, not to assume that they speak for themselves. There were attempts to describe significant resources for offending, features of crime locations and attributes of known offenders in what were generally "victimless" crimes. Moreover, the strategy proposed following the analysis had some logic to it. It involved marrying crackdowns on crack houses and prostitution, which might be expected to yield short-term effects, with longer-term situational and social measures to achieve sustained improvements. No other bid enjoyed this range of positive qualities.

Yet it is not difficult at the same time to cavil with some of the analysis. The relevance of some of the material, for example on deprivation and general offence patterns, was neither self-evident nor explained. Where the data were deemed merely to reflect police activity their relevance was again not certain. Routinely recorded attributes of offenders were summarized, but the significance of these attributes was not, for the most part, explained. The major conclusions could have been drawn from a much more tightly drawn (and briefer) analysis or, indeed, without any formal analysis. The analysis is difficult to summarize, in part because it seems to amount to an account of "all we could find out about" drugs and prostitution in the local authority, rather than a targeted analysis to inform a preventive strategy. No significant efforts were made systematically to break the problems down into sub-types or sub-elements, or to test the hypotheses to emerge from what were essentially exploratory opportunistic analyses of readily available data. Whilst the strategy seemed to make sense, was consistent with the data, and had the advantage of looking to both long and short-term effects, it did not follow *from* the analysis. It simply followed it. The circumstances of the problem were not looked at in ways that suggest whether or not the strategy was a plausible one in the particular conditions in which the problem was manifested.

The criminologist assessors of the bid located the reported findings in a criminological framework, referring to the target neighbourhood as a "zone of transition." They also advocated a number of amendments and extensions to the proposed strategy. These referred to specification of:

- the means to mobilize local resident support especially in schools,

- the provisions to be made for those sex workers and drug users suffering mental health problems, and

- the kind of efforts that were to be made to pre-empt the relocation of further linked drug and sex markets elsewhere, presuming success in dislodging them from the target area.

The assessors also advocated coordination of work by the varying partners to the proposed initiative to avoid the pursuit of conflicting goals. They noted the potentially very high costs that could be incurred through environmental improvements.

The proposers' response to the bid assessors' report included a sharpened and more detailed strategy that covered the gaps that had been highlighted. It provided no further analysis of the problem, but did refer to further work on a full "environmental audit" of the area. The aim of the project was at this point said to be, "To improve the quality of life of the local authority residents by disrupting the local crack market." The specific objectives "following problem analysis" were: "to rid the target area of its connection with prostitution," and "to disrupt the local authority's closed drugs market." The planned initial spending over 18 months was £1.5 million.

This successful bid to the Targeted Policing Initiative might not show the very best problem-oriented policing analysis that can currently be achieved in a British Police Force without external specialist help, but it is certainly amongst the best.

DISCUSSION

Over all the analyses included within the Targeted Policing Initiative of the Crime Reduction Programme have been limited in scope, detail and in some cases relevance to dealing with the problems that were targeted. What was generally missing were efforts to break presenting problems down into sub-types relevant to prevention, or to unpack in detail what went on in the problematic behaviors, or to focus on significant ways in which the mechanisms producing the problems might be impacted. It is sobering to compare these efforts with, for example, the Boston Gun Project (Braga et al., 1999), the Charlotte-Mecklenburg work relating to thefts of appliances from houses under construction (Clarke and Goldstein, 2002), or the Kirkholt Burglary Reduction Project (Forrester et al., 1988, 1990). The latter all produced analyses that honed the definition of the targeted problems, and identified potential points of leverage to impact on their recurrent generation. They did so, though, over a much longer period than was available for the preparation of the bids reviewed here, a matter returned to below.

The problems found here in relation to analyses within the Targeted Policing Initiative are not uncommon. Other parts of the Crime Reduction Programme, though not explicitly linked to problem-oriented policing, called for a similar approach. The Reducing Burglary Initiative (RBI), for example, required bidders to identify areas that exceeded a given threshold rate, analyse the problem and propose responses, preferably innovative ones. The RBI bids likewise used very limited forms of analysis (Tilley et al., 1999) and a report was produced giving case studies that showed what might have been achieved with more thorough and creative analysis (Curtin et al., 2001).

More generally, overviews of problem-oriented policing in the U.K. (Read and Tilley, 2000) and in the United States over the past 20 years (Scott, 2000) have highlighted weaknesses in analysis. Indeed, Scott points out that, "By most accounts from those who observe problem-oriented policing carefully, problem-analysis remains the aspect of the concept most in need of improvement" (Scott, 2000:59). The preceding account of analyses included in Targeted Policing Initiatives within Britain's Crime Reduction Programme likewise finds them to be lacking.

What, if any, are the implications of these consistent shortcomings for the project of problem-oriented policing? Four possibilities are briefly considered here:

(1) that prevailing assumptions about what is possible in analysis for problem-oriented policing have been refuted, and that this undermines the whole approach;

(2) that developing the capacity for strong analysis in problem-oriented policing will take longer than had been hoped, but eventually with help and encouragement shortcomings will be remedied;

(3) that the Targeted Policing Initiative provided an inadequate and inappropriate vehicle for encouraging and enabling problem-oriented policing; or,

(4) that some rethinking is called for relating to the ways in which analysis for and in problem-oriented policing should be conceived and delivered.

Have Prevailing Assumptions about Analysis for Problem-oriented Policing been Falsified, Undermining the Whole Project?

Problem-oriented policing has common-sense appeal. Identifying and defining problems systematically and without prejudice, on the basis of evidence and analysis, sounds right. Devising tailored responses based on grasping the specifics of a given problem setting also seems sensible. Putting this in the hands of police services that pride themselves on a can-do attitude looks as if it should work. Moreover, there are many examples of police work where careful attention to a problem and lateral thinking about responses have produced remarkable achievements. For example, seeing broken windows in a tourist attraction as a problem of loose rubble rather than loose people, as happened in Oakham, required no more than accepting responsibility to address the problem and imaginatively redefining it.[2] In addition, there is nothing to suggest that the critiques of prevailing models of policing that animated the proposals for problem-oriented policing are invalid. Indifference to many community concerns for crime, disorder and feelings of insecurity does indeed miss the point of policing (for an account of the sub-set of community issues relating to crime, security, and protection that are relevant to the police see Goldstein, 1977). Moreover, dependency on traditional patrol and enforcement responses means neglecting many potentially effective ways of dealing with problems. Responding to similar incidents in the same area repeatedly is wasteful and fails to deal with the problem. For these reasons, the case for systematic problem-oriented policing remains as strong as ever.

It is when the problems require more than careful attention and a modicum of lateral thought that weaknesses in analysis in problem-oriented policing create difficulties. And it is this aspect of problem-oriented policing that has become questionable in the light of experience. We may have wrongly assumed that the common sense which can be so effective when used by conscientious officers in relation to specific local problems can readily be scaled up to deal with more substantial and more widespread issues.

Known examples of strong analysis are relatively uncommon and seem to have required something more than raw common sense and the application of standard analytic techniques. Instead, imaginative methods of analysis, often using non-standard data, informed by theory and previous research findings have rarely taken place. This type of activity may be the stock in trade of universities and some government social research groups. It does not seem to be habitual in other public sector organizations, and there is no reason why this should be the case. Theoretically informed, technically sophisticated, open-minded, imaginative analysis involving casting around for alternative data sources where those readily available are not appropriate is a high-order research activity. It calls for unusually able people with advanced education, technical training, and experience in quite basic research. It may be unreasonable to expect these abilities and attitudes to be found widely in police services.

Is Developing the Capacity for Strong Analysis in Problem-oriented Policing Something That Can be Achieved Only in the Long Term, With Help and Encouragement?

Perhaps the weaknesses repeatedly found in analysis in problem-oriented policing simply reflect the extent of the transformation needed for police organizations to become genuinely problem-oriented.[3] It will just take a long time. Moreover, we should be encouraged by small improvements such as those found between Rounds One and Two of the Targeted Policing Initiative.

There are certainly growing numbers of analysts working in British police services. What they currently do, though, appears to be more oriented to a detection and enforcement agenda, and to satisfying performance indicator requirements, than it is to an agenda concerned with dealing with police-relevant community problems. Moreover, the supply of analysts with the theoretical understanding required for systematic problem-oriented policing is currently very limited. Few relevant courses are available.

All these difficulties suggest that, though an increasing number of analysts are employed in police services, they are not yet contributing much to making good the weaknesses in analysis in problem-oriented policing. There are, though, efforts in hand to build their capacity to do so.

First, the Jill Dando Institute of Crime Science at University College, London is furnishing an academic center in Britain where for the first time there will be teaching and research focused on the forms of analysis required of problem-oriented policing. Second, Ron Clarke and Marcus Felson are preparing a handbook for analysis under Home Office auspices. To be published alongside this will be a problem-oriented policing guide for practitioners which will identify strategic and practical issues for those seeking to implement problem-oriented policing. Third, Paul Ekblom has prepared a comprehensive framework intended to guide policy makers, practitioners and researchers through the process of prevention — giving discipline, coherence and structure to their activities — that should guide analysis (Ekblom, 2002). Fourth, Tilley and Laycock have attempted to lay out in some detail the basic questions needed to work out what to do to develop preventive strategies. This gives guidance on the patterns that local analysts could usefully tease out (Tilley and Laycock, 2002). Fifth, the United States Office of Community Oriented Policing Services' *Problem-Oriented Guides for Police* series (COPS Guides) provide detailed problem by problem research-based pointers to the ways local manifestations of those problems should be interrogated to devise promising responses. Moreover, it is planned that these should grow in number and scope. There are 17 at the time of writing. Finally, the Home Office has produced a series of "toolkits" that are designed again to deal with specific problems.

The common thinking behind all these developments is that there is a need to upgrade the analyses occurring in problem-oriented policing, and crime prevention more generally. The common thread running through them all is that analysis of specific local problem patterns needs to be informed by research-based principles. It cannot rely solely on raw common sense. The common assumption is that analysis within police services can be improved, and that with this there will be improvements in problem-oriented policing. We have yet to see whether this is the case. In the long run, the impact of these kinds of developments on analysis and problem-oriented policing will be at least partly dependent on the extent to which they are routinely adopted by practitioners in police forces.

Able, self-motivated individuals, who do develop an orientation to problems and those skills in analysis that can improve understanding of problems and inform the development of appropriate interventions, are liable, however, to enjoy better prospects away from the police. Unsurprisingly, whilst there are often good career paths for talented police officers, they are much more limited for analysts. Experienced, capable analysts will seldom stay long in police agencies in current conditions. High quality graduate analysts currently soon leave.

Did the Targeted Policing Initiative Fail to Provide a Suitable Vehicle to Enable and Encourage Problem-oriented Policing?

The comparisons with the Boston gun project, the Kirkholt burglary prevention project and the Charlotte-Mecklenberg thefts from construction sites work are unfair and inappropriate. In all those exemplary cases the analyses were conducted at much greater leisure. Sharpened problem definitions only emerged after a period of reflection. Sheets remained relatively blank for much longer than a month. What the month available for initial bid preparation offered, at best, in the Targeted Policing Initiative was time for scanning, from which only provisional conclusions could be drawn. A much longer initial period would have been needed to make progress in more adequately defining and understanding the problem for effective response-development purposes.

Nevertheless, even as "scanning," in terms of the SARA (Scanning, Analysis, Response, Assessment) model, the Targeted Policing Initiative bids were disappointing. Moreover they did not generally act as precursors to a more extended process where interventions remained open for a significant period of time. In so far as the funding regime of the Targeted Policing Initiative itself provoked premature closure over problem-definitions and measures to address them, ironically it may, of course, have undermined that problem-orientation it was intended to promote. The Kirkholt Burglary Reduction Project, the Boston Gun Project and the Charlotte-Mecklenburg construction site show that even with the very strong external academic support each enjoyed, quite a protracted period was needed to develop those accounts of the problems addressed, which opened the way to effective responses. The Targeted Policing Initiative bidding timetable may have encouraged the assumption that scanning (and analysis) of complex problems could be undertaken in just a very few weeks.

It should also be pointed out that the bids for support from the Targeted Policing Initiative were made at a time when competitive, opportunistic bidding for funding was commonplace. The initiative constituted one pot of money amongst many for which speculative applications were being made. That it might require anything different by way of analysis from the usual called for to elicit financial support is unlikely to have been apparent to those making the bids. "The usual" would not entail the kinds of detailed work on problem specification and understanding called for within problem-oriented policing.

Is Some Rethinking Required Relating to Analysis for and in Problem-oriented Policing?

It may be useful to distinguish between different categories of problem, which have rather different analytic needs. Four are set out here. These comprise repeat incident prevention, attention to specific local problem generators, generic problems with strong research-based responses, and generic problems without strong research-based responses.

(1) Repeat Incident Prevention: Research on repeat victimisation consistently finds elevated risks of repeat incidents, especially in the short term (Pease, 1998; Farrell and Pease, 2001). This strongly suggests that a preventive orientation to incident scene attendance offers potential dividends; the increasing risks following successive incidents suggests the potential benefits of increasing intensity in attention. Each incident furnishes a relatively targeted opportunity for problem solving. A problem-oriented police service calls for this, maybe with specified forms of intensified attention following successive incidents. Elaborate analysis will not be needed, though some quite advanced data manipulation skills might be required in order that repeat patterns can be identified from police systems in the first

place. Moreover, there is a research base to the cumulative interventions that can be put in place following incidents and their recurrence.

(2) Attention to Specific Local Problem Generators: Some effective local problem-oriented policing relies upon committed and clever police officers focusing on problems and looking at them imaginatively for aspects open to preventive attention. The Oakham Castle case is a good example. It did not require extensive analysis of the problem. Instead it required diligent application of common sense and an ability to look for interventions that do not rely on enforcement. This is not to say that these problems are simple. In retrospect the solution may be obvious (and often elegant), but some inspiration is needed to light on it. Some perspiration may then also be needed to effect the implementation of the measure. Routinely to find these points of crime concentration, to mobilise attention to generators, will require some basic analytic capacity. Moreover, past research and past experience may catalyse/inform thinking about non-standard responses (see, for example, Brantingham and Brantingham, 1984; Felson, 1998; Clarke, 1997).

(3) Generic Problems with Research-Based Responses: The COPS guides comprise outstanding efforts to distil research findings relating to a series of specific, but recurrently encountered problems. They emphatically do not provide blueprints. What they do is to indicate what sorts of questions are relevant to particular types of generic problems, to work out what might be put in place to deal with in their specific local manifestation. The guides already published relating to street prostitution (Scott, 2001) and drug dealing in privately owned apartment complexes (Sampson, 2001), for example, could have informed the analysis for the drugs and prostitution project proposal discussed earlier had they been published at the time of Round Two of the Targeted Policing Initiative.

(4) Generic Problems Without Adequate Research-Based Responses: For many frequently found problems, there is insufficient research-based experience to provide adequate guides. They require strong, original research input to develop an adequate definition of the problem and/or to try to work through potentially effective responses. Problem-patterns themselves can be far from self-evident. Identifying them will require a capacity for original research.

Figure 1 shows the relationship between the four identified orders of problem and their analytic requirements.

Original research helps guide more routine applied analysis to recognize problem patterns. This is no different from the applied analytic services springing from the natural sciences, such as those used in medicine or forensic science. Following pioneering research, standard techniques can be used to recognize case types for inter-pretation and intervention. The arrows going from the original re-search involved in pattern-discernment show the role of this in fo-cusing the (often highly skilled) analysis that will be required to rec-ognize problems. The two "recognition" problem-types describe, on the one hand, individual cases comprising problems calling for at-tention, and, on the other hand, patterns underlying presenting problems that are open to preventive intervention. The substantial volume of research on repeat victimization has revealed the crime preventive potential of targeting victims and repeat victims for prob-lem-solving attention. The COPS guides cleverly tease out ranges of underlying patterns, established by research, that may be present in what at first sight seem similar presenting problems. Case discern-ment may also be facilitated by research, though it is not always nec-essary. Research within environmental criminology and situational crime prevention may help define cases and ways in which they can usefully be examined for problem-solving purposes, but inspired and committed police officers capable of lateral thought may not need such aids. Original research can continuously feed the evidence bases for the forms of applied analysis needed to recognize cases and patterns.

Figure 1: Orders of Problem in Problem-oriented Policing with Varying Analytic Needs

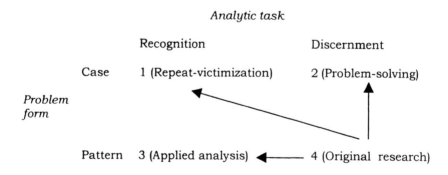

Experience so far suggests that British police services are not yet equipped for basic research, and there is, perhaps, no reason to expect them to be in the future. It requires time, experience, skills and rather distinctive ways of thinking that it may simply not be possible to provide in a police setting. The assumption that strong basic analysis is needed for all problems relevant to problem-oriented policing is dubious. Much good work may take place without it. Expecting it is liable to lead to unrealistic expectations and inappropriate disappointment with what is deemed inadequate, at least by the standards of the research community. The Targeted Policing Initiative may have exemplified this inappropriate expectation, and this paper may reflect the unwarranted disappointment with the qualities of the analyses contained in bids.

When it comes to recurrent generic problems with inadequate research to guide police analysts, the best in the applied research community need to become involved in the original and creative research to feed guides for local analysts, ideally working closely with the police. Indeed, the conclusion within the Targeted Policing Initiative team was that greater direct help with analysis was needed. This explains first the greater use of academic advisors in Round Two to help refine bids, and secondly why the rural crime, Manchester gun and Knowsley projects were operated differently from the rest of the program and included substantially greater researcher involvement. Indeed, the Knowsley project reflected a growing sense that local analytic capacity had generally been found inadequate. It involved putting a very senior researcher (Ken Pease) in a police station for two days a week alongside a full-time post-doctoral researcher (Michael Townsley) to work with the local police in providing problem-oriented policing analytic capacity. These developments also reflected growing recognition that the Targeted Policing Initiative might not have succeeded in encouraging and enabling the problem-oriented work as had originally been intended. They allowed much more time for problems to be defined and analyzed prior to the development of response strategies.

Guides rooted in strong applied research, of the sort currently being produced, can then inform the sort of analysis that will still be needed locally to determine plausible responses to problems. This in turn will still require a population of competent local analysts but not necessarily ones with advanced research abilities. Even this, however, may prove rather taxing. One officer has been heard to describe the COPS guides as ABCs for problem-oriented policing.

CONCLUSION

The main part of this paper has shown the limitations in the analysis included in bids to the Targeted Policing Initiative in the British Crime Reduction Programme, even where there were substantial incentives for strong analysis. Even the best that was produced had some significant weaknesses. Four possible implications were then considered — that the problem-oriented policing project has been shown to be fatally flawed, that the project will take longer than had been hoped or expected, that the Targeted Policing Initiative was inadequate for bringing out strong analyses in funding bids, and that some adjustments to our conception of problem-oriented policing (at least in Britain) are called for.

Over all, though the case for problem-oriented policing remains strong, evidence consistently shows that the prevailing expectations of analysis within police services have been unrealistic. Though the Targeted Policing Initiative focused on in this paper may have failed to provide adequate conditions for strong analyses to be evidenced in bids for funding, the weaknesses revealed in the selection, collection and processing of data suggest that the analytic capacity of the British Police has been rather limited. Recent efforts to increase this analytic capacity, assuming that they are adopted throughout the police service, may produce improvements.

Nevertheless, it is felt unlikely that analysts will ever be able to provide the original research input required for defining and dealing with problems for which there is not already a research literature. For these, much greater strong, applied research input is needed. The products of this could feed guides of the sort being produced by the U.S. COPS office that, in turn, should enable local analysts to examine manifestations of problem types to determine what might be appropriate responses. All this, though, need not exhaust problem-oriented policing. Much relevant work can take place without being burdened by the need for systematic analysis.

There is scope for a wide range of problem-focused work in police services. The literature over the past few years provides strong research grounds for the police to pay increasing, cumulative attention to those who have been victimized and revictimized. There are many examples of talented police officers dealing with specific local problems generating crimes and calls-for-service. These problem-focused activities need to be actively nurtured and encouraged with leadership, training and rewards. They do not, however, require a heavy analytic input. More complex, more widely distributed recurrent problems with multiple and variable causes and conditions require systematic analysis. To the extent that there is an adequate literature to draw on, the analysis may involve diagnosis into relatively well-known problem types and categories with tried and tested menus of interventions. To the extent that the existing literature is inadequate, more pioneering research may be needed.

There are, thus, different orders of activity to be encouraged and enabled across a broad agenda of increased attention to police-relevant community problems. It may be unhelpful to lump all these together. They call on different people and different skills. Whether they should all be put under the umbrella term problem-oriented policing, or whether some should be called problem solving and some problem-oriented, is a moot point. What is more important is to acknowledge that they have differing requirements and that analytic shortcomings inhibit police capacity to develop targeted strategies to define and deal with complex, widespread generic problems.

Address correspondence to: Nick Tilley, 35 Ebers Road, Mapperley Park, Nottingham NG3 5DY, UK. E-mail: <tilley@home-office.swinternet.co.uk>.

Acknowledgments: Special thanks are due to Herman Goldstein, who acted as discussant for this paper at the Norwegian workshop where the papers collected in this volume were discussed. He corrected some significant errors. We would like also to thank other members of the seminar for their thoughtful comments. We are grateful too to Tim Read, Gloria Laycock and Verity Ridgman for commenting on other versions produced before and after the meeting in Norway.

REFERENCES

Braga, A., D. Kennedy and A. Piehl (1999). "Problem-Oriented Policing and Youth Violence: An Evaluation of the Boston Gun Project." Unpublished Report to the National Institute of Justice, Washington DC.

Brantingham, P. and P. Brantingham (1984). *Patterns in Crime*. New York: Macmillan.

Bullock, K., G. Farrell and N. Tilley (2002). *Funding and Implementing Crime Reduction Initiatives*. (On line only publication, 10/02.) London, UK: Home Office.

Clarke, R. (1997). *Situational Crime Prevention: Successful Case Studies*. New York: Harrow and Heston.

—— and H. Goldstein (2002). "Reducing Theft at Construction Sites: Lessons from a Problem-Oriented Project." In: N. Tilley (ed.), *Analysis for Crime Prevention*. (Crime Prevention Studies, vol. 13.) Monsey, NY: Criminal Justice Press.

Curtin, E., N. Tilley, M. Owen and K. Pease (2001). *Developing Crime Reduction Plans: Some Examples from the Burglary Reduction Initiative*. (Crime Reduction Research Series Paper No. 7.) London, UK: Home Office.

Ekblom, P. (2002). "From the Source to the Mainstream is Uphill: The Challenge of Transferring Knowledge of Crime Prevention Through Replication, Innovation and Anticipation." In: N. Tilley (ed.), *Analysis for Crime Prevention*. (Crime Prevention Studies, vol. 13.) Monsey, NY: Criminal Justice Press.

Farrell, G. and K. Pease (eds.), (2001). *Repeat Victimization*. (Crime Prevention Studies, vol. 12.) Monsey, NY: Criminal Justice Press.

Felson, M. (1998). *Crime and Everyday Life* (2nd ed.). Thousand Oaks, CA: Pine Forge Press.

Forrester, D., S. Frenz, M. O'Connell and K. Pease (1990). *The Kirkholt Burglary Prevention Project: Phase II*. (Crime Prevention Unit Paper No. 23.) London, UK: Home Office.

—— M. Chatterton and K. Pease, with the assistance of R. Brown (1988). *The Kirkholt Burglary Prevention Project, Rochdale*. (Crime Prevention Unit Paper No. 13.) London, UK: Home Office.

Goldblatt, P. and C. Lewis (1998). *Reducing Offending: An Assessment of Research Evidence on Ways of Dealing with Offending Behaviour*. (Home Office Research Study No. 187). London, UK: Home Office.

Goldstein, H. (1990). *Problem-Oriented Policing*. New York: McGraw-Hill.

—— (1979). "Improving Policing: a Problem-Oriented Approach." *Crime & Delinquency*: 234-58.

—— (1977). *Policing in a Free Society*. Cambridge, MA: Ballinger.

Her Majesty's Inspectorate of Constabulary (2000). *Calling Time on Crime*. London, UK: Home Office.

—— (1998). *Beating Crime*. London, UK: Home Office.

Irving, B. and N. Dixon (forthcoming). *Hotspotting*. London, UK: Police Foundation.

Leigh, A., T. Read and N. Tilley (1998). *Brit Pop II Problem-Oriented Policing in Practice.* (Crime Prevention and Detection Series Paper No. 93.) London, UK: Home Office.

—— T. Read and N. Tilley (1996). *Problem-Oriented Policing: Brit Pop.* (Crime Prevention and Detection Series Paper No. 75.) London, UK: Home Office.

Pease, K. (1998). *Repeat Victimisation: Taking Stock.* (Crime Detection and Prevention Series Paper 90.) London, UK: Home Office.

Read, T. and N. Tilley (2000). *Not Rocket Science? Problem-Solving and Crime Reduction.* (Crime Reduction Research Series Paper No. 6.) London, UK: Home Office.

Sampson, R. (2001). *Drug Dealing in Privately Owned Apartment Complexes.* (Problem-Oriented Guides for Police Series No. 4.) Washington, DC: Community Oriented Policing Services, U.S. Department of Justice.

Scott, M. (2001). *Street Prostitution.* (Problem-Oriented Guides for Police Series No 2.) Washington, DC: Office of Community Oriented Policing Services, U.S. Department of Justice.

—— (2000). *Problem-Oriented Policing: Reflections on the First 20 Years.* Washington, DC: Office of Community-Oriented Policing Services, U.S. Department of Justice.

Tilley, N. and G. Laycock (2002). *Working out What to Do: Evidence-Based Crime Reduction.* (Crime Reduction Research Series Paper No. 11.) London, UK: Home Office.

—— K. Pease, M. Hough and P. Brown (1999). *Burglary Prevention: Early Lessons from the Crime Reduction Programme.* (Crime Reduction Research Series Paper No. 1.) London, UK: Home Office

NOTES

1. These are charities concerned respectively with rape victims and personal safety.

2. This took place in the Leicestershire demonstration project introducing problem-oriented policing (Leigh et al., 1996, 1998). Prior to removing the rubble, the police response had been periodically to lie in wait for stone throwers within the building and to rush out to arrest them when they began throwing stones. This response was both expensive and ineffective. The rubble-removal evidently solved the problem cheaply and immediately.

3. Important though they are, weaknesses in analysis are, of course, far from the only obstacles to the successful implementation of problem-oriented policing.

PROBLEM ORIENTATION, PROBLEM SOLVING AND ORGANIZATIONAL CHANGE

by

Michael Townsley

and

Shane D. Johnson
Environmental Criminology Research Unit, University of Liverpool

and

Ken Pease
Jill Dando Institute of Crime Science, University College, London

Abstract: *The widespread adoption of problem-oriented policing requires a dramatic and fundamental change in both the organizational focus of the police and the manner in which day to day policing is performed. The focus of this article is on the factors that have limited the implementation of problem-oriented policing. These are partitioned into two groups; those inhibiting the problem orientation of the organization and those inhibiting the problem solving of police officers. The key principles of successful organizational change are discussed, drawing upon the relevant psychological literature. Examples are given with an emphasis upon public sector agencies. Finally, solutions for overcoming the apparently intractable implementation problems are presented* *that draw on the principles identified in the change management litera-ture.*

INTRODUCTION

Just over two decades have passed since Herman Goldstein's seminal article introducing problem-oriented policing (POP) was published. Since then, much effort has been expended on instituting change in police organizations to render them congruent with the approach espoused by Goldstein (1979).

A parsimonious definition of problem-oriented policing is that it aggregates individual events, with a common characteristic, into problems. Rather than deal with individual incidents, police are encouraged to respond to problems by identifying the underlying causes and address these. A broader definition is that problem-oriented policing is a systematic approach for police to constantly improve their ability to fulfill the range of needs expressed to them by the community and the government. Goldstein (1990) recognized the limit of the police organization's authority, and that transferring the unit of analysis from individual incidents to problems was the only rational approach to crime management.

Despite problem-oriented policing's wide appeal amongst senior officers, its implementation appears piecemeal in extent and halting in pace. The widespread transformation of problem-oriented policing rhetoric into practice cannot be expected anytime soon. Reviews of POP implementation reveal that across different police jurisdictions problem-oriented policing principles are applied to varying degrees, but that in most cases implementation involves a small number of officers, is highly focused in terms of geography or the scope of problem examined, and reports mixed success, according to a somewhat informal assessment (Leigh et al., 1996).

Recently, two published reviews of have described the rate of progress toward the problem-oriented policing ideal in the last 20 years. Scott (2000) details how Goldstein's framework has purportedly been implemented and to what degree these attempts deviate from the original model. A number of obstacles facing the advancement of problem-oriented policing are outlined, such as the limited nature of POP training offered by typical police organizations, knowledge being disseminated orally and rarely documented. In consequence, no body of knowledge related to effective problem solving exists, police rarely conduct problem analysis at the policy level, and police-researcher alliances have not developed to the degree anticipated. The last obstacle helps perpetuate some of the other limitations. The tension between researchers' apparent conservatism and the emergency-driven, action-oriented environment of the police is a critical stumbling block for problem-oriented policing. The dividend available from reconciling these opposing perspectives remains attractive.

Read and Tilley (2000) explored the extent of problem solving across all 43 police forces in England and Wales. The study represents an ambitious examination of the extent of problem-oriented policing implementation in the U.K. at both extremes of the rank structure. By examining examples of successful and unsuccessful problem solving, selected by the police themselves, the authors identified factors common to successful and unsuccessful problem solving. Unsurprisingly, successes were found to:

- exhibit detailed analysis in defining and "pulling apart" problems;

- involve the community in identifying effective responses; and

- select responses based on their likely impact on the stated problem.

Read and Tilley (2000) also examined what factors operate on an organizational level that facilitate or inhibit problem-oriented policing implementation and routinization. Factors identified as facilitative include a committed and involved leadership, incentives for problem solving, and access to practical help and methods of disseminating good practice. Organizational factors that limited problem-oriented policing included not devoting time to problem solving, concentrating on local, low-level problems and a lack of attention to evaluation.

Considering the paucity of comprehensive problem-oriented policing implementations to date, some consideration needs to be given to the nature of the change that problem-oriented policing advocates seek to engineer. As highlighted by Eck and Spelman (1987), a thorough implementation of problem-oriented policing requires two levels of change: the organization needs to become problem-oriented, and frontline officers need to become problem identifiers/solvers (or at least problem identifiers/allocators or identifiers/alleviators).[1] At present, in the U.K., the Performance Indicator (PI) culture is predominant. The one thing guaranteed to change operational priorities is for an area commander to hear that, "crime is up" or "detections are down", or "we are failing to meet our targets." This creates a flurry of activity designed to elicit some "quick wins," routinely with no real thought behind what is driving the volume of crime.

The organizational philosophy (reactive, proactive, or a mixture of both) drives the demand profile of rank and file police officers. If this is changed (from reactive to proactive, say) different outputs are expected from management. However, merely changing the vision of a police organization will not ensure that police officers will be equipped to identify or solve problems. A manager can empower someone, but if that individual does not have the necessary tools to complete their task, the empowerment is merely setting someone up for failure.

The remainder of this article is structured in the following way: First, some of the problems of problem-oriented policing implementation are discussed, partitioned into two levels of analysis: organizational and front-line. Second, organizational psychology's change management literature is briefly reviewed and a model of change is explored. Last, solutions to the implementation barriers are developed which are consistent with the organizational psychology framework.

OBSTACLES TO LACK OF IMPLEMENTATION

The following list has been developed from the authors' collective experience in working with a number of police forces in the U.K., Australia and North America. Some of the obstacles outlined have been mentioned by others (Read and Tilley, 2000; Scott, 2000), some have not. Most researchers who have spent any time with police officers will recognize the obstacles listed here. Nor is this list a definitive collection. Other problems exist which hinder the efforts of implementing problem-oriented policing, but we consider the ones discussed to be the most prominent.

We have partitioned the obstacles into two groups: those that operate on an organizational level, and those that influence individual problem-solving efforts. This reflects our view, as well as others (Eck and Spelman, 1987 and less explicitly Read and Tilley, 2000), that problem orientation is distinct from problem solving. We feel that problem-oriented policing implementation will only be successful when problem orientation and solving are combined.

Problem Orientation Obstacles (organizational factors)

Rapid Turnover of Staff

The aim of programs such as the Accelerated Promotion Scheme for Graduates (APSG) in the U.K. is to allow talented individuals to rise quickly through police ranks to occupy positions of influence. However, the unintended consequence of fast-track promotion schemes has been that ambitious individuals spend short periods in each role occupied. This results in some officers, arguably those best suited to creative approaches to problem solving, not having enough time to acquire local knowledge about their community or, worse, having gained valuable experience and then being transferred to another role where lessons learnt may not inform policing action. Sustainable problem solving, either initiatives that require long term commitment or those which rely on the experience of separate but related problems, will be difficult to foster when lessons need to be continually re-learnt, or a body of knowledge is not accumulated.

Where problem-oriented policing has been applied successfully, front line officers are often passionate about what they do and are willing to perform duties outside their job description and/or work extended hours (Braga et al., 2001; Queensland Criminal Justice Commission, 1996). They frequently have contacts in other agencies, built up over time, which they can use to lever in external agency support.

Middle Management Paying Lip Service to Problem-oriented Policing

Police middle management is responsible for translating force policy into local action. In other words, officers in such ranks operationalize strategy into tactical deployment. They wield considerable influence over the direction of police activity and can almost absolutely determine the prospects of success through tacit endorsement or discouragement of new practices.

As a management style, problem-oriented policing suffers from the policing reform treadmill; the observation that reform has been linked to policing for so long that its meaning has been eroded (Goldstein, 1990). To many police officers, problem-oriented policing is the latest in a series of management fads that have promised fundamental change, have been implemented superficially and have produced inconsistent change. Worse, the term problem-oriented policing sounds like management jargon. Problem-oriented policing appears to work when police officers think it is important.

Any change in operational policing will need the approval of local area commanders and other middle managers if they are to be effective or implemented as envisaged (Zhou et al., 1999). Problem-oriented policing is a difficult strategy to oppose, but an easy one to neglect. Can anyone say they are not, or should not be, oriented towards problems? In practice, problem-oriented policing takes its place with community and neighborhood policing as a style that is vapid rather than rigorous. This is the basic reason why partnership is so often taken to be an element in problem-oriented policing in the U.K., because both belong in the fluffy corner of the policing enterprise.

Left unchecked, efforts to convert a reactive organization into a problem-oriented one are susceptible to breakdown because they require constant, even vigilant, monitoring. Front line officers still operate largely unsupervised, with wide remits of responsibility. On the other hand, recording the extent of problem-solving efforts is difficult without becoming overly bureaucratic.

Re-prioritizing of Police Resources Is Too Easy

Police prioritize crime problems according to a variety of criteria such as risk to the public, severity and community interest. These criteria are operationalized, along with political rhetoric, by central government into performance indicators. Local idiosyncratic bureaucratic priorities are also reflected in a second set of performance indicators devised by force headquarters. The sets are combined to measure how well each local area is performing. In effect, these become a set of rods for a police commander's back. Typically, if a performance in one area is good, attention can be diverted to the areas that are under-performing. This is natural. But when resource diversion occurs frequently, policing becomes similar to a dog chasing its tail, in the sense that police attention vacillates from performance indicator to performance indicator depending on areas of poor performance. The momentum gained during the "old" set of priorities is lost as attention is focused on "new" problems. If priorities are further changed relatively quickly, no momentum is built up. Pressure to change priorities comes from headquarters, in local versions of COMPuterised STATistics (COMPSTAT) meetings (Bratton, 1998). The feedback given to area commanders varies but attention is drawn to under-performing performance indicators, irrespective of the number of performance indicators on target. While the intention is to preclude slacking off, the result is often an unrealistically high standard, where praise for good work is sparse. This is an unfortunate situation as accurate feedback is a key determinant of job satisfaction and motivation (Arnold et al., 1998:231).

The rationale for using performance indicators makes sense, but when they are applied incorrectly the result hinders effective police work. Some police forces apply annual targets uniformly across each month, despite the fact that some crime categories exhibit dramatic seasonal variation. Thus, target setting is unweighted. If crime categories have a seasonal component, target setting should be weighted according to each month's share of the total (based on historical trends), perhaps relative to that observed across the wider force area.

Pressure to re-prioritize police resources can come from outside the organization (see, for example, Scott's discussion in this volume on police constituencies and how these can manipulate policing). Letters from elected representatives are notorious offenders, as are single-issue lobby groups. Occasionally, a high-profile incident will occur to divert police attention away from other problems.

SARAs Are Not Considered Part of "Real" Police Work

The method of problem solving widely used within police organizations is the Scanning, Analysis, Response and Analysis (SARA) model. This model is a stripped down version of the scientific method — an iterative process of testing hypotheses and rejecting or modifying them. The intention of the SARA model is to systematize the process of thought that good police officers use intuitively.

The effort and time devoted to instigating a SARA can be substantial. Even for relatively small-scale problems, the length of time spent in the scanning and analysis phases could be as much as two months. The time required for collating and analyzing crime or disorder data is considerable, even if all the information is contained in-house. Depending on how many external agencies are involved, organizing partnership meetings can add weeks to the exercise, to say nothing of the time taken in obtaining tangible agreements for collaborative initiatives.

The inevitable time buffer between conception and implementation allows SARAs to be viewed by some police officers as a delaying mechanism. The hot potato of the crime problem can be passed to a crime analyst for a few days or even weeks before returning to be delegated to someone else. With any luck the crime levels will have regressed to the mean by the time any initiative will need to be commenced. The initiative will then be "condemned to succeed" unless the evaluation is unusually careful. While this may appear overly cynical, and there is no suggestion that this is a widespread view amongst police officers, the quality of problem solving encountered by the authors, and most independent evaluators (see Read and Tilley, 2000), is extremely variable.

The time delay in the rigorous development of quality analysis tends to erode the importance of the SARA process in officers' eyes. The converse is true for police operations, a traditional facet of police work. Operations are launched when incidents exceed some threshold. To illustrate police officers' perceptions of SARAs, an example from an area familiar to the authors will now be discussed. When crime figures rose sharply recently, an operation was launched before any consideration was given to existing initiatives. When someone looked, there were three SARAs currently operating in the area. While it is apparent that the SARAs were not addressing the problem, the operation was conceived and launched without any knowledge of what initiatives were not working.

To some, SARAs are what you do day-to-day, operations are something you do when you are serious, or when the pressure for action exceeds some threshold — in line with our assertion that problem-oriented policing implementation fails because the police do not consider it important. In further support of this, a small-scale survey conducted by the authors revealed that 77% of officers who completed the survey had not initiated a SARA in the previous six months, although those that had initiated a SARA reported being significantly more motivated by their job than those who did not (t_{58}=2.89,p<.01).

Problem-Solving Obstacles (front line factors)

Critical Thinking Impacts Reactive Decision Making

Police officers find themselves in situations that require decisions to be made quickly, often in stressful environments. Therefore, methods of decision making that allow a limited range of alternatives are desirable. For this reason, officers who operate in this way seem to be favored over those who do not. The reactive nature of policing has produced police officers who tend, or need, to see problems in one dimension.

Problem-oriented policing requires officers to examine problems carefully, to separate problems into their discrete components. Most importantly, it obliges officers to devote time to working a problem through in order to save time by eliminating or reducing future incidents. Once exposed to critical thinking, one tends to notice the confounding forces which produced the observed phenomena. In other words, the multiple dimensions of problems are seen. This may retard the speed of decision making.

A slower rate of decision making, due to a more complex view of scenarios requiring deliberation, can be mistakenly attributed to indecision, which can jeopardize promotion chances. Policing is action-oriented and emergency-driven. Therefore, broader ways of thinking, largely endorsed and recommended by researchers and policy makers, appear unattractive to police officers as they feel their career prospects may be compromised by appearing less operationally competent.

This is not to say that every deliberating police officer is an indecisive wreck. Some officers are extremely adept at making decisions in an operational setting and maintain a catholic view of problems. But there are individuals who find it difficult, once exposed to analytic ways of thinking, to make decisions at the same speed as they did in their pre-analytic life. This is not meant to suggest that reading criminological texts will be akin to a Road to Damascus experience for every police officer, merely that once a person's point of view has been modified, adjusting to an operational setting may not be straightforward.

Lack of Imagination of Responses

The variety of solutions offered by police officers to remove or reduce problems can be quite small. This would not be so bad if the solutions were effective, but there is little credible evidence to suggest they are effective in the longer term.[2] There appears to be three reasons why there is a limited repertoire of responses to crime problems. First, the understanding of the problem is not at a level at which "pinch points" (Read and Tilley, 2000) can be identified. This is usually a symptom of using police descriptions (e.g., youths causing annoyance or violence) to define problems. If problems can be defined in terms of the offending behavior that generates the problem (Scott, 2000), the analysis can be refined to a level that allows identification of pinch points.

The second reason for a limited range of solutions to crime problems is that a great deal of problem solving involves only the police. When solutions to problems are generated by the same pool of people, invariably the responses produced will have a limited range. This is one reason why partnership work is highly regarded, because, among other advantages, fresh minds are exposed to old problems. Indeed, evidence from the Home Office's Burglary Reduction Initiative suggests that the success of crime prevention action is positively associated with the number of partners involved (Hirschfield et al., 2002). Nonetheless, evidence of partnership work is often used in a superficial way to demonstrate adherence to central government dogma. Partnerships should only occur in appropriate contexts for specific outcomes. It would be counterproductive to engage in partnership work purely to satisfy the desires of interests external to a geographic area.[3]

The most important reason for unimaginative responses to crime problems is that police officers are not aware of the plethora of examples of crime prevention. In support of this claim, our survey of police officers revealed that 58% had not read any Home Office reports within six months of the survey. While we argued in the previous point that an exposure to academic thinking/critical thought can influence decision making, so too can a lack of exposure.

Inability/Unwillingness to Involve Partner Agencies

One of the strengths of problem-oriented policing is the identification of those individuals, groups or agencies best placed to deal with the factors that contribute to problem generation. Despite this, effective multi-agency work is exceptional. Reasons for the attractiveness of intra-agency work vary: everyone "sings from the same hymn sheet," activity can be scrutinized via familiar in-house information systems and the rank structure facilitates compliance. Enthusiasm for partnership work can become strained when one organization is relatively dynamic (the police) and others are incapable of matching its speed of action. Differential work speed, the rate at which decisions are made and acted upon within an organization, is arguably the most potent source of frustration for front-line officers, and management, in their attempts to tackle particular community problems.[4]

Local authority departments appear to progress slowly compared to the police, perhaps inevitably given the break-neck speed at which police organizations are obliged to operate. The time lag of response could be explained by a multitude of factors — poor communication, outdated information systems and a lack of analytical ability — none of which is limited to police agencies.

"I Don't Know" Phobia and "I Know Best" Syndrome

Crime prevention initiatives are only as effective as the accuracy of the analysis on which they are based. In other words, proper understanding of the problem is vital. This will not occur when police officers persuade themselves that they understand more about a problem than they really do. When this does occur, they either overstate their knowledge of the problem ("I know best" syndrome), which results in a set of inappropriate responses; or cannot be specific enough about underlying causes, but deliver a series of responses anyway to appease superiors ("I don't know" phobia). Both are the result of a lack of analysis.

The "I know best" syndrome is a trait prevalent in all officer ranks. A lack of appreciation for the value of analysis, a lack of exposure to quality analysis, prior experience with similar crime problems, the reactive nature of the job and personal predilections contribute to a superficial diagnosis of the causes of crime problems (c.f., Eck's [2001] comment about officers who skip the "A"s in SARA). Examples of this are abundant. Using the proximity of homeless shelters or halfway houses as an explanation for areas of high crime and disorder is a classic case. Generally the responses generated in this case are quite specific and detailed, but they do not address the underlying causes of the problem.

"I don't know" phobia is displayed when someone is unwilling to admit not knowing the answer to a question but answers it anyway. There appears to be reluctance by *some* police officers to admit they do not know details about some feature of the problem they had not considered.[5] Whether the inability to admit a lack of knowledge is due to professional embarrassment or a lack of diligence is hard to say. They may anticipate the consequence of an "I don't know" answer: a request, possibly forceful, to find out. If this is true, "I don't know" phobia masks either laziness, insecurity regarding analysis (e.g., "I don't know and I don't know how to find out"), or a lack of interest in analytical precision. In any case, problem-solving efforts are scuppered due to individuals not being honest about the extent of their knowledge. Initiatives generated by "I don't know" phobia are usually not prescriptive enough to address the underlying causes of the problem.

For scientists, being able to say, "I don't know" is one of their greatest attributes.[6] Perhaps this is one of the contributory reasons why the widespread implementation of problem-oriented policing has been retarded; scientists are content to admit they know nothing; the excitement of discovering or empirically demonstrating hypotheses is sufficient. Police, on the other hand, insist they "know" crime and how to control it; they know about offender networks, prolific offenders, hot spots and crime trends. Yet there is a body of knowledge that suggests they do not (Ratcliffe and McCullagh, 2001; Townsley and Pease, 2002).

It needs to be stressed that we are not implying that every police officer is reactionary or too scared to admit he or she is ignorant. Many officers do decompose problems into their discrete units, untangling seemingly intertwined phenomena in imaginative ways. Others do admit they do not have sufficient knowledge to act, but know how to advance the agenda. However, as discussed above, it is important to stress that for any organizational change to be successful, officers' perceptions of the importance of accurate intelligence are paramount.

LESSONS FROM ORGANIZATIONAL PSYCHOLOGY

Fundamental changes in the way in which the police deliver services will undoubtedly require considerable changes in their organizational systems and internal structures. Unfortunately, the process of organizational change may be challenging as the task involves the interaction of both driving and impeding forces (Lewin, 1958). For instance, although a vision for change may be identified, this may only be realized if all those involved can be motivated to embrace the new ideal. In the sections which follow, we will discuss some of the lessons from the field of organizational psychology that may inform the process that may be necessary within police forces if the problem-oriented policing ideology is to be fully embraced. Specifically, we will discuss one model of organizational change and illustrate some of the factors that are important in effecting change. Although there is a paucity of research concerned with organizational change within public sector organizations, findings from studies concerned with changes in the U.K. National Health Service (NHS) and local government will be drawn upon where possible.

Organizational psychology is a field that incorporates research involving assessment of workers (recruitment, performance appraisal), physical work environment (ergonomics, occupational health and safety), development of individuals and groups (training), employee satisfaction and nature of work and organization (organizational change and management) (Arnold et al., 1998). For the purposes of this chapter, only the change management literature is considered. We are only interested, at this stage, in making comments on the systematic approach to executing fundamental change in organizations. While the other branches of organizational psychology are useful (Lefkowitz, 1977), their relevance in the context of this article is marginal.

A Short Note on Police Organizational Change

Research into police organizational change has produced mixed results. Despite a great deal of sustained effort in making a variety of police agencies more equitable, inclusive, accountable and effective, independent *empirical* results of change programmes are sparse. The systematic application of organizational psychological methods to police organizations has occurred rarely (Zhou et al., 1999).[7] This could be in part because it is only recently (1970s) that they have begun to be applied to public sector agencies (Alderfer, 1976), and possibly because the aspects of the organization needed to be changed were perceived to be obvious.[8]

The volume of research devoted to changing police organization in the criminal justice literature far exceeds that published in organizational psychology research circles. The bulk of studies in criminal justice that describe changing an organization rely heavily on anecdotal evidence (e.g., Geller and Swanger, 1995; Seagrave, 1996; Stevens, 2001). By itself, this is not terrible, but the fact that findings are not underpinned by theory weakens their utility and generalizability.[9]

Accounts of the attempts to implement team policing (Eck and Spelman, 1987; Schwartz and Clarren, 1977 and Sherman et al., 1973) and community policing (Schafer, 2000; Zhao et al., 1999) imply that a number of conditions fundamental to the concept being pilot tested were only temporarily present or not all. The importance of the change was widely held as peripheral to the mission of the organization and, as such, the exercises were under-resourced, not enough effort was exerted to bring in the structural changes required, or the project not given long enough to produce outcomes (Eck and Spelman, 1987; Zhou, 1996). The variation in the level of implementation was usually attributed to variation in management commitment to the change process (Wycoff and Skogan, 1994).

This chapter will not draw on the research published within criminal justice on the grounds that it does not explicitly communicate with a systematic body of knowledge on organizational change. Neither are we wedded to the body of knowledge derived from organizational psychology, although it informs and structures what follows. While change management may not demonstrate high rates of success (see a review of reviews in Arnold et al., 1998:485-486), and qualifiers regarding the amorphous nature of the task need to be stressed, it is, nonetheless, an attempt to collect a systematic body of knowledge about the change management process. Utilizing a relevant body of knowledge and theories will yield better results than basing a programme of change on experience or conjecture. It is perhaps ironic that scholars attempting to engineer a change process in a police agency without consulting the change management literature may be guilty of the very thing they accuse the police profession: adherence to practices that have not been evaluated.

There are two schools of thought in change management: the planned approach and the emergent approach (Arnold et al., 1998). The planned approach to organizational change describes changes that are discrete or "one-off," whereas the emergent approach describes change endeavors that are incremental or continuous. Advocates of the second school are linked more by their mutual skepticism of planned change than by a common theoretical stance. The body of knowledge for emergent change is dwarfed by that of planned change. For these reasons, the planned approach is chosen for exploration in greater detail here.

The planned approach to change derives from the work of social psychologist Kurt Lewin. Lewin was responsible for conceiving the action-research model (1946), which later led to the formalized three-step model for change (see Arnold et al., 1998), which has remained a fundamental approach to planned change management (Lewin, 1958). Hendry (1996:624) remarks that if you "scratch *any* account of creating and managing change and the idea that change is a three-stage model which necessarily begins with a process of unfreezing will not be far below the surface" [emphasis added].

Lewin's three-stage model (1958) of organizational change comprises the following steps:

(1) *unfreezing* the present way of working,

(2) *changing* to a new way of working, and

(3) *re-freezing* the new way of working.

Unfreezing involves challenging the existing way of working and demonstrating that it is no longer suitable in the current context, with the primary motivation of creating a readiness for change. To achieve this aim, the model contends, it is important to show that some salient goal remains unmet, or that an ideal is not fully realized. In policing, one approach for a change to problem-oriented policing would be to convince officers that mostly reactive styles fail to address the underlying causes of crime, and to challenge the common perception that the role of the police is to simply "catch the criminals." The literature attributes many organizations' failure to realize change to unsatisfactory completion of the unfreezing process (Schein, 1987). Unfreezing is held to be easiest when the organization is in crisis (Goldstein, 1990). There is, of course, the danger of circularity in the argument that failure to change is attributable to incomplete unfreezing, emphasizing the need for unfreezing to be measured adequately and independently of change success.

Unfreezing refers to the perceptions of individuals. Communicating a rationale for organizational change to individuals is essential if it is to be successfully implemented. Moreover, each stage must be achieved by all involved rather than senior management only — although the latter must be seen to believe in and actively lead the new style of working.

A formula developed by Jacobs (1994) is useful for conceptualizing readiness to change:

$$D*F*V>R$$

Where   D=Dissatisfaction with the current situation;
V=Vision of what the future could/should look like;
F=real and achievable First Steps people can take toward the vision, and;
R=Resistance to change.

The key point of the formula relevant to problem-oriented policing implementation is that the product of D, F and V needs to be greater than R for change to occur. If D, F or V are absent, the organization will not change, regardless of the levels of the complement arguments of the formula.

Once the unfreezing phase is completed, the focus of the change process turns to articulating and demonstrating the new method of operating. The Lewin model requires identification of behaviors central to the new style of working. In policing, while the overall vision of problem-oriented policing is clear, the individual implied behaviors under problem-oriented policing must also be.

For this process to be comprehensive and substantive, it is essential that the specific aims and objectives be clarified, and that suitable management and internal structures are developed. For instance, research concerned with organizational change in local government in the U.K. has highlighted the problem of focusing on externally-driven agendas without addressing the need to establish the appropriate infrastructure. Asquith (1997) examined the extent to which organizational change was realized in eight local authorities. Local authorities that had carefully identified organizational aims and objectives, and that had an appropriate and flexible operational management designed to achieve them, were those for which change had been most successful. Thus, while it is important to focus on the vision of the organization, it is also essential to develop the necessary systems and internal structures which ultimately facilitate organizational change.

If a defining characteristic of problem-oriented policing is its being evidence-based, it would be necessary to ensure that adequate resources are allocated to intelligence units so that different forms of evidence can be assembled and triangulated, and that the members of these units acquire "problem-oriented policing heads": i.e., ways of organizing the data optimal for problem-oriented policing-derived analyses. How are "problem-oriented policing heads" acquired? It would be important for staff with the right experience and qualifications to be recruited for intelligence posts. Alternatively, in keeping with the first steps advocated by Jacobs (1994), the appropriate training should be provided.

There will be resistance to change. Officers may be fearful of losing their jobs, being swamped by work or being unable to carry out their new roles, concerns that were expressed by staff during reforms of the NHS during the early 1990s (e.g., see Deluca, 2000). For such reasons, potential problems should be anticipated and appropriate counter-moves implemented. For instance, funding may be allocated to provide training or education to assist officers in carrying out their new roles. Ensuring that officers are confident in their continuing competence is crucial if they are to embrace the new way of working.

Rumors and gossip abound in police environments. These may subvert any of the three change phases. Layton et al. (1998) stress the importance of communication of facts throughout the process. Research conducted by the Wyatt Company in the United States involved asking 531 organizations what they would change about the way they implemented organizational change. The most frequent answer was "The way I communicated with my employees" (cited in Garside, 1993). Moreover, a small scale survey (N=60) conducted by the present authors indicated that police officers' degree of motivation in their roles was (significantly) positively associated with the extent to which they perceived information to be communicated effectively, a finding also reported in a study of nurses by Davidson et al. (1997).

A further important consideration during this stage is that of maintaining the momentum generated during the early phase of implementation. A clear problem is reversion to the old ways of doing things. In fact, a review of change within the NHS cited commitment and conviction for the project from the chief executive and senior clinicians and management as the most important factor in its success (Garside, 1993).

It is important that senior management is constantly seen to support and be enthusiastic about the new way of working. Clearly, to do this, it is necessary to convince them of the benefits of the new approach so that they advocate it rather than simply paying it lip service. Arnold et al. (1998) cite an example from private industry. A company introduced a new computer system. Its previous experience of implementing changes had identified difficulties with senior management and production supervisors. As the full endorsement of these two groups would be essential if changes were to be properly implemented, the company specifically targeted these two groups. Both groups received extensive training on the computer system beyond that required. The aim of this exercise was to make them fully aware of the capabilities of the system and the problems associated with implementing the changes. The result, as described by the project manager, was "remarkable." Thus, one of the key factors in implementing changes is in convincing those who lead the organization of the benefits of the new way of working.

Having changed the current way of working, the final stage of Lewin's model is that of re-freezing, the aim of which is to solidify the revised practices. The challenge is to ensure that the organization really has adopted the new way of working, rather than simply giving the illusion of embracing it. People or organizations apparently tend to revert to the old style of working immediately after the process of change has been implemented and there is no one to monitor their behavior. The process of refreezing may be particularly difficult if the work environment does not appear to support the new vision, although this difficulty will be in indirect proportion to how well the first two steps have been executed. For instance, problem-oriented policing strategies may take some time to yield significant results. Even when these techniques may be more sustainable than traditional policing because they seek to address underlying causes, officers may become disillusioned with the approach and revert to more uniformly reactive forms of policing believing these to be more immediately effective.

Unsurprisingly, the process of refreezing is frequently achieved through the use of positive feedback regarding the effectiveness of the new practices. Successes need to be emphasized and the long-term effects of the new styles highlighted and contrasted with the problems associated with the old style. Senior management needs to remain clear on, and promote, the benefits of the new style. This may involve the acknowledgement of the fact that changes may take some time to impact upon measures of success, especially traditional performance indicators such as simple counts of crime. Thus, it would be wise to develop alternative ways of reacting to changes in performance indicators in the short term to discourage officers from becoming disaffected with the new style simply because they, and their superiors, have unrealistic expectations of the successes that may be achieved in the short term. Indeed, one of the problems with both the Lewin model and SARA is the illusion that it is a one-off process, rather than an iterative process approximating ever more closely to an optimum.

HOW TO TACKLE OBSTACLES

The following section contains a number of remedies to the barriers to implementation identified in the preceding sections. Each aims to mitigate the influence of one or more of the implementation barriers. The ideas presented here are consistent with the lessons distilled from the previous section. They therefore have the advantage of drawing on systematized experience, but remain provisional.

Utilizing Performance Indicators in a Positive Way To Leverage Action

Problem orientation can be fostered through the use of performance indicators, but not the way these indicators are traditionally employed by police organizations. Most performance indicators are counts of criminal matters and detection ratios.[10] These make sense only to police organizations and central government, the latter purely from a motive of wanting less crime and more detections (at least up to the point when the courts are overloaded and the prisons full). Police officers attempting to engage either subordinates or external partners usually point to crime levels and try to argue the other party into action. We feel that this is an ineffective technique, and other methods are available which would provide greater possibility of action. Two examples are provided here. Both are designed to be more meaningful to their intended target audience than orthodox crime counts.

Problem identification can be enhanced by the use of the "number of officer hours" statistic.[11] This is calculated by aggregating the signing on and off times for incidents to which officers respond. A matrix of places against incident types can be constructed to compare how much time is spent by officers at a location (for all crime), on particular crime types (at all locations) or specific problems at certain locations. The cell entries can be simple summations of time elapsed, or rates or weightings could be applied to the number of hours (hours per officer, hours per incident). Table 1 is an example of such a matrix using one month of patrol deployment data.

Table 1: Observed Officer Hours for One Month

Call type	Area 1	Area 2	Area 3	Area 4	Area 5	Area 6
Minor disorder	62.15	98.17	107.55	101.42	27.28	46.73
Susp indiv.	16.25	45.15	29.20	44.02	16.97	18.15
Traffic accident	39.15	36.87	10.40	21.42	5.33	8.75
Abandoned car	20.73	27.70	11.62	6.27	16.52	10.82
Other theft	13.95	25.55	20.02	10.87	11.98	2.87
Found stolen car	3.47	11.62	19.95	18.28	23.78	5.53
Other	2.95	29.62	31.00	8.60	5.48	2.32
Dom. Violence	12.30	22.73	18.18	12.17	6.40	5.75
Stolen car	21.32	19.67	9.50	5.87	7.92	3.07
Assault	0.80	9.97	21.45	1.90	19.18	4.13
Burglary Dwell	12.67	3.97	21.23	2.75	12.95	2.33
Misc. (46 call types)	53.00	190.52	90.05	89.08	103.62	64.62
Total	274.32	523.88	400.63	334.25	268.87	177.33

The cell entries are the summation of observed officer time spent on calls. Shaded cells indicate where the observed amount of officer hours is greater than the expected number of officer hours (calculated using marginal row and column totals). The cumulative time represented by the shaded cells is over 130 officer hours per month. This equates to an extra officer for three weeks out of four.

Table 1 naturally elicits questions about resource allocation. These will vary depending on whether a manger is convinced of the merits of problem-oriented policing (i.e., if they've been "unfrozen" or not). Frozen managers will compare the picture presented with their expected resource allocation. Pointing out the number of repeat calls, and the amount of time expended responding to these matters, will further force managers to realize current practices are wasteful and ineffective. Most importantly, it provides objective proof of recurring incidents and the need to address them.

The power of the "number of officer hours" statistic is that the units used are the hard currency of police managers. In other words, it is in the manager's best interest to "reclaim" more officer hours from recurring problems. This can be done by solving or alleviating problems identified by the statistic. For managers unable to see the benefits of being problem-oriented, the "number of officer hours" statistic provides an excellent impetus to focus on problem resolution or reduction. In other words, problem orientation becomes the route through which one must pass to proceed from an undesirable situation (lots of officer time spent at a few addresses) to a desirable one (less officer time devoted to preventable calls). Thus, problem orientation can be marketed as relevant, and therefore important, on the grounds that repeated preventable incidents tie up officers and compromise their ability to respond swiftly in the event of a real emergency. This is a desirable goal not only for the community, but also for officer safety.

Unfrozen managers, those who have accepted problem-oriented policing in principle but do not know where to begin, will use the table as a scanning tool (in the SARA sense). The analysis cannot be gained from the matrix, but it is an excellent management tool that restricts a reader's attention, objectively, to problems that deserve further exploration. This form of demand profile can be extremely illuminating for police managers as a starting point for identifying problems.

When dealing with other agencies or groups, the "number of officer hours" statistic will buy little support. The same can be said of using crime counts as a means of engaging partnership work. For audiences external to the police agency, performance indicators are required which individuals will understand and be motivated by. One approach that does gain support relatively easily, particularly among taxpaying residents, is calculating the cost of crime and disorder incidents for the community. This could be done by quantifying the financial cost to the police of the calls generated by particular addresses, with a footnote implying that better use could be made of public resources, or the financial cost to society as a whole. Comprehensive models of economic costs of crime and techniques for calculating meaningful cost-benefit analyses (see Mallender et al., 2002) are being developed (Brand and Price, 2000) and should be used by police organizations as a means of gaining support from external agencies (examples of intra-agency support through this tactic also exist, see Queensland Criminal Justice Commission, 1997).

In Green Bay, Wisconsin, police officers identified a number of bars that did not observe proper serving practices and served intoxicated individuals who had extensive histories of public drunkenness. Common opinion was that a homeless shelter in the area was responsible for problems at the bars in the area. Closer examination of the incidents revealed that the two bars closest to the shelter — both were equidistant — displayed dramatic differences in calls for police service. In order to persuade the city council of substandard serving practices at particular bars, the officers, rather than presenting the volume of calls for the two bars, quantified the total time spent responding to calls for both bars and multiplied this by the hourly cost of police services. These figures greatly impacted the council's decision not to renew a number of licences (Bongle, 2002). [12, 13]

Expressing the impact of offending behavior in financial terms is a powerful persuader for potential partners to provide support because it is easily understood, has more impact than counts of crime and is easily calculated.

Body of Knowledge

This section deals with two types of knowledge: parochial and catholic. Parochial knowledge encompasses crime analysis and crime reduction initiatives performed at the local level, along with a set of useful contacts from other agencies and the community. Intelligence on what contextual factors differentiate one area from another is of paramount importance. Catholic knowledge consists of the universe of criminological research applicable to crime reduction.

In a perfect world, the list of problem-solving initiatives (e.g., SARAs) put into action comprise the body of parochial knowledge. Unfortunately, routine documentation of initiatives is generally not of sufficient quality to be used by other individuals. The valuable minutiae of specific problems seem to exist almost exclusively within the memory of the officer involved. Much relearning occurs within an area when problems recur and effective prior responses are forgotten. Without the systematic collection of parochial knowledge, areas are reliant on the presence of individuals involved in problem solving in the past.

A frequent comment made of the criminal justice system, and of the police in particular, is that little is known about what procedures are effective. Until recently, little scrutiny of established practices occurred, but there is now a great deal of activity invested in the development of evidence-based policy and practice. Adding insult to injury, however, are instances when effective practice exists but front-line officers are oblivious to it. As Davies and Nutley (2002) argue, the creation and development of a cumulative body of knowledge will only serve a purpose if there is effective dissemination and access to knowledge as well as a means to increase the uptake of evidence-based practice.

Much work has served to build up a body of knowledge about what is effective in reducing crime. One of the earliest attempts was the ambitious "What works, what doesn't and what's promising" report commissioned by the U.S. Congress (Sherman et al., 1997). The U.K. Government has specified "evidence" as one of the central characteristics of policy, one of the results of which are the Crime Reduction Toolkits — interactive templates for specific problems authored by experts to be used by practitioners. In a similar vein, but more comprehensive, are the U.S. COPS Problem Oriented Guides for Police series. The Campbell Collaboration, a collection of systematic reviews concerned with social policy, but primarily criminal justice, has been founded in order to advance the dissemination and uptake of evidence-based policy and practice.

So far, our experience relates only to the extent that police officers use the Home Office Crime Reduction Toolkits.[14] Officers are grateful for the resource, but they are not using them as they were envisaged. Generally a problem only appears on their radar at the last minute, when they need to devise an approach to tackle a problem in a very short space of time. Proper use of the toolkits requires a substantial period of time, which is often unavailable to police. This is not a criticism of the toolkits, just an operational reality for police officers.

A potentially more effective way to disseminate the results of systematic reviews would be to incorporate the existing knowledge of "what works" within an expert system. Expert systems are a programming paradigm based on "rules of thumb" and are typically used as diagnostic tools. A series of closed questions is put to a user and the answers are matched against a suite of symptoms. Once a match is found, the database of remedies is cross-referenced and supplied to the user. Common applications of rule-based tools are found in medicine, industry (machinery failure) and finance (mortgage applications, asset management). The likely reason that expert systems have not been applied to police problems is that it has only been relatively recently that a body of systematic and reliable knowledge has been compiled.

Using such a system, police officers would answer a set of questions about the problem they seek to address. At the end of the process they would be given a set of applicable initiatives that have been demonstrated to work elsewhere, with hypertext links for literature or contact information of involved individuals. If there are no appropriate initiatives, perhaps secondary analysis of an appropriate victimization survey could provide a starting point (risk levels of vulnerable groups, say).

The strengths of such an application would be: (a) that officers would be prompted to think of aspects of problems they may not have considered otherwise; (b) it would be the equivalent of having a problem-solving expert "on demand;" (c) much of the work has already been done (expert systems are not difficult to programme and we are beginning to know "what works"); (d) it would be a comparatively quick problem solving exercise compared to the toolkits; (e) it would be as explicit and context-oriented as desired without forcing the user to become too academic; and (f) it could be used by agencies other than the police (crime and disorder partnerships, for example). In other words, not only would the quality of problem solving be heightened, but the process would also be made simpler and more straightforward.

Making Promotions Problem-oriented Policing-based/related

A method of positively reinforcing organizational change is to restrict career advancement to only those individuals who exhibit attributes consistent with the stated organizational vision. This means that an area commander who wishes to instill the need for problem orientation in other officers can achieve this by making problem-oriented policing the route through which one must pass to be promoted. To be promoted to any rank, two things need to be demonstrated (in addition to the existing set of characteristics and qualifications): a thorough understanding of the problem-solving policing ethos, along with evidence of problem-solving participation. Making these two a requisite condition for applying for other posts transforms problem orientation and solving from a vague notion or activity into a relevant and attractive one, and provides encouragement to translate a vision into reality. Once officers deem problem-solving policing important, more attention will be devoted to identifying and dealing with the conditions which give rise to groups of similar incidents.

Two important qualifiers should be stressed. First, a policy of this sort would obviously need to be widely promoted so that officers were aware of the importance that management places on problem-solving policing. Second, the problems listed in the first organizational obstacle (rapid turnover of staff) need to be kept in mind, as it would be counterproductive to lose quality staff continually. The recommendations of the collection of local bodies of knowledge (see the second solution of this section) would be applicable here.

Training Sessions

An explanation for the slow penetration of critical thinking into everyday police work is that reactive decision making becomes compromised by exposure to wider perspectives. The more options available, the greater the deliberation; so the theory goes. However, rapid decision making is not restricted to the police. Astronauts, the military, pilots, surgeons and emergency rescue workers all need to make decisions in stressful situations, involving large amounts of risk. In these careers, the margin for error is mostly infinitesimal.

The difference between the careers mentioned above and the police is that the former group routinely undergoes strategy and review sessions in an attempt to learn more efficient methods of operating or to highlight critical errors. These simulations might involve hypothetical scenarios and provide the luxury of assessing the situation from a variety of perspectives. In this way, the "heat of the moment" factor is taken out of the decision-making process. Other features of routine "re-training" sessions are overviews of basic theory complemented by emerging developments.

Professional sports teams also regularly review tactics and strategy. Geller (1997) provides a neat comparison between the police and professional football teams. Analysis of games (opponents and themselves), learning new set plays (often tailored to exploit a particular weakness of the opposition), and training out poor technique comprise a considerable amount of time compared to the time spent using that knowledge. The motivation for professional sports teams to constantly monitor, adapt and improve performance is largely financial, a motivation inapplicable to police organizations.

If police organizations ran a problem-solving policing retraining scheme, similar to the ones that other professionals oblige their members to undertake, for all front-line officers on a frequent basis, basic problem-solving policing principles would be reinforced, promising developments could be highlighted and case studies of problem solving could be scrutinized. This would keep the body of professional knowledge of crime reduction more up to date than the current situation and allow some evolutionary learning to occur. More importantly though, the allocation of time to re-training would reiterate the organization's commitment to problem solving policing. Regular training courses are only offered for those skills which are considered important, either for officer safety or litigation minimization. By stipulating retraining as compulsory would raise the status of problem solving considerably.

CONCLUSIONS

Clearly, if police organizations are to become "learning organizations" (Geller, 1997), there is much ground to cover. The present philosophies and set of priorities adhered to by police forces are not consistent with problem solving policing, at least as advocated by Goldstein (1990). We have tried to avoid sounding pessimistic at the evidence of sporadic and isolated instances of rigorous problem-oriented policing despite police organizations' universal espousal of the merits of problem-oriented policing. In this vein, it should be of perverse comfort to researchers and practitioners that other fields struggle to make substantive ground toward routinizing evidence-based practice. Medicine, with its high educational entry standards, numerous journals, and requirements for practitioners to keep abreast of the latest developments and procedures, suffers from similar orientation obstacles as the police (Goldstein, 1990; Scott, 2000; Sherman, 1998).

The field of organizational psychology is a potentially powerfully source of information for how best to engineer fundamental change within organizations. To our knowledge, this literature has not been explicitly consulted for the purposes of implementing problem-oriented policing, at least not on a routine basis. In this article, we have outlined Lewin's model for change, which has been proved to be effective for a variety of organizations, including those in the public sector. The model consists of a three-step process of justifying a basis for change, recalibrating the organization to reflect the new vision, and reinforcing the new vision. The feature common to each process is effective and targeted communication.

Proposals for change will be best received when they are expressed in terms that are consistent with or reinforce principles considered important by officers. In the unfreezing process, for example, to persuade officers into acknowledging the need for a new vision, appeals should be delivered in such a way that they do not conflict with the police subculture (Goldstein, 1990; Reiner, 1985). Resistance to proposed changes will also be minimized if the benefits of the new vision can be directly related to eliminating or alleviating conditions that are universally unfavorable to officers (such as too many calls for service, or not enough officers).

Obstacles to the widespread implementation of problem-oriented policing were partitioned into two groups, based on the level at which they operated. The obstacles were interdependent, but there are opportunities to exploit this mutual reinforcement. A number of remedies for obstacles have been discussed, each directly addressing one of the stated obstacles with an anticipated "diffusion of benefits" for weakening other obstacles.

Two recurring themes emerged in this article: (a) police officers will not devote much energy to activities they do not consider important, and (b) effective communication will mitigate many of the obstacles that have bedeviled other problem-oriented policing projects. Widespread, substantive implementation of problem-oriented policing is possible, but will not occur until senior officers are psychologically committed to substantive change and are willing to develop a comprehensive communication strategy to supplement the intended changes. By clearly justifying a reason to change, communicating methods of problem solving and developing systems that reinforce good practice, a system of disseminating successful problem-solving initiatives will place the police much closer to the Goldstein ideal of problem-oriented policing. In short, the path of least resistance for orchestrating an organizational shift involves clearly emphasizing, through communication and promotion, how the new paradigm is consistent with, and will provide greater attention toward, that which officers deem important.

If problem-oriented policing is to be truly implemented throughout an organization, not just "bolted on" or restricted to small subunits of the agency as has occurred in the past, then advocates need to concentrate their energies into "changing" rather than "change."

Address correspondence to: Michael Townsley, Environmental Criminology Research Unit, University of Liverpool, The Gordon Stephenson Building, 74 Bedford Street South, Liverpool, L69 7ZQ, United Kingdom. Email: <mtownsle@liv.ac.uk>.

REFERENCES

Alderfer, C.P. (1976). "Change Processes in Organizations." In: M.D. Dunnette (ed.), *Handbook of Industrial and Organizational Psychology*. Chicago, IL: Rand McNally.

Arnold, J., C.L. Cooper and I.T. Robertson (1998). *Work Psychology: Understanding Human Behaviour in the Workplace* (3rd ed.). London, UK: Financial Times Pitman Publishing.

Asquith, A. (1997). "Achieving Effective Organisational Change in English Local Government." *Local Government Studies* 23(4):86-99.

Bongle, B. (2002). Personal communication, March 7, 2002.

Braga, A.A., D.M. Kennedy, A.M. Piehl and E.J. Waring (2001). *Reducing Gun Violence: The Boston Gun Project's Operation Ceasefire*. Washington, DC: U.S. National Institute of Justice.

Brand, S. and R. Price (2000). *The Economic and Social Costs of Crime*. (Home Office Research Study No. 217.) London, UK: Home Office.

Bratton, W.J. (1998). "Crime is Down in New York City: Blame the Police." In: N. Dennis (ed.), *Zero Tolerance: Policing a Free Society*. London, UK: Institute of Economic Affairs, Health and Welfare Unit.

Davidson, H., P.H. Folcarelli and S. Crawford (1997). "The Effects of Health Care Reforms on Job Satisfaction and Voluntary Turnover among Hospital-Based Nurses." *Med Care* 35:634-45.

Davies, H. and S. Nutley (2002). *Evidence-Based Policy and Practice: Moving from Rhetoric to Reality*. (Discussion Paper 1.) St. Andrews, SCOT: Research Unit for Research Utilisation, University of St Andrews.

Deluca, M.A. (2000). "Transatlantic Experiences in Health Reform: The United Kingdom's National Health Service and the United States Veterans Health Administration." PriceWaterHouseCoopers Endowment for The Business of Government end of grant report, (http://endowment.pwcglobal.com/).

Eck, J.E. (2001). "Ducks, Dens and Wolves." Plenary address, 2001 British POP Conference, Leicester, September, 2001.

—— and W. Spelman (1987). *Solving Problems: Problem Oriented Policing in Newport News*. Washington, DC: Police Executive Research Forum.

Feynman, R. (1999). *The Meaning of It All*. London, UK: Penguin Books.

Garside, P. (1998). "Organisational Context for Quality: Lessons from the Fields of Organisational Development and Change Management." *Quality in Health Care* 7(supplement):8-15.

—— (1993). *Patient-Focused Care. A Review of Seven Sites in England*. London, UK: NHS Management Executive.

Geller, W.A. (1997). "Suppose We were Serious about Police Departments Becoming 'Learning Organizations'"? *NIJ Journal* (December)234:2-8.

—— and G. Swanger (1995). *Managing Innovation in Policing: The Untapped Potential of the Middle Manager.* Washington, DC: Police Executive Research Forum.

Goldstein, H. (1990). *Problem Oriented Policing.* New York, NY: McGraw-Hill.

—— (1979). "Improving Policing: A Problem-Oriented Approach to Improving Policing." *Crime & Delinquency* 25:236-258.

Hendry, C. (1996). "Understanding and Creating Whole Organizational Change through Learning Theory." *Human Relations* 49:621-641.

Hirschfield, A., S. Chenery and N. Davidson (eds.), (2002). *The Home Office Reducing Burglary Initiative in the North East and North West Regions: Final Evaluation Report.* London, UK: Home Office.

Jacobs, R.W. (1994). *Real Time Strategic Change: How to Involve an Entire Organization in Fast and Far Reaching Change.* San Francisco, CA: Berrett-Koehler.

Langhoff, N.T. (1982). "Planning and Change: The Need for a Theoretical Bridge." *Viewpoints in Teaching and Learning* 58(4):41-47.

Layton, A., F. Moss and G. Morgan (1998). "Mapping Out the Patient's Journey: Experiences of Developing Pathways of Care." *Quality in Health Care* 7(supplement):8-15.

Lefkowitz, J. (1977). "Industrial-Organizational Psychology and the Police." *American Psychologist* May:346-364.

Leigh, A., T. Read and N. Tilley (1998). *Brit POP II: Problem-Oriented Policing in Practice.* (Crime and Detection and Prevention Series Paper 93.) London, UK: Home Office.

—— T. Read and N. Tilley (1996). *Problem-Oriented Policing: Brit POP.* (Crime and Detection and Prevention Series Paper No. 75.) London, UK: Home Office.

Lewin, K. (1958). "Group Decisions and Social Change." In: G.E. Swanson, T.M. Newcomb and E.L. Hartley (eds.), *Readings in Social Psychology.* New York: Holt, Rinehart and Winston.

—— (1946). "Action Research and Minority Problems." *Journal of Social Issues* 2:34-36.

Mallender, J., A. Richman and R. Kingsworth (2002). "Burglary Reduction Initiative, Evaluating Costs and Benefits, Liverpool Strategic Development Project: A Case Study." Submitted to the Home Office.

Queensland Criminal Justice Commission (1997). *The Cost of First Response Policing.* (Research Paper, vol. 4(2).) Brisbane, AUS: author.

—— (1996). *The West End Police Beat: An Evaluation*, Brisbane, AUS: Criminal Justice Commission.

Ratcliffe, J.H. and M.J. McCullagh (2001). "Chasing Ghosts? Police Perception of High Crime Areas." *British Journal of Criminology* 41(2):330-341.

Read, T. and N. Tilley (2000). *Not Rocket Science? Problem Solving and Crime Reduction*. (Crime Reduction Research Series Paper No. 6.) London, UK: Home Office.

Reiner, R. (1985) *The Politics of the Police*. London, UK: Harvester Wheatsheaf.

Schafer, J.A. (2000). "The Challenges of Implementing Successful Organizational Change: A Study of Community Policing." Doctoral dissertation, Michigan State University.

Schein, E.H. (1987). *Process Consultation Volume II: Lessons for Managers and Consultants*, MA: Addison-Wesley Publishing Company.

Schwartz, A.I. and S.N. Clarren (1977). *The Cincinnati Team Policing Experiment: A Summary Report*. Washington, DC: Police Foundation

Scott, M.S. (2000). *Problem-Oriented Policing: Reflections on the First 20 Years*. Washington, DC: Office for Community Oriented Policing Services.

Seagrave, J. (1996). "Defining Community Policing." *American Journal of Police* 15(2):1-22.

Sherman, L. (1998). *Evidence-Based Policing*. (Ideas in American Policing series.) Washington, DC: Police Foundation.

—— D. Gottfredson, D. MacKenzie, J. Eck, P. Reuter and S. Bushway (1997). *Preventing Crime: What Works, What Doesn't, What's Promising*. Washington, DC: National Institute of Justice.

—— C. Milton and T. Kelly (1973). *Team Policing: Seven Case Studies*. Washington, DC: Police Foundation.

Stevens, D.J. (2001) "Community Policing and Managerial Techniques: Total Quality Management Techniques." *Police Journal* 74(1):26-41.

Tan, T.K. and L. Heracleous (2001). "Teaching Old Dogs New Tricks: Implementing Organizational Learning in an Asian National Police Force." *Journal of Applied Behavioral Science* 37(3):361-380.

Townsley, M. and K. Pease (2002). "Hot Spots and Cold Comfort: The Importance of Having a Working Thermometer." In: N. Tilley (ed.), *Analysis for Crime Prevention*. (Crime Prevention Studies, vol. 13.) Monsey, NY: Criminal Justice Press.

Wilkinson, M., M. Fogarty and D. Melville (1996). "Organizational Culture Change through Training and Cultural Immersion." *Journal of Organizational Change Management* 9(4):69-81.

Wycoff, M.A. and W. Skogan (1994). "Community Policing in Madison: An Analysis of Implementation of Impact." In: D. Rosenbaum (ed.), *The Challenges of Community Policing: Testing the Promises*. Thousand Oaks, CA: Sage.

Zhao, J. (1996). *Why Police Organizations Change: A Study of Community-Oriented Policing*. Washington, DC: Police Executive Research Forum.

—— N.P. Lovrich and Q. Thurman (1999). "The Status of Community Policing in American Cities: Facilitators and Impediments Revisited." *Policing: An International Journal of Police Strategies and Management* 22(1):74-92.

NOTES

1. The term problem solving implies that problems are always eliminated. Use of the term restrictively could raise the bar too high. Eck and Spelman (1987) outlined five possible results of problem solving: elimination, reduction in volume, reduction in harm, better processes to deal with the problem, and assigning responsibility to other agency or group.

2. During a review of problem solving in one neighborhood, the bulk of the initiatives consisted of only two tactics: (i) high visibility police for a period of about two weeks, and (ii) the production and dissemination of crime prevention literature in the area.

3. Exceptions exist of course. Offenders who reside in one jurisdiction but offend in another create a thorny problem.

4. As a wit once remarked, police organizations operate with the philosophy "Ready, Fire, Aim," and local governments operate with the philosophy "Ready, Aim, Aim, Aim...."

5. To illustrate, we have encountered a number of SARAs dealing with auto crime, which includes such offences as theft from motor vehicles, theft of motor vehicles, and unlawful taking of motor vehicles. The problem here is that auto crime can describe joyriding, acquisitive crime, professional car theft (parts or "ringed" vehicles) and even insurance fraud. The responses generated rarely reflect the range of problems present.

6. Richard Feynman, Nobel prize winner in physics and considered to be the greatest physicist in the second half of the twentieth century, gave three public lectures in 1963 regarding science and society. A great deal of the first was devoted to the "nature of science" and the existence of doubt and uncertainty within its practice. In it, he proposed that a sci-

entist's ability to admit ignorance was a powerful tool. He claimed that, "to solve any problem that has never been solved before, you have to leave the door to the unknown ajar... Because we have the doubt, we then propose to look in new directions for new ideas" (Feynman, 1999:26-27).

7. Exceptions exist, notably Langhoff (1982), Tan and Heracleous (2001) and Wilkinson et al. (1996).

8. This may be true, but executing the necessary adjustment is where organizational psychology could most contribute to a programme of change.

9. The uniqueness of a police organization is taken as given by researchers, yet there is no evidence that factors contributing to resistance to change are exclusive to the police.

10. Repeat victimization is an obvious exception.

11. Credit for this concept should go to Sgt. Paul Firth, of North Wales Police.

12. The number of calls did not include those made from inside the bar. The officers wanted to avoid the owners thinking they would be penalized if they asked for police assistance.

13. Several other approaches were made to convince the council not to renew licenses, such as encouraging residents to attend meetings and voice concerns over license renewal.

14. See: www.crimereduction.gov.uk/toolkits/index.htm.

REPEAT VICTIMIZATION: LESSONS FOR IMPLEMENTING PROBLEM-ORIENTED POLICING

by

Gloria Laycock

**Jill Dando Institute of Crime Science
University College, London**

and

Graham Farrell

**University of Cincinnati and Jill Dando Institute of
Crime Science**

Abstract: *This paper discusses some of the difficulties encountered in attempting to introduce ideas derived from research on repeat victimization to the police services of the United Kingdom. Repeat victimization is the phenomenon in which particular individuals or other targets are repeatedly attacked or subjected to other forms of victimization, including the loss of property. It is argued that repeat victimization is a good example of the kind of problem solving envisaged by Goldstein and discussed in his original conception of problem-oriented policing.*

The paper first briefly describes the U.K. research program on repeat victimization and a chronology of the action taken to implant the ideas into the routine of policing. It then pinpoints some of the structural features of policing in England and Wales which facilitated the process described. These features are missing in many other jurisdictions, which have a fundamentally different policing structure and call for a different approach in introducing research-based evidence to tackle problems. The implications for repeat victimization in particular, and problem-oriented policing in general, are discussed.

INTRODUCTION

Herman Goldstein's (1990) original conception of problem-oriented policing (POP) was that it would involve a fairly high-level analysis and response to a persistent problem. Identified problems would be sufficiently significant as to require the attention and support of senior police officers in dealing with them. There are relatively few examples of what Goldstein had in mind as high-level problems, but arguably repeat victimization is one. In the U.K. Home Office, repeat victimization was seen as an example of the kind of higher-order problem that Goldstein promotes. Research in a number of countries and in different policing contexts has consistently shown the presence of repeat victimization in relation to a range of offences. Developing ways of successfully reducing the incidence of repeat victimization is a major challenge for police agencies — it is, in other words, a significant problem in Goldstein's sense.

For example, at its highest level we might consider a group of individuals who are "repeat victims." They may suffer from burglary, car theft and street robbery. They may live in a high-crime area; they would be part of the group identified within the British Crime Survey as the 4% of people who suffer from about 44% of crime. In adopting a problem-solving approach, we may need to address their routine activities and try to determine what is was about their lifestyle that made them so particularly vulnerable. This is not the normal offence centred approach, but it is, we feel, a "problem-solving approach." In contrast, and at a lower level, a more detailed analysis of particular types of repeat victim might lead to the usual crime-focussed problem solving — burglary, car theft, domestic violence and so on. We might, for example, wish to address repeat commercial burglary, and find that this breaks down into burglaries involving stores, which require one type of response, and those involving small factories in a defined area, which suggest a completely different approach. Thus it could be argued that repeat victimization is the kind of higher-level problem that POP should be focussed upon, but whether or not that is accepted, the attempt to persuade the U.K. police to focus on repeat victimization as an operational strategy holds lessons for future attempts to bring POP into the policing mainstream. The U.K. experience in doing this is described in this chapter.

The British Home Office first began supporting research in this area in the early 1980s and has continued ever since. In the first part of the paper the research program is briefly described. It became clear during the course of this work that the publication of quality research was, of itself, having relatively little effect on the delivery of policing, despite some striking examples of its power as a focus for prevention. Consequently, a series of further initiatives were then taken by the Home Office to promote the implementation of the work across the U.K. police forces.[1] These are described in the second section of the paper. The implementation program was facilitated by the structural arrangements in England and Wales for the delivery of local policing, and these are discussed in the third section. They were seen as significant in assisting the introduction of research-based evidence to the police (Laycock and Clarke, 2001), although questions remain as to the depth of real understanding. These issues are considered in the fourth section. The concluding section examines the implications for future efforts to infiltrate problem-oriented approaches into police delivery mechanisms.

THE RESEARCH

Laycock (2001) describes both the program of Home Office research on repeat victimization, and the measures taken to introduce it to the U.K. police. Farrell et al. (2001) provided an estimation of the extent and nature of the implementation of repeat victimization policies by U.K. police forces by the year 2000.

The program of research on repeat victimization began with a project designed to reduce burglary on a particularly high-crime housing area in the North of England known as the Kirkholt Estate (Forrester et al., 1988). A detailed analysis of the burglary problem, as would be required for any problem-oriented approach, showed that individual premises were more likely to be burgled if they had already been burgled. In other words, there was a concentration of victimization. The problem then became reformulated as one of reducing repeat victimization, and this proved to be a particular challenge for the police and other agencies in the area. The approach taken was to protect victims by whatever means necessary to ensure that they were not revictimized. In practice, this involved a range of measures, which proved highly effective in reducing repeat victimization to zero in seven months, and reducing burglary over the whole estate by almost 75% over the following three years (Forrester et al., 1988; Pease, 1998).

The Kirkholt project marked the beginning of a substantial program of work looking at the extent to which repeat victimization featured in a range of other offences. Farrell and Pease (1993) listed a number of the key characteristics of repeat victimization that made it an attractive general crime prevention strategy. A synthesis of that work with more recent research and practice resulted in 17 reasons why the prevention of repeat victimization is an attractive strategy for policing (Table 1).

Table 1: Seventeen Reasons for Policing To Prevent Repeat Victimization

(1) Preventing repeat victimization is a crime prevention activity and hence pursuant to the most fundamental of police mandates (as defined since Robert Peel's original list of principles).

(2) Targeting repeat victimization is an efficient means of allocating, in time and space, scarce police resources to crime problems.

(3) Preventing repeat victimization is an approach that is relevant to all crimes with a target. It has been shown to be a feature of crimes including hate crimes, domestic and commercial burglary, school crime (burglary and vandalism), bullying, sexual assault, car crime, neighbor disputes, credit card fraud and other retail sector crime, domestic violence and child abuse. Even murder can be the repeat of attempted murder.

(4) Police managers can use repeat victimization as a performance indicator (Tilley, 1995). These can range from the national to the local level.

(5) Preventing repeat victimization naturally allocates resources to high crime areas, crime hot spots, and the most victimized targets (Bennett, 1995, Townsley et al., 2000).

(6) Preventing repeat victimization may inform the allocation of crime prevention to nearby targets (near-repeats) and targets with similar characteristics (virtual repeats; Pease, 1998).

(7) Preventing repeat victimization is a form of "drip feeding" of prevention resources (Pease, 1992). Since all crime does not occur at once, police resources need only be allocated as victimizations occur from day to day.

(8) Preventing repeat victimization is even less likely to result in displacement than unfocused crime prevention efforts (Bouloukos and Farrell, 1997).

(9) Preventing repeat victimization may be even more likely to result in a diffusion of crime control benefits (Clarke and Weisburd, 1994) than more general crime prevention. Offenders will be made uncertain and more generally deterred by changed circumstances at the most attractive and vulnerable targets.

(10) Preventing repeat victimization can generate common goals and positive work between police and other agencies (such as housing, social services, and victim organizations), which may in turn facilitate broader co-operation.

(11) Focusing on repeat victimization empowers police officers to do something tangible and constructive to help crime victims and for policing to become more generally oriented towards victims, who are arguably its core consumers (Farrell, 2001).

(12) Efforts to prevent repeat victimization can lead to positive feedback from victims. This is still a relatively rare reward for police in the community. It may promote good community relations.

(13) Preventing repeat victimization is triggered by a crime being reported. Since victims can be asked about prior victimizations, a response does not necessarily require data analysis.

(14) Preventing repeat victimization can sometimes — but not always — use off-the-shelf prevention tactics rather than requiring inventive problem solving.

(15) Preventing repeat victimization can be used to enhance the detection of serious and prolific offenders. Police officers like detecting offenders.

(16) Preventing repeat victimization presents possibilities for preventing and detecting organized crime and terrorism that focuses on vulnerable and, for offenders, lucrative victims and targets — including protection rackets, forced prostitution, loan-sharking, repeat trafficking via certain low-risk locations, art and other high-value thefts and robberies. (The 1993 terrorist attack on the World Trade Centre was a precursor of the 2001 attack.)

(17) Targeting repeat victimization can inform thinking on repeat crimes typically perceived as "victimless," where the repeatedly victimized target is the state or nation.

By way of illustration, Table 2 is taken from a report on commercial burglary (Webb, 1994). It shows the way in which, as the number of repeatedly burgled premises falls, the probability of repeat victimization increases. It demonstrates the cost-effectiveness of concentrating effort on the decreasing population of repeatedly targeted premises. The data illustrate the potential role of detection in the prevention of crime and open up a whole range of possibilities for the enthusiastic detective. For example, if the 27 places burgled four times could be effectively protected, perhaps by a set of judiciously placed silent alarms linked to the nearest police station, then for this sample there is a 63% probability of a further offence being prevented and perhaps an offender being captured. But it took a fair amount of professional research effort to extract the data in this form. It is not something that police data systems can routinely do, although they do not necessarily need to if the police routinely ask victims about recent prior victimizations. Other research has shown that of the order of 80% of repeat burglary victims are likely to have been re-victimised by the same offender (Pease, 1998). Concentrating effort on repeat burglary victims has the effect, therefore, of concentrating effort on repeat offenders.

Table 2: Probabilities of Repeat Commercial Burglary

Number of potential victims	Number who report at least:				
	One burglary	Two burglaries	Three burglaries	Four burglaries	Five burglaries
1,125	250	97	47	27	17
	22% (of 1,125)	39% (of 250)	48% (of 97)	57% (of 47)	63% (of 27)

Source: Table taken from Webb, 1994, data from Tilley, 1993a.

The studies described by Farrell and Pease (1993) appeared to have identified a powerful means of controlling crime, but they also highlighted some serious problems in the provision of services to victims. For example, prior to these results being published the victim support literature was reassuring victims that lightning did not strike twice; if they had been burgled once then it was unlikely to happen again, and they did not really need to take any additional precautions. This literature had to be rewritten to make it clear that although the probability of being revictimized remained low, it was higher than it otherwise would have been. Similarly the way in which the British Crime Survey results were presented was misleading in saying that people might expect to be burgled once every 40 years. In fact, most people will not be burgled at all. We now appreciate from the British Crime Survey that in any one year 95% of people are not burgled, but of those who are, 12% are burgled twice and 6% three or more times. Over all 18% of burglary victims suffer 35% of all domestic burglaries. As so often when measuring repeat victimization, due to aspects of the survey method these are conservative estimates of the extent of repeat burglary.

On the positive side, the research showed that by concentrating effort on victims, crime could be reduced. This was made easier by the observation that there was a period of heightened risk after the last offence, and the more times the person or place had been victimised, the shorter that time would be. Relatively expensive options for detection, such as mobile alarms or closed-circuit television (CCTV) cameras, thus became viable.

It is worth describing the burglary strand of the research in a little more detail, since it is of significance to the program on implementation that followed. The success of the Kirkholt project was widely reported at a time when the U.K. Government launched the Safer Cities Program (Ekblom, 1992). In its first round, this program involved supporting 20 cities around the U.K. with extra resources to develop crime prevention locally. Crime prevention co-ordinators in a number of the cities noticed the Kirkholt outcome and decided to replicate the project. Their attempts are described by Tilley (1993b), who reported mixed success largely because, he argued, the replications had misunderstood the mechanism that had made the Kirkholt project the success it was.

On the basis of Tilley's report, and other contemporaneous observations that moving from a localised but successful small project to a larger scale was not common, the Home Office funded another burglary project that used the Kirkholt approach more systematically. Ken Pease, who had been so influential in the original project, directed it. The success of Kirkholt hinged, as Pease (1998) later described it, upon protecting victims by the most appropriate means. There was, in other words, no off-the-shelf package to be applied to all the burglary victims, but a range of possible options needed to be systematically appraised. These ideas were taken and developed in the next project, which was based in West Yorkshire Constabulary and covered the whole of a police division — Huddersfield. The task was to reduce burglary (and car crime, although this part of the project is not discussed here), across the whole Division by concentrating on reducing repeat victimization. The Home Office published two reports on the work. The first (Anderson et al., 1995) described the research phase of the project, and the second (Chenery et al., 1997) outlined the results, which showed a 30% reduction in domestic burglary. The research team, of which some police officers were an integral part, adopted a phased response to burglary victims. An early iteration of this approach is set out in Table 3, but the report stresses that the responses remained flexible and changed as the police learned which were the more effective or practical. This general approach came to be known as the Olympic Model because of the bronze, silver and gold phases to prevention that it advocated.

Table 3: Measures Taken To Protect Domestic Burglary Victims

Bronze response (After first burglary)	Silver response (After second burglary)	Gold response (After third or subsequent burglary)
Victim letter with postcode pen for property marking	Further victim letter	Further victim letter
Informant checks	Search warrant	Priority on police fingerprint search
Early check of known outlets for stolen goods	Insurance incentives	Home Office portable alarm installed
Target offenders	Crime Prevention Officer visit	Police Watch (minimum daily)[b]
Crime prevention advice	Police Watch (minimum twice per week)	
Rapid repair service	"Police Aware" stickers	
Security upgrade	Mock occupancy devices	
Victim support	Audible or dummy alarm	
Cocoon Watch[a]	Improved lighting	

Adapted from Chenery et al., 1997.

a) Cocoon Watch was developed in the Kirkholt project and involved close protection of victims of burglary by their immediate neighbours, subject to agreement. It is akin to a "mini" neighbourhood watch.
b) Police Watch is a form of focused patrolling at regular and specified intervals during the six weeks after an offence during the time interval when the original offence occurred. For example, if the original offence occurred around 3pm, then that is the approximate time that the Police Watch would be carried out.

The publication of the Farrell and Pease (1993) report, and in particular the broader discussion of the significance of repeat victimization as a means of preventing crime, begged the question of how these research results could be integrated into the routine activity of the relevant agencies. What was the most effective means of disseminating the results of the work and to whom?

It was decided to focus on the police as the most appropriate agency to develop and deliver a strategy to protect victims. This was because they had the data with which to identify victims, and also had the authority to engage other agencies in the task. This was facilitated in the U.K. by pressure from central government over a number of years for a "partnership approach" to crime prevention, which culminated in the Crime and Disorder Act (1998). Under the Act, the police and local authority are required to carry out a local crime audit, prepare a crime strategy in response, and obtain agreement to the plan from the local community. This can be compared with the approach taken in the U.S.A. where there is enthusiasm for partnership between the police and "community."

THE IMPLEMENTATION PROGRAM: ENGAGING POLICE PRACTITIONERS

A number of measures were taken by the U.K. central government to raise the profile of repeat victimization as an approach to crime prevention and detection. These included:

(1) Six "roadshows" on repeat victimization, which were held across the country, and drew the research and its implications to the attention of relevant agencies, including the police. The extent to which tackling repeat victimization offered a cost-effective strategy in dealing with crime was emphasised to the senior staff invited to attend. As an aside it is worth mentioning that attending these events was cost-free to the delegates. The roadshows were fully funded by central government. In hindsight this was a mistake, as a number of invitees did not attend. If such an exercise were to be repeated, we would recommend at least a small charge as a means of ensuring that people come!

(2) A "task force" on repeat victimization was established within the central government research agency. This grand title amounted to a task force head and a seconded police officer. The head of the task force was a specialist in organisational development and had some marketing expertise. These skills proved crucial to the subsequent success of the task force, which despite modest resources was able to make a significant impact (Laycock, 2001; Laycock and Clarke, 2001).

(3) A police officer was designated as repeat victimization liaison officer in each of the 43 forces in England and Wales, whose task it was to ensure that the research was properly disseminated — in effect a local champion. It may be assumed that the police would be fully familiar with the notion that some victims are particularly vulnerable, but this was not so; nor had the implications of this for the prevention of crime registered. Indeed, in some cases the more a victim complained

about being victimised, the less inclined were some police officers to respond, a classic example being domestic assaults.

(4) Following the example of Pease in encouraging police officers to work on the projects directly and to co-author reports, the police were encouraged to present reports on their work at both practitioner and academic conferences. The police generally appear more accepting of advice from their colleagues than they are from academics, whom they may see as remote or unrealistic in their expectations of what can be delivered.

(5) Continued investment was obtained in a research program designed to demonstrate that reducing repeat victimization could reduce crime.

(6) Reducing repeat victimization was included as one of the Home Secretary's performance indicators for the police. This followed an important report by Tilley (1995) that discussed the potential performance indicators for crime prevention. Tilley argued that success in crime prevention is particularly difficult to measure because you are trying to measure non-events. He suggested that although not ideal for many offences, reducing repeat victimization was a useful first step in measuring the performance of the police in this area. Acknowledging that the police were poorly placed to even measure repeat victimization in the U.K., let alone reduce it, a staged process was adopted to develop performance measurement in this area, as set out in Table 4.

In the event, the performance regime as set out operated until 1997/98. By the end of 1998, the research department, which had been driving the crime prevention performance agenda, lost control of it and the pressure on the police to maintain their efforts in this area was reduced.

The report by Farrell et al. (2001) showed that by 1999 all forces *claimed* to have a system in place to identify repeats. It was not possible in their brief review to determine the extent to which the identification of repeats by forces was accurate or properly carried out. The requirement for the period 1996/97 was that forces should have developed a strategy to tackle repeat victimization, and most chose to concentrate upon residential and other forms of burglary. This was probably because most of the published research had been centred on domestic burglary reduction, and reducing burglary was, by then, one of the central government priorities.

Table 4: Police Performance Regime — Reducing Repeat Victimization

Year	Performance requirement	Commentary
1995 - 1996	Demonstrate capability of identifying repeat victims.	This performance indicator (PI) was chosen because in the mid-1990s most forces did not have the technical capability of measuring repeat victimization in relation to any specified offence, but many were in the process of upgrading their computer systems. This PI helped to ensure that the ability to measure repeat victimization was taken into account.
1996 - 1997	Develop a strategy to reduce repeat victimization for any locally relevant offence.	We were concerned not to specify an offence centrally. These PIs are assumed to operate at the basic command level in forces where local concerns are more relevant than central prescription. In some areas domestic violence might be a major issue, in others domestic burglary might feature. An important consequence of this approach is that it precludes the creation of simplistic lists comparing the performance of one police area with another.
1997 - 1998	Implement the strategy.	This was intended to reinforce the point that strategies need to be delivered. This is an obvious point but one often ignored by managers, whose interest stops with the articulation of a strategy.
1998 - 1999	Set targets for reduction?	It was intended that targets should be set locally as part of the strategic development.

Taken from Laycock, 2001.

The national picture showed great variation in the progress being made. The stages of policy implementation were always intended to be gradual and to allow for individual variation between forces, but the discrepancies were quite wide, with some forces appearing to do far more than others. Significantly, however, most forces (37 of 43, or 86%) reported that they had developed some form of graded response to burglary. This is the response based on the Huddersfield model described above, where crime prevention resources are allocated according to risk as determined by the number of prior victimizations (Anderson et al., 1995). For example, a victim who reports his or her third burglary within a year is likely to receive a higher-level response, perhaps including the more costly elements of detection and security hardware, than a first-time victim. This is on the assumption that such a household remains at greater risk of a further crime in the near future. In Table 5, the grade of response ranges from A (the least resource-intensive) to D (the most resource-intensive). The naming of specific graded response systems varied between forces, so that some called it "gold, silver, bronze," others "red, amber, green," others "A, B, C" etc. (This re-labelling of what are essentially the same responses, reflects the U.K. police's disinclination to adopt an approach that was not invented in their force — commonly called the "not invented here" syndrome.)

Table 5: Number of Forces Adopting Graded and Other Responses

Tactic	% of Forces (N=43)
Graded Response:	
Graded response/activity after 1st crime (Level A).	77%
Preventive activity after 2nd crime (Level B).	84%
Preventive activity after 3rd crime (Level C).	70%
Preventive activity after 4+ (Level D).	2%
Other Responses:	
Linking repeat victimization prevention to detection activity.	40%
Linking repeat victimization prevention to problem solving.	33%

Adapted from Farrell et al., 2001, page 10.[2]

The Forces could also report more than one level of graded response, so Table 5 contains double counting of forces. Of the 43 forces, 29 reported having a specific response to each of a first, a second and a third victimization. Three forces reported a response to only a first or second victimization (unfortunately the survey did not ask why), five reported a response to a combination of both of a second or third burglary, and six forces reported not having a graded response. The graded responses were sometimes integrated with other efforts as part of an overall repeat victimization strategy. Seventeen forces (40%) reported combining offender detection efforts with the prevention of repeat victimization, since repeat victimization can predict where prolific offenders are likely to be. Fourteen forces (33%) reported combining the prevention of repeat victimization with a problem-solving approach. Problem solving is a methodology that can usefully complement other efforts to prevent repeat victimization (Farrell and Sousa, 2001; Bullock and Tilley, this volume).

The penetration of these ideas into forces seems substantial, but it is worth questioning the depth of understanding underpinning the responses. Although it was not specifically addressed by the questionnaire, the interest in the Huddersfield project was expressed not by an increasing demand for the research report, but by a stream of police officers visiting the Division to hear for themselves what was done. There were also a number of conference presentations on the research, which were popular with the police and their partners. The U.K. police, in common with many of their colleagues in other places, have a reputation as a "can do" organisation. One consequence of this is that they prefer the spoken word to the written word as a means of communication. Reading slows them down, and they would rather spend their time visiting a project or program to reading about it. In addition, the "Olympic Model" was "catchy" — it was memorable, and made intuitive sense. Although perhaps more by good fortune than design, the representation of the initiative was marketable.

Farrell et al. (2001) conceded that on the basis of their survey they could not determine to what extent the strategies which forces claimed to have in place had actually been implemented as planned. Furthermore, although forces claimed to have launched a wide range of tactics as part of their repeat victimization strategies, some of the tactics looked suspiciously like the run-of-the-mill force crime prevention activity that had been going on for some time. Neighbourhood Watch (NW) is a good example. There was no sense from the responses from forces that NW had in any way been modified to make it more relevant to the needs of existing victims.

It seemed clear from the review that forces were trying to respond to the requirement that they address repeat victimization. Unfortunately, it also seemed likely that the tactics were not obviously targeted to the protection of victims, and many had a weak preventive mechanism (Pawson and Tilley, 1997; Tilley and Laycock, 2002). It is largely assumed that police officers know — either from training, experience or from research literature such as the Home Office publications — of the full and wide range of prevention possibilities and the mechanisms that underlie them. This assumption may well be wrong. Indeed the review by Pease (1998) was addressed to the many police officers with whom he had discussed repeat victimization over the bulk of the last decade, but who were not familiar with the research. As Pease (1998, Executive Summary, page v) says:

> Many believed they knew about the available research, but were familiar with only a small proportion of it. Neither had they encountered anything which sought to locate recent repeat victimization research in thinking about crime prevention more generally.

The success with which the ideas associated with repeat victimization, as a crime reduction strategy, have penetrated the routine of U.K. police thinking is therefore debatable. Nevertheless, when compared with other jurisdictions, the U.K. police appear to be well ahead of the game. This has been facilitated by the committed and well-informed central government research agency that managed the process of research and dissemination, and also by the controls over policing which are available from the centre, as discussed in the next section.

RELEVANT U.K. POLICING STRUCTURES

There are 43 police forces covering England and Wales, all of which are overseen by the Home Office at central government level. The Home Secretary, the most senior member of the Government in the Home Office, is responsible to Parliament for the efficient and effective delivery of policing in England and Wales. This responsibility is shared with the locally accountable "police authority" and the force's Chief Constable, whose operational independence is strictly guarded. This tripartite structure gives the police a significant degree of independence from central control. In this respect the U.K. forces (the same system essentially operates in Northern Ireland and Scotland), are very different from the police agencies of continental Europe, where generally a more centralised and militaristic approach is taken.

It would, however, be a mistake to characterise the 43 forces as totally independent of the centre. Quite apart from the Home Secretary's powers to set a performance regime for forces, there are a number of other levers over which the Home Office has control and which they can and do use to influence policing. These are set out in Table 6.

Table 6: Centrally Available "Levers" over Policing in England and Wales

Category	Lever	Commentary
Financial	General police funding	The Home Office provides 51% of the funding for the 43 police forces.
	Project money	The Crime Reduction Program (Tilley et al., 1999) has provided a major injection of funds in the crime reduction field, which are being used to influence the delivery of policing.
Legal	Police Inspectorate	There is a high profile central Police Inspectorate in the U.K., which regularly inspects forces and reports publicly on performance. It has completed two recent inspections on crime reduction.
	Legislation	The Crime and Disorder Act requires the police to work with local government and develop a strategy to tackle local crime and disorder based on a crime audit and consultation with the community.
Managerial	Training	There is considerable central influence over police training in the U.K. Crime prevention training through a specially designated college, for example, is under direct Home Office control.
	Audit Commission	The Audit Commission has a statutory responsibility to report on the extent to which the police are carrying out their responsibilities in an effective and efficient manner. It carries out regular inspections of forces on various themes and publishes its reports.
	Performance regime	Police performance against a range of criteria is assessed on an annual cycle. The Home Secretary sets some of the targets for crime reduction.
Intellectual	Research results	The free availability and wide dissemination of Home Office research papers has had increasing influence over U.K. policing since the early 1990s.
	Persuasion	Advice and guidance is provided to police forces on a regular basis from central government. Although much of this has no statutory force, it is often seen to be setting out good practice.

Although the police and their local authorities regard the central power of the Home Office as a potential threat to independence (which it is), it does offer some advantages in disseminating research and encouraging the spread of good practice, which a totally localised system would not enjoy. Because there are only 43 forces, it is feasible to circulate research reports to them all, hold meetings with all forces represented and inspect them on a regular basis.

To take the United States of America as an extreme example, there are relatively few levers available to the federal government other than money and perhaps those in Table 4 under the "intellectual" heading. And the fragmentary nature of U.S. policing means that such levers as there are, are fairly indirect. It is true that the majority of U.S. police agencies now claim to be community-oriented (U.S. Bureau of Justice Assistance, 1997), and many are trying to "solve problems," but there is still very little hard evidence that what they are doing under these headings is having any real effect or that the claims to problem solving are any more than rhetorical (Goldstein, this volume; Scott, 2000). The resistance of the police on the front line to problem solving is considerable, as U.K. research has shown (Leigh et al., 1998).

INTRODUCING RESEARCH-BASED EVIDENCE INTO POLICING

Problem-oriented policing, like the work on repeat victimization, which is a particular and common problem facing police agencies, stemmed from an academic base. Goldstein's original ideas were set out in a book (Goldstein, 1990), in various academic papers and during numerous presentations to police audiences over the years. There is no denying that the ideas have penetrated police thinking. The annual Problem-Oriented Policing Conference held in the United States each year, and its more recently established equivalent in the U.K., are both well attended by serving police officers. There are also some outstanding examples of work being done by front-line officers, and interest in the annual Goldstein Award for problem-oriented policing excellence remains high. The equivalent in the U.K., the Tilley Award, is also fairly well subscribed with about 70 applications each year.

Placing this in perspective, however, leads to a more pessimistic view. Although over 1,000 delegates typically attend the annual U.S. conference in San Diego, there are currently about 17,000 police agencies in the U.S.A. with almost 1 million sworn and civilian full-time staff (U.S. Bureau of Justice Statistics, 2001). As a proportion of the whole, the attendance at the POP Conference is not quite so impressive. Furthermore the quality of some of the presentations is variable. Many of the projects presented lack rigorous analysis and there remains an emphasis on enforcement as the response of choice. Attendance at some of the sessions can also be variable — San Diego has a number of attractive distractions!

The argument in the remainder of this paper is that the assumptions made by those academics, keen to encourage this approach over so many years, were wrong. The assumptions, essentially, revolved around the belief that problem-oriented policing was offering a more rational approach to policing, with a multitude of advantages to victims, the general public and the police themselves. Goldstein has made the case most eloquently for many years and continues to do so. His chapter in this volume is a good example. It is difficult for a rational reader to disagree with the case he makes.

This argument in support of problem-oriented policing was strengthened by the belief that the present system of policing does not work well. Reactive policing can be seen as inefficient and ineffective. On these grounds, combined with the obvious logic of the case in favour of problem-oriented policing, it was assumed that the police, including senior managers, would embrace it and change the fundamental nature of policing, away from reaction and toward a more data-driven empirical approach. In essence, it was assumed that "problem-oriented policing will sell itself."

This has not happened. Despite continued research in the area, along with innumerable books, research papers and conferences, the police remain doggedly wedded to their more traditional ways of doing business. Why has it proved so difficult to change these organisations? It may be easier to address the question of why should the police change rather than why have they not.

Apart from an ongoing wish to continually improve service delivery, which it has to be assumed would be at the margins of what is generally being done, there is no sensible reason for any organisation to radically change its approach. The introduction of repeat victimization into U.K. policing did not challenge anything fundamental about the routine of police service delivery. On the contrary, it called for an improvement in what they claimed to be doing anyway — protecting victims, preventing crime and catching offenders. This has not been the case with attempts to introduce problem-oriented policing into policing. Those wishing to promote problem-oriented policing have criticised the way in which policing is currently delivered: in particular there has been a criticism of incident-driven policing — in effect a fundamental criticism of the status quo.

We should however concede that 78% of people in the 2000 BCS said that their local police did a very or fairly good job, and that levels of confidence in the police remained virtually unchanged throughout the 1990s (although these have decreased slightly since the 1998 BCS) (Sims and Myhill, 2001). There is simply no criticism of incident-driven policing by the public. On the contrary the police are, not unreasonably, expected to respond to calls-for-service as quickly and efficiently as possible. Although this expectation is seen to stem from the public, it is reinforced through the democratically elected agencies that pay for the police, monitor their performance or report on their activities. It includes the media. Indeed, not only is incident-driven policing expected, it is applauded. Many police agencies are measured against their ability to answer the emergency calls quickly, and get to the location of the problem rapidly. (There the interest ends. There is little discussion or criticism of what happens when the call is responded to, other, perhaps, than the failure of the police to arrest someone.) So criticising incident-driven policing, and using it as an argument for change, is not likely to win the day.

The argument from the supporters of problem-oriented policing, of course, is not that responsive policing is unacceptable in the sense of responding to urgent calls-for-service, but that the continued response to calls-for-service to the same location, or in response to the same persistent problem, is not the best way of doing business. The evidence for the inefficiency of the approach, which might lead to criticism of police performance, is buried within the police data systems. It is difficult to access this evidence without considerable interrogation of data that were collected for other purposes (largely to count incidents).

Interestingly, the *experience* of the public in higher-crime areas is perhaps more sensitive to this lack of police efficiency. Repeated calls-for-service from the same people to the same place arguably do not lead those individuals to a positive view of policing. But because high-crime areas are relatively rare, and are populated by people with less capacity to challenge policing delivery, there remains no fundamental criticism of revisiting the same place and essentially doing nothing to solve the problems. A report by Bradley (1998) provides some support for this view. His research involved a series of focus group discussions with members of the public living in different areas and from different socio-economic groups. He concluded (Bradley, 1998:11):

> ...people who are the most exposed to crime problems and to their perpetrators are far more inclined to prioritise police resources toward direct/proactive/targeted actions. In contrast members of the public who are far less directly exposed to, or more geographically distant from, crime problems are inclined to seek reassurance through visible patrol....

The emphasis by those "in the know" on "direct/pro-active/ targeted actions" probably meant that the police should make more effort to arrest known offenders. We might hope this was being prioritised not because of a fundamental wish on the part of the individuals involved to encourage the use of the criminal justice system but because of their deeply held view that this was how to deal with offenders. They saw no alternative. The problem-oriented policing approach would be to deal with the problem as efficiently and fairly as possible, ideally without recourse to the criminal justice system. At its most charitable, we might argue that those vulnerable people on the high-crime estates were actually asking that the problems be solved. Arrest was the only way they knew how.

Further support for this view comes from the British Crime Survey (Sims and Myhill, 2001), which shows that satisfaction levels appear to be directly influenced by the practical outcomes of police investigations. Seventy-seven percent of victims were very or fairly satisfied with police handling of the case if charges were brought, compared with 39% if the police knew who the offender was but brought no charges.

There is, therefore, no substantial criticism of present policing *style*. When the police are criticised, it is usually because there has been a major ethical disaster, because they are not seen to be responding quickly enough to calls-for-service, not arresting enough people, and not getting them through the criminal justice system and into prison. Despite these particular criticisms, police performance in most advanced Western democracies is consistently judged to be good. Failing to solve problems in a more fundamental sense is, for most members of the public, the police themselves, and politicians, simply not an issue.

Furthermore, the fact that the present system does not work is somewhat difficult to justify in the context of persistently falling crime rates across the advanced western democracies over at least the past decade. Of course, we can all argue that these falls are attributable to a whole range of factors, only one of which is police performance (Blumstein and Wallman, 2000), but the fact that they have fallen does not play to a significant reform agenda for policing. Nor, as we noted above, is there a head of steam from the public to see radical police reform on the scale suggested by problem-oriented policing advocates.

Finally, the argument for the advancement of problem-oriented policing, either along-side current policing styles or more typically as a radical alternative to them, has not been based on a powerful or clear-cut demonstration of the efficacy of the approach. Despite the fact that problem-oriented policing has been around in some form for

decades, there are still relatively few large-scale examples of its having "worked." Attempts to demonstrate to the police through research
that there are other, more efficient ways of doing business have not
been sufficiently attended to by academics (a point made by Goldstein in this volume). Partly as a consequence of this, there have
simply not been a large or dramatic enough set of well conducted
demonstration projects showing that the approach works. The work
on reducing repeat victimization provides one solid and persistent
example of the efficacy of the approach, but it has not been "pack-
aged" as a problem-oriented policing initiative.

One reason for the scarcity of good problem-solving examples is
that there are relatively few police agencies with the skills to develop
the projects or programs. In order to carry out the problem-oriented
policing process as envisaged by Goldstein and others, existing crime
data have to be collected, analysed and interpreted, and there may be
a need for additional information. Some sort of response then has to
be developed and the solutions implemented. The specific skills to
carry out these tasks, particularly if this involves thinking beyond
the usual arrest and prosecution options, are not well developed in
police departments.

CONCLUSIONS

The case for the police adopting a problem-oriented approach remains strong. Nobody has yet challenged the logic of the argument.
But we may need to aim lower than radical reform of the whole police
delivery mechanism. There is no reason why problem-oriented policing cannot live alongside other policing styles. Indeed there are good
reasons to suggest that it should. Incident-driven policing cannot
and should not go away, and it is obvious that the police will retain
their enforcement role. The issue is rather one of balance. How much
resource should be devoted to responding to calls, and to supporting
the criminal justice system, and how much should be diverted to
problem-oriented policing and a much broader set of crime and disorder control options?

At this stage in the development of problem-oriented policing it is
not possible to answer that question. But it is fairly clear that the
current balance is not correct. There are far too many cases where
persistent problems are ignored and where, even when the police do
think about solving a problem, they fall back on the standard approach of arrest and prosecution. They do not naturally consider alternatives.

Even if only modest progress is to be made in introducing problem-oriented policing, then we need to look more systematically at

the range of levers that are available to change the police way of working. The recent massive investment in the U.S.A. through the 1994 Crime Act will take some time to "bite," but the extent of the investment was such as to potentially make a difference (Roth et al., 2000). And for the first time research publications of relevance, which might actually be read and used, are coming from the COPS Office (the *Problem-Oriented Guides for Police*).

In parallel, there have been major developments in the style of police management at basic command level. The most well known is the Compstat process introduced in New York City and widely copied elsewhere in the United States and in other countries. At its worst, Compstat is an excuse for bullying management and staff harassment. At its best, however, it draws the local command team's attention to the incidence of crime and disorder in their areas and raises expectations that something will be done about reducing the extent of the problems that are illustrated by the data. This process is beginning to create a policing context within which police commanders will be looking for creative solutions to persistent problems. Better understanding of data and its interpretation, and a more sophisticated menu of potential responses to problems, should develop as a consequence.

This process can be facilitated by improvements in the training of problem analysts, or the development of the role of crime analysts, so that they are not only able to collect and analyse data on presenting problems, but can go beyond that and provide a reasoned justification for a range of potential solutions.

Specific Conclusions from the Repeat Victimization Story

The U.K. repeat victimization story holds several key lessons for problem-oriented policing generally.

- It should not be assumed that any change in policing style will sell itself.

- The success of the approach needs to be demonstrated through a robust research program. The work on repeat victimization from the U.K. has been described as "hypothesis based" (Laycock, 2001), and as such contributed to the development of a significant body of knowledge on the repeat victimization phenomenon.

- Any proposed change will be resisted if the *status quo* is seen as enjoying wide support.

- A proactive approach to marketing change needs to be developed and levers need to be identified.

- The more direct the leverage, the more likely that changes will be made.

- Reducing repeat victimization could be used as a spearhead for changing policing style toward problem-oriented policing. The 17 reasons for policing repeat victimization (Table 1) give hope to the possibility that policing will become more conducive to broader victim-oriented, and through that problem-oriented efforts. Reducing repeat victimization in general, or in its more specific manifestation as it relates to particular offences, plays to the existing police agenda of reducing crime, catching offenders and protecting victims. It can be specifically sold as such. It does, therefore, offer the possibility of introducing problem solving through the back door as it were. In order to reduce repeat victimization the police would, necessarily, solve problems.

To end on an optimistic note, the final lesson is that, although much still remains to be done in the U.K., policing can be significantly shifted towards a problem-oriented agenda, and that a hypothesis-based research and evidence-driven agenda can be systematically introduced.

Address correspondence to: Professor Gloria Laycock, Director, Jill Dando Institute of Crime Science, University College London, 3rd Floor, 1 Old Street, London EC1V 9HL. E-mail: <g.laycock@ucl.ac.uk>.

REFERENCES

Anderson, D., S. Chenery, and K. Pease (1995). *Biting Back: Tackling Repeat Burglary and Car Crime.* (Crime Detection and Prevention Series Paper 58.) London, UK: Home Office.

Bennett, T. (1995). "Identifying, Explaining and Targeting Burglary 'Hot Spots.'" *European Journal on Criminal Policy and Research* 3:113-123.

Blumstein, A. and J. Wallman (eds.), (2000). *The Crime Drop in America.* (Cambridge Studies in Criminology.) Cambridge, UK: Cambridge University Press.

Bouloukos, A.C. and G. Farrell (1997). "On the Displacement of Repeat Victimization." In: G. Newman, R.V. Clarke and S.G. Shoham (eds.), *Rational Choice and Situational Crime Prevention.* Aldershot, UK: Dartmouth Press.

Bradley, R. (1998). *Public Expectations and Perceptions of Policing.* (Police Research Series Paper 96.) London, UK: Home Office.

Chenery, S., J. Holt and K. Pease (1997). *Biting Back II: Reducing Repeat Victimization in Huddersfield.* (Crime Detection and Prevention Series Paper 82.) London, UK: Home Office.

Clarke, R.V. and D. Weisburd (1994). "Diffusion of Crime Control Benefits: Observations on the Reverse of Displacement." *Crime Prevention Studies* 2:165-184.

"Crime and Disorder Act" (c.37) (1998). London, UK: Her Majesty's Stationery Office.

Ekblom, P. (1992). "The Safer Cities Program Impact Evaluation: Problems and Progress." *Studies on Crime and Crime Prevention* 1:35-51.

Farrell, G. (2001). "How Victim-oriented is Policing?" In: A. Gaudreault and I. Waller (eds.), *Xth International Symposium on Victimology: Selected Symposium Proceedings.* Montreal, CAN: International Symposium on Victimology.

—— and W. Sousa (2001). "Repeat Victimization and Hot Spots: The Overlap and its Implications for Problem-oriented Policing." In: G. Farrell and K. Pease (eds.), *Repeat Victimization.* (Crime Prevention Studies, vol. 12.) Monsey, NY: Criminal Justice Press.

—— A. Edmunds, L. Hobbs and G. Laycock (2000). *RV Snapshot: UK Policing and Repeat Victimization.* (Crime Reduction Research Series Paper 5.) London, UK: Home Office.

—— and K. Pease (1993). *Once Bitten, Twice Bitten: Repeat Victimization and its Implications for Crime Prevention.* (Crime Prevention Unit Paper 46.) London, UK: Home Office.

Forrester, D., S. Frenz M. O'Connell and K. Pease (1990). *The Kirkholt Burglary Prevention Project: Phase II.* (Crime Prevention Unit Paper 23.) London, UK: Home Office.

—— M. Chatterton and K. Pease with the assistance of R. Brown (1988). *The Kirkholt Burglary Prevention Project, Rochdale.* (Crime Prevention Unit Paper 13.) London, UK: Home Office.

Goldstein, H. (1990). *Problem-Oriented Policing.* New York: McGraw Hill.

Laycock, G. (2001). "Hypothesis Based Research: The Repeat Victimization Story." *Criminal Justice: The International Journal of Policy and Practice* 1(1):59-82.

—— and R.V. Clarke (2001). "Crime Prevention Policy and Government Research: A Comparison of the United States and the United Kingdom." *International Journal of Comparative Sociology* XLII(1-2):235-755. (Special issue: "Varieties of Comparative Criminology," edited by Gregory Howard and Graeme Newman.)

Leigh, A., T. Read and N. Tilley (1998). *Brit Pop II: Problem-oriented Policing in Practice.* (Crime Detection and Prevention Series No. 93.) London, UK: Home Office.

Pawson, R. and N. Tilley (1997). *Realistic Evaluation.* London, UK: Sage.

Pease, K. (1998). *Repeat Victimization: Taking Stock.* (Crime Detection and Prevention Series Paper 90.) London, UK: Home Office.

—— (1992). "The Kirkholt Project: Preventing Burglary on a British Public Housing Estate." *Security Journal* 2(2):73-77.

Problem-Oriented Guides for Police. Series is available from: www.cops.usdoj.gov.

Roth, J.A., J.F. Ryan, S.J. Gaffigan, C.S. Koper, M.H. Moore, J.A. Roehl, C.C. Johnson, G.E. Moore, R.M. White, M.E. Buerger, E.A. Langston and D. Thatcher (2000). *National Evaluation of the COPS Program — Title I of the 1994 Crime Act.* (National Criminal Justice Report 183643.) Washington, DC: Office of Justice Programs, U.S. Department of Justice.

Scott, M. (2000). *Problem-Oriented Policing: Reflections on the First 20 Years.* (Final Report to the Office of Community-Oriented Policing Services.) Washington, DC: U.S. Department of Justice.

Sims, L. and A. Myhill (2001). *Policing and the Public: Findings from the 2000 British Crime Survey* (Research Findings No 136.) Research, Development and Statistics Directorate, London, UK: Home Office.

Tilley, N (1995). *Thinking About Crime Prevention Performance Indicators.* (Police Research Group Paper 57.) London, UK: Home Office.

—— (1993a). *The Prevention of Crime Against Small Businesses: The Safer Cities Experience.* (Crime Prevention Unit Paper 45.) London, UK: Home Office.

—— (1993b). *After Kirkholt: Theory, Methods and Results of Replication Evaluations.* (Crime Prevention Unit Paper 47.) London, UK: Home Office.

—— and G. Laycock (2002). *Working Out What To Do: Evidence-based Crime Reduction.* (Crime Reduction Series Paper 11.) London, UK: Home Office.

—— K. Pease, M. Hough, and R. Brown (1999). *Burglary Prevention: Early Lessons from the Crime Reduction Program*. (Crime Reduction Research Series Paper 1.) London, UK: Home Office.

Townsley, M., R. Homel and J. Chaseling (2000). "Repeat Burglary Victimisation: Spatial and Temporal Patterns." *Australian and New Zealand Journal of Criminology* 33(1):37-63.

U.S. Bureau of Justice Assistance (1997). *Crime Prevention and Community Policing: A Vital Partnership*. (NCJ Monograph 166819.) Washington, DC: Office of Justice Programs, U.S. Department of Justice.

U.S. Bureau of Justice Statistics (2001). *Local Police Departments, 1999*. Washington, DC: Office of Justice Programs, U.S. Department of Justice.

Webb, B. (1994). "Tackling Repeat Victimization: Getting it Right." Paper presented at the National Board for Crime Prevention regional Conferences, May, 1994.

NOTES

1. This paper refers to the "U.K. police" although most of the initiatives were taken in relation to the 43 police forces of England and Wales, which have a particular relationship with the Home Office. The work was, nevertheless, also relevant to the police in Scotland, Northern Ireland, The Channel Isles and the Isle of Man, and research reports were also circulated routinely to them.

2. Aspects of this table were revised from the original and it includes new analysis for the present study.

ADVANCING PROBLEM-ORIENTED POLICING: LESSONS FROM DEALING WITH DRUG MARKETS

by

Rana Sampson
Problem-oriented Policing Consultant

Abstract: In the early 1990s, American policing, applying a problem-oriented approach, displayed much creative energy in closing drug markets. This has not translated to a wider range of quality efforts in tackling other common crimes, such as burglary, auto theft, and shoplifting. While few of the factors that combined to fuel wide exploration of creative solutions in drug markets are present for other crime and safety problems, there may be some simple ways to engage the police to further study and target other crimes. Three strategies are offered: identifying, understanding, and responding to snowball crimes; using a situational crime prevention approach to graded responses for repeat victimization; and examining privately-owned properties for disproportionate demands on police service with an eye towards shifting responsibility for crime-place management to these owners.

INTRODUCTION

During the last two decades, largely as the result of Herman Goldstein's work (1979, 1990), a number of police leaders have advocated that police should take a problem-oriented approach to their work and that police organizations should shift from a reactive, call-driven operation to proactive problem-based policing (Scott, 2000). However, at the 20-year mark, quality police problem solving, as well as full reform of policing operations to maximize the ability of departments to systematically examine and more effectively respond to community safety problems, still remains more of an idea than an accomplishment. Response time is still the measure of policing that local political leaders favor, crime-clearance rates are still dismally low (even after a decade-long decline in crime), and arrests, summonses and car stops remain the main tools of proactive American policing.

There were times in the last decade when effectively and creatively addressing specific public safety problems was of high priority for the police. This was particularly true when police focused on open-air drug markets (Kleiman and Smith, 1990; U.S. Bureau of Justice Assistance, 1993; Sampson and Scott, 2000).

This paper attempts to develop a set of lessons from police and community efforts at tackling drug markets as a means for further advancing the application of effective problem solving to other crime and safety problems. The first section of the paper examines the range of tactics that police and communities developed to close drug markets. The second section of the paper explores possible reasons the police explored so many ways to close these markets and whether similar spurs exist to attract police to tackle other crime and safety problems. The third and final section of the paper discusses some of the lessons that can be drawn from work on drug markets, and attempts to capture straightforward steps (based on these lessons) that police can take to tackle other, more complex, crime and safety problems.

THE ROLE OF ILLICIT OPEN-AIR MARKETS IN ADVANCING PROBLEM-ORIENTED POLICING

During the early 1990s, at least initially, interest in problem-oriented policing spread beyond a handful of police departments, picking up momentum with the emergence of open-air drug markets (particularly involving crack) in predominately poor, urban U.S. neighborhoods and then in suburban enclaves (Sampson and Scott, 2000).

Experimentation in closing drug markets, particularly in apartment complexes, produced a wide array of new police tactics and involved much more analysis than police were accustomed to (Sampson, 2001a). However, as will be argued later in this paper, the analysis was less than is required to understand most other crimes, such as prostitution, auto theft, burglary and even shoplifting.

For purposes of this paper, the range of responses that officers and communities developed in addressing drug markets in apartment complexes is organized under the four situational crime prevention categories developed by Clarke (1997): increasing risk, reducing reward, increasing effort, and removing excuses. It will be apparent from the list below that a very wide range of responses was adopted.

Increasing Perceived Risk

- Meeting with property owners and outlining the costs associated with permitting drug dealing on the property.
- Credit checks of prospective tenants.
- Verifying prospective tenants' income sources.
- Doing a criminal history check of all prospective tenants.
- Police surveying of tenants to gain more accurate information.
- Encouraging tenants to document illegal activity.
- Encouraging property managers to keep "in-house" log of illegal activity on property and actions taken to resolve the problem.
- Having legitimate tenants attend court hearings (court watch).
- Enforcing building code violations.
- Using surveillance cameras.
- Obtaining a temporary restraining order against the property owner from operating the property as a public nuisance.
- Informing mortgagors that the property will lose value because it is being used as a drug market.

Decreasing Perceived Reward

- Using asset forfeiture.
- Enforcing tax laws concerning unreported income.
- Taking civil action for monetary damages against property owners who fail to take action to stem dealing on property.
- Applying nuisance abatement.

Increasing Perceived Effort

- Establishing a no-cash policy for deposits or monthly rent.

- Preventing access to vacant apartments used for dealing or using.

- Controlling access to property and restricting parking to "tenants only."

- Limiting potential buyers' ability to cruise through the area in search of open drug markets.

- Prohibiting or limiting on-street parking.

Removing Excuses[1]

- Establishing tenancy rules.

- Evicting dealers.

- Sending a letter to property owners from the police chief alerting them to the consequences of failing to take action.

- Supplying owners with calls-for-service data for their properties, and with comparison data for well-run nearby properties.

- Establishing a landlord training program.

- Establishing a crime-free multi-housing program.

- Engaging an apartment managers' association to work with the owner.

- Doing reference checks of prospective tenants' prior tenancies.

- Adding a "no drug" addendum to lease agreements.

- Enforcing city ordinances or state laws requiring owners to address conditions that foster drug markets on private property.

- Posting "no trespassing" signs.

- Asking owners to require property managers to address illegal activity.

- Using vertical prosecution for arrests coming from a particular property (one prosecutor handles all arrests from a single property).

- Persuading prosecutors to seek court-ordered treatment of chronic users who buy at the apartment complex.

- Providing space for alternative legal activities on the property.

- Launching a media campaign against slumlords whose properties house drug markets.

- Encouraging tenants to petition property owners to rid the complex of drug dealing.

- Holding community anti-drug marches in front of the property owner's home.

Possible Reasons for Extensive Police Exploration of Creative Ways To Close Drug Markets

First, why did police so broadly explore ways to close drug markets? Second, why then did police efforts to stem drug markets not translate into equal levels of enthusiasm for other problem-solving projects, for crimes such as auto theft, commercial or residential burglary or even shoplifting?[2]

- *Police Perceived Open-Air Drug Markets as a Refutation of Their Power.* Police experienced open-air drug markets as a personal rebuff to their authority. Markets were often visually blatant, communicating an "in your face" taunt to patrol officers and visually exploding the myth that police control the streets. This is not true of many other crimes, such as auto theft, burglary, shoplifting, and robbery, which most often occur when police are not present.

- *Problem-oriented Policing in Drug Markets Still Allowed for Traditional Policing Tactics.* Taking a more comprehensive problem-oriented approach to the market did not preclude cops from making arrests. A single, active drug property even in a small city could generate 100 arrests in one year. As a result, policing drug markets, even using a problem-oriented approach, continued to feel, in part, like "real police work." For other types of crimes (auto theft, burglary, shoplifting and robbery), fewer arrests are likely to be involved creating an even greater contrast to traditional policing.

- *Communities Supported the Closing of Drug Markets.* Communities complained about open-air markets, which, in part, drove police to intensively focus on them. This is not true of many other crimes. As a result, police may not view these other crimes as a priority.

- *Drug Markets Contained Guns.* Some drug dealers carried guns to protect themselves from robbery attempts made by competing dealers or predatory criminals. Officers could make gun, not just drug arrests, and gun arrests are highly prized in American policing. Many other crimes involve less danger to police, and other officers may perceive tackling these crimes as less worthwhile.

- *Drug Market Analysis is Relatively Straightforward.* Analysis generally required that police possess only basic analytic skills, predominately in identifying property ownership, conducting surveillance, gathering information from nearby residents, and reviewing calls-for-service data. By comparison, analyzing a problem such as residential burglary can involve sifting through hundreds of past burglary reports, comparing entry points, articles stolen, conducting environmental surveys to determine differences in lighting and visibility of entry points, and conducting literature reviews on effective anti-burglary efforts.

- *Tackling Drug Markets Involved Gamesmanship.* Open-air drug markets allowed police to engage in a game of "outfoxing" the opponent. This involved a competition between officers and dealers — each time dealers changed their tactics, officers had to change theirs so as not to be outdone by the dealers (Lengel, 2000). Perhaps this "game" helped to engage officers. Crimes such as shoplifting and auto theft will have little to offer in this regard.

- *Assessing Impact in Drug Markets is Relatively Uncomplicated.* Once responses are in place, the impact is more easily determined in open-air drug markets than for most other crimes. In drug markets, an assessment might include visually appraising the market, resurveying of nearby residents, and reviewing current calls-for-service. For a problem such as auto theft from public parking facilities, an assessment may involve recalculating risk rates by parking lot, an activity totally unfamiliar to police.

- *Drug Markets Allowed Police to Maintain a Paramilitary Image.* In drug markets, officers could believe that they were part of a war — "the war on drugs" — reinforcing the police paramilitary image and justifying, in some departments, practices such as donning camouflage and staging masked jump-outs to capture dealers.[3]

- *Little Organizational Assistance is Required to Close a Drug Market.* One patrol officer, with community help, can close a drug market, particularly if laws are already in place that can assist in that process, such as nuisance abatement laws. Reducing other types of crime problems often requires the assistance of trained crime analysts — in some cases researchers — and to a greater extent than in drug markets, the involvement of mid-and upper level police managers to steer, manage and contribute their skills to the effort.[4]

- *Communities Agreed to Hold Property Owners Accountable for Drug Markets.* Communities could be persuaded that property owners of drug-infested properties had to take responsibility for actions on their land. It helped that a number of these owners were slumlords, engendering little support in the community. It is harder, perhaps, to convince community members that police should shift responsibility for other safety problems, such as false alarm responses,[5] or to convince corporations and industry that they have the bulk of responsibility for reducing auto theft, shoplifting (Clarke, 2001a), gas drive-offs, burglary, and phantom wireless 911 calls (Sampson, 2002).

The elements that allowed for police innovation — the profusion of dangerous open-air drug markets, community activism around them, and the ability of police to retain strong elements of traditional policing (arrests, citations, car stops) — are unlikely to present themselves in the same form for other crime and safety problems. How then do we persuade police to use problem-oriented measures in addressing the myriad of these other problems? In the next sections, three lessons from the work on drug markets are explored.

LESSON 1: OPEN-AIR DRUG MARKETS AS "SNOWBALL" CRIMES

One crime produces opportunities for another. Burglary produces the opportunity for fencing stolen goods, and pickpocketing produces the opportunity for identity theft. One offense also produces opportunities for a crime chain (Felson and Clarke, 1998). Auto theft produces the opportunity for: (1) stealing the contents of the vehicle (CDs, stereo), (2) taking parts from the vehicle such as airbags, and (3) selling the car to someone else who then, (4) exports the car. All of the crimes along a chain may not occur, but they can. Some offenders will intentionally move along the chain, and some do so unintentionally: e.g., a convenience store robbery turns into a serious assault on the clerk when a gun goes off accidentally (Felson and Clarke, 1998).

So, one crime can produce a crime chain, but beyond that, it may be that certain *crime markets*, such as open-air drug markets, produce even wider crime links, a "snowball" of crime, not just a chain. For instance, open-air drug markets appear to create opportunities for all those who frequent them to engage in additional crime.[6] As a result, for purposes of this paper, these are called snowball crimes, *crimes that can bring a series of crimes to a location.* Figure 1 depicts a drug market creating opportunities for other crimes at the same location.

If the snowball analogy holds, it is clear that closing drug markets is a worthwhile activity for police because this can reduce the opportunity for many other crimes. This may also be true of prostitution markets that have similar snowball qualities. Prostitution markets may produce less crime, but they may spread venereal diseases and AIDS. In addition, prostitutes are frequently drug dependent and spend much of their earnings on drugs, fueling a drug market (perhaps nearby) to satisfy their addiction.[7] An active prostitution market may look like Figure 2.

Identifying snowball crimes can help police determine priorities for problem-oriented projects. In addition, mapping crimes, as these illustrations depict, may also convince community members and the police to explore more creative solutions than directed patrol, stings and repetitive arrests. In the case of prostitution markets, these solutions should involve nearby businesses, health and social service agencies, as well as lawmakers.[8]

LESSON 2: FOCUSING EFFORTS WHERE CRIME IS CONCENTRATED IS PRODUCTIVE

Policing drug markets taught police that focusing their efforts where crime was concentrated was highly productive. However, crime does not only concentrate at hot spots but also on repeat victims, and concentrating on repeat victims could also bring significant gains for the police.

Figure 1: Mapping Snowball Crimes at a Drug Market

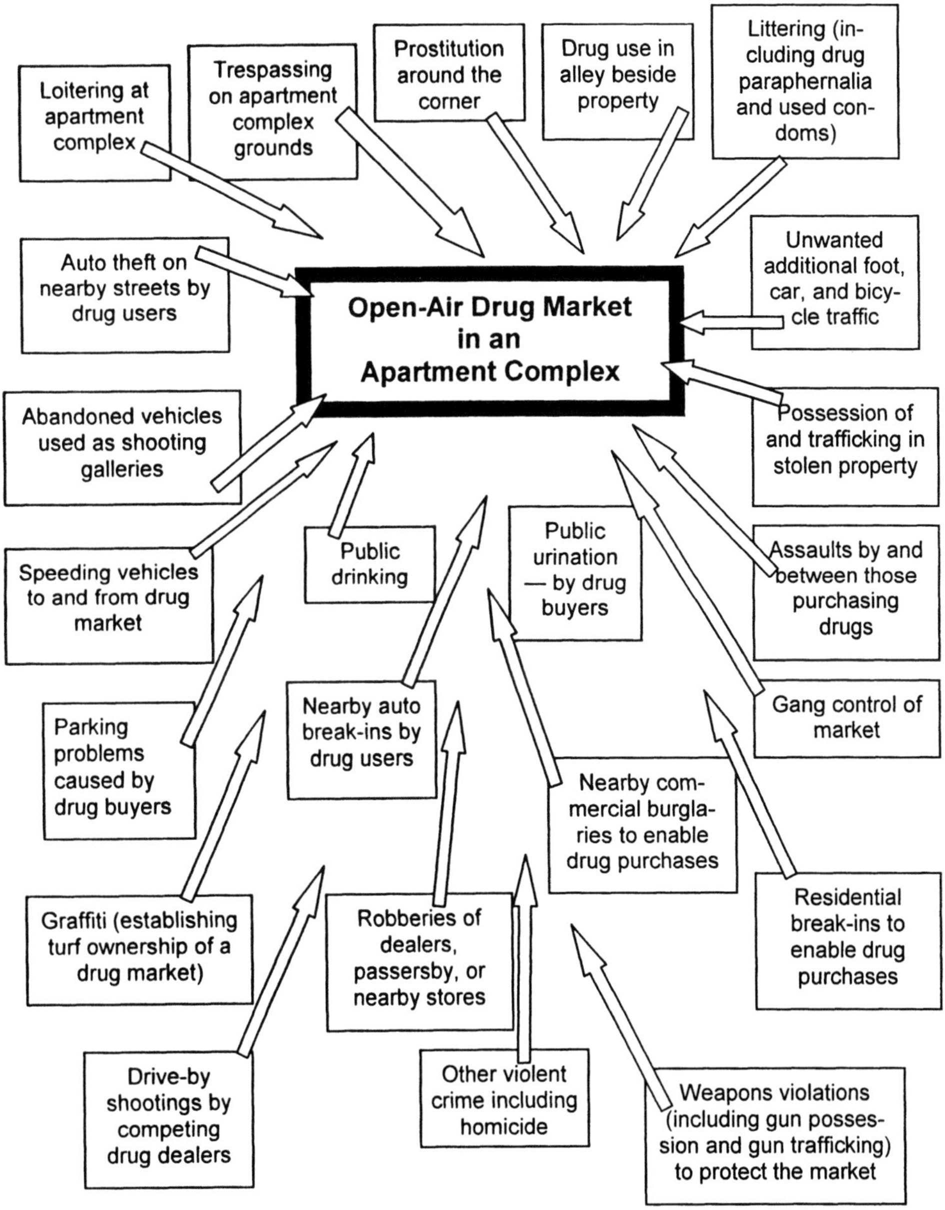

Prostitution around the corner

Drug use in alley beside property

Littering (including drug paraphernalia and used condoms)

Trespassing on apartment complex grounds

Loitering at apartment complex

Auto theft on nearby streets by drug users

Open-Air Drug Market in an Apartment Complex

Unwanted additional foot, car, and bicycle traffic

Abandoned vehicles used as shooting galleries

Possession of and trafficking in stolen property

Public drinking

Public urination — by drug buyers

Assaults by and between those purchasing drugs

Speeding vehicles to and from drug market

Parking problems caused by drug buyers

Nearby auto break-ins by drug users

Gang control of market

Nearby commercial burglaries to enable drug purchases

Graffiti (establishing turf ownership of a drug market)

Robberies of dealers, passersby, or nearby stores

Residential break-ins to enable drug purchases

Drive-by shootings by competing drug dealers

Other violent crime including homicide

Weapons violations (including gun possession and gun trafficking) to protect the market

Figure 2: Mapping Snowball Crimes at an Active Prostitution Market

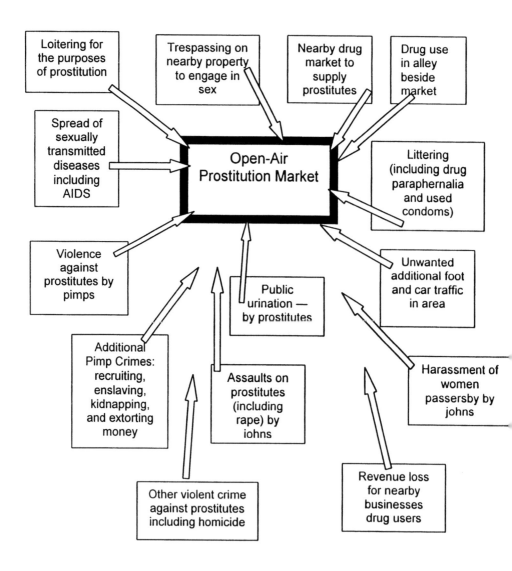

Loitering for the purposes of prostitution

Trespassing on nearby property to engage in sex

Nearby drug market to supply prostitutes

Drug use in alley beside market

Spread of sexually transmitted diseases including AIDS

Open-Air Prostitution Market

Littering (including drug paraphernalia and used condoms)

Violence against prostitutes by pimps

Public urination — by prostitutes

Unwanted additional foot and car traffic in area

Additional Pimp Crimes: recruiting, enslaving, kidnapping, and extorting money

Assaults on prostitutes (including rape) by iohns

Harassment of women passersby by johns

Other violent crime against prostitutes including homicide

Revenue loss for nearby businesses drug users

In the U.K., a number of Home Office publications provide police with research and good practice related to understanding and reducing elements of repeat victimization (Pease, 1998; Anderson et al., 1995; Chenery et al., 1997; Bridgeman and Hobbs, 1998). However, in the U.S., police have shown little interest in targeting this population with problem-oriented efforts and graded responses based on the extent of the revictimization.[9] Graded response, based on the level of revictimization, is a good use of police resources, just as taking on emerging drug markets before they draw additional crimes, is also cost-effective.

Perhaps the easiest framework American police can use in developing graded responses to repeat victimization are the four situational crime prevention categories developed by Clarke and described earlier in this paper: increasing risk, reducing reward, increasing effort, and removing excuses. If a victim is revictimized, police can use these categories as a framework for tailored interventions. On the first victimization, police interventions should do one or more of the following:

(1) Increase the offender's risk;

(2) Reduce the offender's reward;

(3) Increase the effort the offender must take to revictimize the victim; and/or,

(4) Remove excuses the offender has to revictimize the victim.[10]

On the second victimization, police interventions should further tighten these four elements so that risk and effort will be greater and reward and excuse are lessened.[11] If a third victimization occurs, further tightening is required.

An example is provided by stalking. If a woman finds an anonymous, obscene letter under her car's windshield and calls the police because it scares her, police may do little other than take a report (and may not do that in some cases). The police in all likelihood will also tell the woman to call again if there is a second annoyance. However, they are unlikely to do much further unless the victim is sure of the identity of the letter writer.

A week later, the woman receives an anonymous phone call from a man who says he is the letter writer. He tells her he likes her and wants to meet her and reminds her of the obscene thoughts he has about her. The caller declines to identify himself. She hangs up and calls the police a second time. At this point, a repeat victimization response tightening the situational matrix should kick in. Perhaps it might be such as this:

(1) *Increase the offender's risk* — Police help the victim obtain caller I.D. and, in fact, the police may even want to pay for it for one month. Police request that the victim maintain a log of any calls from the offender.

(2) *Reduce the offender's reward* — Police advise the victim to park her car in the apartment complex's locked garage, and not the open street so that the offender cannot use the car to convey his messages.

(3) *Increase the effort the offender must take to revictimize the victim* — Police advise the victim to tell the caller to stop calling and then to hang up immediately.

If the victimization does not stop — for example the offender places a bouquet of roses outside her door and he follows up with another obscene phone call — police would put a tighter revictimization plan in place, such as the following:

(1) *Increase the offender's risk* — Police run a criminal history check on the offender, based on caller I.D. information, then try to locate the offender. If they are unable to locate him, police give the victim a temporary personal alarm or cell phone that dials 911 directly.

(2) *Reduce the offender's reward* — Police may arrange for call blocking so that the victim will not receive calls from the offender's home phone.

(3) *Increase the effort the offender must take to revictimize the victim* — Police, with the consent of the victim, advise her neighbors and work colleagues of the offender and ask them to watch over the victim and immediately alert the police if they see something of note. Police request that no one let strangers into the apartment complex or the victim's workplace.

(4) *Remove the offender's excuse* — If the police can locate the offender, they arrest him if there is enough evidence that a crime has been committed.

Addressing repeat victims, just like addressing repeat locations, is a productive police strategy, and applying the situational matrix during graded responses provides an easy way to conceptualize opportunity-blocking tactics.

LESSON 3: POLICE MUST SHIFT OWNERSHIP OF CERTAIN CRIME PROBLEMS

Many of the interventions developed to close drug markets (as described earlier in this paper) rely on property owners exercising better controls over their property and their tenants' and visitors' behaviors. When crime occurs on private property other than apartment complexes, police will also likely find that property owners are better able to stem the crime than police themselves (Felson, 1995). This is true for auto theft from parking facilities, motel crime, commercial and residential burglary, shoplifting, crime in bars, and crimes occurring at convenience stores. However, owners may not welcome this responsibility, particularly if it involves a financial commitment (redesigning parking lots, limiting access to hotels, upgrading door and window locks, hiring well-trained bouncers, keeping beer locked up in evening hours).

Where owners do not welcome this responsibility, how can police persuade them to accept it when this is warranted?[12] The key here is "when warranted." A problem-oriented analysis of crime at different types of private property — whether police are looking at one particular property (a single convenience store) or all properties of that type (all convenience stores in town) — should involve some analysis of whether the level of crime is disproportionate, and if not, if it places a disproportionate demand on the police. If so, there is a good case for shifting responsibility to the property owner.

If one apartment complex results in 100 calls-for-service to police in one year, one of the analysis questions in a good problem-oriented project will be: Are 100 calls-for-service disproportionate? Sometimes this can be answered through comparisons to nearby, well-run apartment complexes as to their management practices and calls-for-service per apartment unit (Sampson, 2001a). For some other types of crimes, police will need to know what types of property management practices reduce or limit crimes for particular property types. In the case of auto thefts from a mall parking lot, two of the key questions will be: What management practices prevent auto crime in parking lots and what is the risk rate of auto theft in this parking lot compared to others (Clarke, 2001b)?

As they did in drug markets, police should identify those privately owned places that make disproportionate demands on police resources. This will help police provide better service to the public and give them a strategy for managing their ever increasing workload.[13]

SUMMARY

While few of the factors that combined to stimulate exploration of creative solutions in drug markets are present for other crime and safety problems, there may be some simple ways to help the police to address these other problems. In this paper, three suggestions are offered: identify, map, and address snowball crimes; adopt a simplified situational crime approach to graded responses for revictimization; and shift responsibility to property owners for dealing with factors that disproportionately raise levels of crime on their properties. While other approaches are also needed, police and communities will benefit from beginning with these three steps.

Address correspondence to: Rana Sampson, 4817 Canterbury Drive, San Diego, CA 92116. E-mail: <ranasampson@aol.com>.

REFERENCES

Anderson, D., S. Chenery and K. Pease (1995). *Biting Back: Tackling Repeat Burglary and Car Crime*. (Crime Detection and Prevention Series Paper 58.) London, UK: Home Office.

Bridgeman, C. and L. Hobbs (1998). *Repeat Victimization: The Police Officer's Guide*. London, UK: Home Office.

Chenery, S., J. Holt and K. Pease (1997). *Biting Back II. Reducing Repeat Victimization in Huddersfield*. (Crime Detection and Prevention Series Paper 82.) London, UK: Home Office.

Clarke, R.V. (1997). *Situational Crime Prevention: Successful Case Studies* (2nd ed.). Albany, NY: Harrow and Heston.

—— (2001a). *Shoplifting*. (Problem-Oriented Guides for Police series.) Washington, DC: Office of Community Oriented Policing Services, U.S. Department of Justice.

—— (2001b). *Theft of and From Cars in Parking Facilities*. (Problem-Oriented Guides for Police series.) Washington, DC: Office of Community Oriented Policing Services, U.S. Department of Justice.

Felson, M. (1995). "Those Who Discourage Crime." In: J. Eck and D. Weisburd (eds.), *Crime and Place*. (Crime Prevention Studies, vol. 4.) Monsey, NY: Criminal Justice Press.

—— and R.V. Clarke (1998). *Opportunity Makes the Thief: Practical Theory for Crime Prevention.* (Police Research Series Paper No. 98.) London, UK: Home Office Policing and Reducing Crime Unit.

Goldstein, H. (1990). *Problem-Oriented Policing.* New York: McGraw Hill.

—— (1979). "Improving Policing: A Problem-Oriented Approach." *Crime & Delinquency* 25(2): 234-258.

Lengel, A. (2000). "Struggle with a Stubborn Drug Trade: Closing D.C. Open-Air Markets Isn't Easy." *Washington Post*, Jan. 31.

Kleiman, M. and K. Smith (1990). "State and Local Drug Enforcement: In Search of a Strategy." In: M. Tonry and J. Wilson (eds.), *Crime and Justice: A Review of Research,* vol. 13. Chicago, IL: University of Chicago Press.

May, T., M. Edmunds and M. Hough (1999). *Street Business: The Links Between Sex and Drug Markets.* (Police Research Series Paper 118.) London, UK: Home Office.

Pease, K. (1998). *Repeat Victimisation: Taking Stock.* (Crime Detection and Prevention Series Paper 90.) London, UK: Home Office.

Sampson, R. (2002). *Misuse and Abuse of 911.* (Problem-Oriented Guides for Police series.) Washington, DC: Office of Community Oriented Policing Services, U.S. Department of Justice.

—— (2001a). *Drug Dealing in Privately Owned Apartment Complexes.* (Problem-Oriented Guides for Police series.) Washington, DC: Office of Community Oriented Policing Services, U.S. Department of Justice.

—— (2001b). *False Burglar Alarms.* (Problem-Oriented Guides for Police series.) Washington, DC: Office of Community Oriented Policing Services, U.S. Department of Justice.

—— (2001c). "Problem Ownership." Presentation at U.K. Problem-Oriented Policing Conference. Leicester, England. (Copies available from author.)

—— and M. Scott (2000). *Tackling Crime and Other Public-Safety Problems: Case Studies in Problem-Solving.* (Problem-Oriented Guides for Police series.) Washington, DC: Office of Community-Oriented Policing Services, U.S. Department of Justice.

Scott, M. (2001). *Street Prostitution.* (Problem-Oriented Guides for Police series.) Washington, DC: Office of Community Oriented Policing Services, U.S. Department of Justice.

—— (2000). *Problem-Oriented Policing: Reflections on the First 20 Years.* (Problem-Oriented Guides for Police series.) Washington, DC: Office of Community-Oriented Policing Services, U.S. Department of Justice.

Spelman, W. and J. Eck (1989). "Sitting Ducks, Ravenous Wolves, and Helping Hands: New Approaches to Urban Policing." *Public Affairs Comment* vol. 35, No. 2. Austin, TX: Lyndon B. Johnson School of Public Affairs, University of Texas at Austin.

Tilley, N., K. Pease, M. Hough and R. Brown (1999). *Burglary Prevention: Early Lessons from the Crime Reduction Programme.* (Crime Reduction Research Series, Paper 1.) London, UK: Home Office.

U.S. Bureau of Justice Assistance (1993). *Problem-Oriented Drug Enforcement: A Community-Based Approach for Effective Policing.* Washington, DC: U.S. Department of Justice.

NOTES

1. Some of the tactics described cross over categories. So a strategy such as lawfully evicting dealers removes the dealer's excuse for being on the property while also increasing the effort the dealer must expend to deal drugs on the property. If a strategy achieves more than one goal it is, in all likelihood, a more robust opportunity-blocker.

2. American police have produced hundreds of good quality drug problem-solving projects, however, one has to dig deeply to find even a handful of quality projects for any of the other crime and safety problems communities face. In collecting quality case studies for "Tackling Crime and Other Public Safety Problems: Case Studies in Problem-Solving," the authors, Sampson and Scott, found scores of drug problem-oriented policing efforts, but had to search much further for even a few quality projects on prostitution, theft from auto, homeless-related crime, cruising, graffiti, alcohol-related crime, mental illness-related safety problems, false alarms, group home crime, college-related crime, park crime, burglary, robbery, domestic violence, and gang crime. This imbalance is also evident in the yearly submissions for the Annual Goldstein Award for Excellence in Problem-Solving. From 1993 through 1995, drug-dealing projects represented the largest single problem type among award winners, as well as among those surviving the first cut during the years 1996 through 1999 (Scott, 2000).

3. The emergence of open-air drug markets with well-armed dealers even allowed police to adopt semi-automatic weapons.

4. Mid- and upper-level police managers only rarely get involved in the actual analysis of community safety problems. Some of this is the result of undue administrative burdens, perhaps also the result of lack of training and accountability.

5. Shifting ownership for false alarm response to the alarm industry is a particularly thorny issue for police because they are often the ones who, as part of their crime prevention outreach, advised homeowners to purchase these systems.

6. As with snow, an individual flake is not that harmful but when compacted with thousands of other snowflakes, it becomes a snowball, and can be significantly more harmful.

7. In England, a study of three drug markets where prostitution occurred found that "sex markets can play a significant part in the development of drug markets (and vice versa)" (May et al., 1999). The researchers noted that "professionals estimated that between two-thirds and three-quarters of street workers might be drug-dependent," and found that many of the prostitutes spent much of their daily earnings on drugs.

8. The recently published street prostitution problem-oriented guide (Scott, 2001) can be helpful in examining prostitution markets and applying creative solutions to them.

9. There are a few exceptions. For instance, in Fremont, CA, Sergeant Mike Eads studied repeat domestic violence victims and developed a graded police response tailored to the level of repeat victimization (Sampson and Scott, 2000).

10. Whether to do one or all will depend upon the circumstances of the initial victimization and the potential harm that could be incurred in a subsequent victimization.

11. In Chenery et al. (1997), graded responses were described with an Olympic design — bronze, silver and gold. Bronze responses were the first level of intervention, silver for the second revictimization, and gold for the third revictimization. Tilley et al. (1999) divide burglary interventions as: offender-related; victim-related; situational; and locality-related. The distinction between these frameworks and those described in this paper is that the latter all derive from the situational matrix, making it perhaps easier for police to keep focused on the end goal for any developed tactic: increase offender risk, decrease offender reward, increase offender effort, and removing offender excuses. This is not to suggest that American police need a simpler version of graded response; rather, a simpler version is more likely to be used.

12. It is less convincing for police to argue that crime in public spaces should be shifted, unless the argument is that nearby residents or frequent (legal) users of these spaces must take some ownership of the problem. Some of the problems in public spaces come from failures in governmental systems, and may manifest themselves in crimes or inci-

vilities by the homeless or the mentally ill, who may be drawn to public places for different reasons.

13. Examining disproportionate demand on police resources is an important mechanism for police to manage its workload and control opportunities for crime. Properties that require a disproportionate share of police response draw police resources to one place at the expense of others. This is also true for private enterprises that unfairly burden the police, such as the private alarm industry with false alarms (Sampson, 2001b) and certain cellular phone manufacturers whose phones produce staggering numbers of 911 phantom calls (Sampson, 2002).

THEFTS FROM CARS IN CENTER-CITY PARKING FACILITIES: A CASE STUDY IN IMPLEMENTING PROBLEM-ORIENTED POLICING

by

Ronald V. Clarke
Rutgers University

and

Herman Goldstein
University of Wisconsin

Abstract: *This paper describes a problem-oriented policing project, extending over a period of more than two years, which was designed to reduce thefts from cars parked in the center-city of Charlotte, NC. A progressive tightening of focus led to a detailed analysis of the risks of theft, and the associated security features, in the 39 decks and 167 surface lots in the center city. This analysis showed: (1) that risks of theft were much greater in lots than in decks, and (2) that higher risks of theft in lots were associated with inadequate fencing, poor lighting and the absence of attendants. These data played an important part in obtaining the agreement of lot owners and operators to make security improvements. Before most of these improvements had been made, however, thefts in the lots began to decline, possibly as the result of more focused patrolling by police and security personnel. The paper concludes with a discussion of the difficulties encountered by police in undertaking problem-oriented projects, and of ways to help them meet these difficulties.*

Crime Prevention Studies, vol. 15, (2003), pp. 257-298.

INTRODUCTION

The concept of problem-oriented policing (Goldstein, 1979, 1990) has been widely endorsed by the American and British police. In the United States, federal grant programs, supported by the 1994 Crime Act, have promoted the concept, and many police departments have made a commitment to it in one form or another (Scott, 2000). The annual problem-oriented policing conference sponsored by the Police Executive Research Forum (PERF) attracts between 1,000 and 1,500 delegates per year, while submissions for the Herman Goldstein Award for Excellence in Problem-Oriented Policing total about 100 per year (Scott and Clarke, 2000). In England and Wales, all 43 police forces claim to be undertaking some form of problem-oriented policing (Read and Tilley, 2000). The British police also have an annual conference devoted to advancing problem-oriented policing projects, and have the Nick Tilley Award to recognize outstanding projects.

Despite these endorsements, advocates of problem-oriented policing, we included, have continued to express disappointment with the projects reported in its name (Clarke, 1997, 1998; Goldstein, 1994a,b, 1996a,b; Read and Tilley, 2000; Scott, 2000; Scott and Clarke, 2000). Many are little more than well-intentioned efforts to improve community relations, barely recognizable as problem-oriented policing. Where they do include problem-solving elements, the problems may be small-scale (sometimes confined to a single address), analysis may be perfunctory, and evaluation often consists of testimonials from citizens or the local newspaper. In the few reported cases of larger-scale projects fitting the definition of problem-oriented policing, analysis seldom goes deeper than looking at calls-for-service data or statistics of reported crimes, responses frequently depart little from traditional enforcement strategies, and evaluation rarely explores alternative explanations for any drops in crime.

The commentators cited above have not been led to conclude that this experience negates the value of the concept or is indicative of "theory failure" — perhaps because a sufficient number of successful problem-oriented projects have been published to sustain faith in the concept.[1] Rather, they have assumed that the disappointing experience of applying problem-oriented policing results from "implementation failure," which they attribute to a variety of sources. We will not be departing from this position, but will anchor our discussion of implementation difficulties in a detailed description of one problem-oriented project in which we have been involved as consultants — an effort to reduce theft from cars in the center city of Charlotte, North Carolina.

It is rare that those who contribute to the development of theories and concepts have the opportunity to play as active a role as we did in an actual effort at implementation, and to observe the entire implementation process so closely. Such a relationship has some drawbacks and hazards. Our involvement made the project atypical. One cannot, as a result, generalize from the project, either in weighing the results or in planning a replication, without allowing for this involvement. And while we tried to remain objective, we are vulnerable to the charge that our involvement compromised our objectivity. But the relationship had its unique benefits. By joining with the project team in muddling through the many complex issues that were encountered, we had the opportunity to gain unique insights into the difficulties of implementation. Thus, while we offer this case study as one more commentary on the state of problem-oriented policing, we believe it offers a somewhat unique and different perspective. As will be seen, it claims mixed results — some successes and some failures — both of which have lessons for the future.

PROJECT BACKGROUND

Our involvement in this project began with a request by Chief Dennis Nowicki to Goldstein, who was serving as an in-house adviser to the Charlotte-Mecklenburg Police Department (CMPD) under a grant from the U.S. Department of Justice's Office of Community Oriented Policing Services (the COPS Office). As part of his work with the CMPD, he was asked to review the department's efforts to implement problem-oriented policing. The department had invested substantially in training in problem-oriented policing and in urging line officers to identify and address problems. Goldstein's review led him to conclude that more progress would be made in implementing the concept if time and resources could be focused on just a few projects in which an intensive, careful effort would be made to address a specific substantive problem. These projects could then be used as illustrations of the type of problem-oriented policing project to which others could aspire.

Captain Jerry Sennett and his officers in the David One district, which encompasses Charlotte's center city,[2] suggested that a suitable candidate for this kind of intensive effort would be a project focused on thefts from parked cars in their district. These "larcenies from autos" (or LFAs) constituted a large proportion of all crimes reported in David One, and bringing them down would make a substantial dent in the district's crime statistics. This was an important objective not only for the district captain, but also for the CMPD, given the significance attached to controlling crime in the recently redeveloped and revitalized center city (known locally as Uptown). LFAs had been resistant to control through conventional police operations and, in fact, were increasing at a rate faster than economic growth. Between 1998 and 1999, they jumped from 1,011 to 1,313. The District One officers knew that these statistics were likely to underestimate the problem because victimization surveys have consistently found that only about 30-50% of LFAs are reported to the police. Moreover, they also believed that LFAs fueled drug and alcohol use by the offenders involved.

Goldstein agreed that the David One LFAs could provide a suitable focus for the kind of project he had in mind and, soon after, he invited Clarke to join him in helping with the analysis and in identifying possible preventive measures. In a series of short visits extending over more than two years, Clarke and Goldstein met regularly with Captain Sennett and several of his officers and the crime analysts assigned to the district — a group that came to be referred to as the project team.[3] Also attending most of these meetings was Steve Ward, a senior assistant district attorney who was assigned to work as an adviser within the CMPD and who was supportive of efforts to increase the effectiveness of the police while making more discrete use of the criminal justice system. The role played by Goldstein and Clarke was essentially consultative: to explain the process of problem-oriented policing, to help talk through the difficulties encountered during the project, to discuss the experience gained elsewhere in dealing with theft from vehicles, to raise points for further inquiry or action, and to make suggestions about data analysis. In tandem with the project team, this work resulted in refining the focus of the project; obtaining a better understanding of the problem; selecting and gaining agreement to solutions; and assessing effectiveness.

DEFINING THE PROBLEM

The first meetings of the project team were largely taken up with defining the problem. It was soon decided to focus on the Uptown where, in 1998, just over 50% of David One's LFAs were reported and where, despite heavy levels of policing,[4] most of the increase in LFAs had occurred. Uptown is a clearly defined geographical area of about one square mile, encircled by a freeway system. The area covers about 170 city blocks, which mostly hold office buildings, hotels and associated retail and parking facilities. In the northern corner is a well-established, affluent residential district, and in the eastern corner is a second residential district, consisting of newly-built condominiums, on land which had been cleared of low income housing that had deteriorated in its quality. The west corner holds the Ericsson Stadium, home of the Carolina Panthers. A trolley line, that had fallen into disuse, but is now being restored, runs across the area in a North-east/South-west direction (see Figure 1).

Each business day, Uptown accommodates some 50,000 commuters who travel into the city by car. Most of these cars are parked in decks or surface lots scattered throughout the area. This pattern is reflected in LFAs, of which 83% in 1998 occurred in decks or lots, and only 17% in residential property or on the streets. Hot spot mapping (see Figure 2) by Monica Nguyen, the crime analyst originally assigned to the project, showed that LFAs were concentrated in the center of Uptown where residences and street parking are largely absent, but where, in support of the businesses and nightlife, there are many decks and lots. In light of these facts, it was decided to tighten further the project's focus to deal only with Uptown LFAs occurring in lots and decks.[5]

The Police View Of The Problem

In the course of dealing with the problem over the previous few years, the police had developed their own view of the causes and potential solutions. They tended to blame a combination of careless victims, lenient courts, and offenders who were supporting drug or alcohol habits. In more detail, their diagnosis comprised the following elements:

(1) LFAs are quick and easy to commit. Most LFAs in Uptown are committed by breaking a window (which is often shattered using a spark plug) and taking items left inside the car. Thefts may take less than 30 seconds to commit and may not be discovered until several hours later when commuters return to their cars. Without having any need to touch the car, fingerprints are rarely left at the scene. Because of the large area to be patrolled, police rarely catch an offender in the act.

(2) In a congested criminal justice system, LFAs are not considered serious offenses by the courts and tend to be treated leniently. The few arrests that are made, therefore, rarely result in offenders being taken off the streets, which means they are free to repeat the same offense.

Figure 1: Uptown Charlotte – the Area Selected for the Study of LFAs

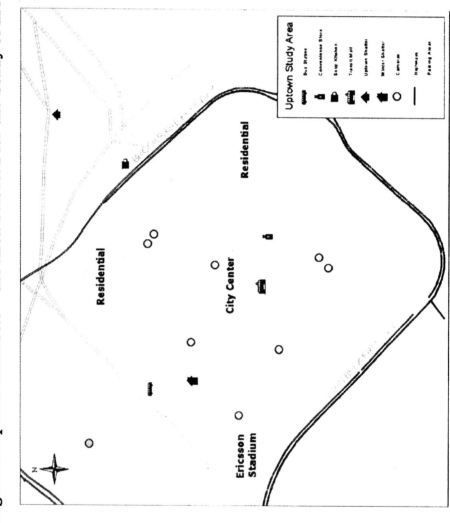

(3) The victims are office workers in the day and customers of clubs and restaurants at night. Many victims must share the blame for LFAs because they leave items, such as cell phones, compact disks and clothes, inside the car in plain view.

(4) Offenders can find a ready market for items they steal in the numerous pawnshops and known street drug markets located in areas close to the Uptown. (Officers spoke of having identified 14 such locations.)

(5) Offenders fall into three main groups: (1) habitual street criminals with drug habits; (2) petty offenders with alcohol problems who spend their days hanging around Uptown; and (3) transients from the city's homeless shelters, many of whom are also alcoholics.

(6) The transients comprise the largest group of offenders and LFAs are committed as part of their daily routine. This begins with their trek from the winter homeless shelter, in the west of the Uptown area, along the trolley line (which, until recently, was not in use), to the soup kitchen, on the other side of Uptown, where they eat their lunch (see Figure 1). Numerous surface lots and decks border the trolley line and it is easy for transients to find something worth stealing in a car and then escape along the trolley route. They sell items they have stolen to drug dealers and pawnshops in the general location of the soup kitchen, and use the proceeds for alcohol. After midday, the transients follow the reverse course and sell stolen items at locations near the homeless shelter. En route they might detour to the convenience store just south of the trolley line to purchase cheap alcohol.

This view governed the strategies pursued by the police. They had worked with cooperating suspects to identify other suspects for arrest. They had attempted to use territorial restrictions as part of sentences for convicted parking lot thieves. They had tried to build cases to enable them to prosecute certain persistent offenders as career criminals, which could result in lengthy prison sentences. They had performed surveillance at high-risk locations. And they had encouraged the placement of "no trespassing" signs in parking facilities to allow the opportunity for officers to detain and question suspects. Apart from these enforcement efforts, they had prompted media stories about not leaving valuables in cars, they had sought to initiate a "business watch" program in the downtown, and they had placed warning notices on cars with tempting items left in plain view.

Figure 2: Concentration of the LFA Problem in Uptown as Determined by Traditional Hot Spot Analysis, 1999.

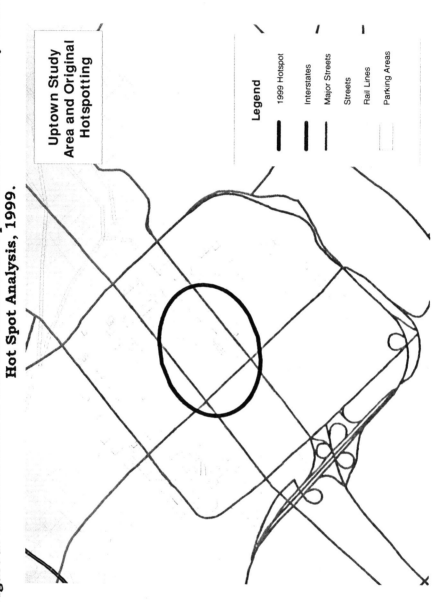

Uptown Study
Area and Original
Hotspotting

Legend

1999 Hotspot

Interstates

Major Streets

Streets

Rail Lines

Parking Areas

These efforts had met with little success. Few offenders were ar- rested and successfully prosecuted, and LFAs in Uptown continued to rise (from 513 in 1998 to 814 in 1999). Even so, some of the David One officers argued that more vigorous pursuit of the strategies would lead to better results. In particular, they wanted to see a more intensive media campaign directed to careless victims, greater efforts to arrest offenders through more direct surveillance and through work with cooperative suspects, and a stronger commitment from the district attorney's office to prosecute alleged offenders and seek harsher sentences for those convicted.

Most of the David One officers initially hoped that the attention focused on the problem through the project would strengthen their hands in pressing for these strategies. They expressed some frustra- tion when their proposed solutions were questioned and an effort was launched to deepen the analysis. In the subsequent discussions that opened that analysis, the ability of the police to substantially in- crease arrests for LFAs was challenged (see Hesseling, 1995), and the likelihood that the district attorney's office could secure harsh sen- tences was questioned.[6] Studies were described that had found few benefits from local "lock-your-car" campaigns (Barthe, 2000; Bur- rows and Heal, 1980; Riley, 1980). In terms of the classic crime tri- angle (Spelman and Eck, 1989), it was pointed out that the police view of the problem was focused mostly on offenders and victims, rather than on the locations, i.e., the parking facilities and, in par- ticular, the security of those facilities.

As a result of these initial discussions, it was agreed that, while the officers would continue to pursue the strategies they had devel- oped, they would, at the same time, assist with analysis of parking security.

FROM MAPPING HOT SPOTS TO PINPOINTING RISKS

The "hot spot" mapping that showed LFAs were concentrated around parking facilities in the center of Uptown was of limited value in further analysis because each hot spot covered several blocks, containing not only a number of parking facilities, but facilities that were quite diverse as well. However, in discussing the maps, officers would occasionally identify particular facilities that they believed ac- counted for most of the LFAs. Many of these were simply the largest facilities, where, because of their size, one might expect to encounter more LFAs, but some facilities identified as troublesome were quite small. This suggested that there were features of the design, location or management of the facilities that might make the vehicles parked in them especially vulnerable to LFAs.

It therefore became important to learn more about the parking facilities, but many of these were not even shown in the CMPD maps of Uptown, which had become outdated as a result of the construction boom driven by the city's thriving banking industry. New lots had been created as old buildings had been demolished pending redevelopment, and new buildings had sprung up on the sites of former lots. Even the maps maintained by the city's planning department did not show every facility. Consequently, it was decided to undertake a comprehensive inventory of parking facilities and to count the spaces in each.

This was a major undertaking, absorbing the resources available to the project for a considerable period of time. The crime analyst who had taken over responsibility for the project, Matthew White, supplemented the available information from the planning department with the detailed knowledge of the David One officers regularly assigned to the area and with information obtained from a new aerial survey of the uptown area. This resulted in the identification of 206 separate parking facilities with more than 20 parking spaces — 39 decks and 167 surface lots.

Table 1: Deck and Lot Size, Charlotte's Uptown, 2000

Spaces	Decks	Lots
0-49	0	52
50-99	2	39
100-199	5	43
200-299	3	17
300-499	10	14
500-999	12	1
1000+	7	1
	39	167

The David One officers assigned to the project, Anthony Crawford and Veronica Foster, and the analyst, White, undertook to count all of the spaces in all of the parking facilities — a laborious enterprise. Eventually it was established that there was a total of 42,574 spaces in the 206 facilities, 22,373 of which were in decks and 20,201 in lots. Table 1 summarizes information about the size of the parking facilities.

With these figures in hand, it should have been easy to calculate the rate of LFAs per facility, but unfortunately LFAs were not recorded for individual parking facilities, but only for the block on which these stood (though location codes distinguished LFAs occurring in parking facilities from those occurring from cars parked on the street or on private property). This was because victims making reports could usually identify the block where the car was parked, but not the particular parking facility. There was no difficulty in assigning the theft to that parking facility when it was the only one on the block. Nor was there any difficulty in assigning thefts to particular facilities where the block contained a lot and a deck because the location code permitted these to be distinguished. Rather, the difficulty arose when blocks contained more than one lot or more than one deck, which was the case for more than half of the blocks. In these cases, LFAs were sorted, using their location codes, into those occurring in lots and those occurring in decks before calculating separate rates of LFAs, per parking space, for the decks and for the lots. This meant that all the lots on the block shared the same rate of LFAs, which might be different from the rate for the decks (or deck) in that block.

Once the rate of LFAs per parking space had been determined for each facility, comparisons could be made of their theft risks. Two facts stood out in the results of this exercise. First, it was apparent that the parking facilities bordering the trolley line and the disused rail tracks to the west of uptown had generally higher rates of theft (see Figure 3). This lent support to the police analysis, which had implicated these as conduits for the transients in their daily movements about the city. Second, it was found that the rate of LFAs per parking space was much higher for lots than for decks. In 1999, 93 LFAs occurred in decks, which between them had 22,373 spaces (a rate of 4.1 LFAs per 1,000 parking spaces). But 510 LFAs occurred in lots, which had a total of 20,201 spaces (a rate of 25.3 LFAs per 1,000 spaces). The risk of LFAs per parking space for lots was thus about six times greater than for decks.

Figure 3: Concentrations of the LFA Problem in Uptown, by City Block, as Determined by Relating the Incidence of Theft to the Number of Available Spaces in Off-Street Parking Facilities (Theft Rate), 1999

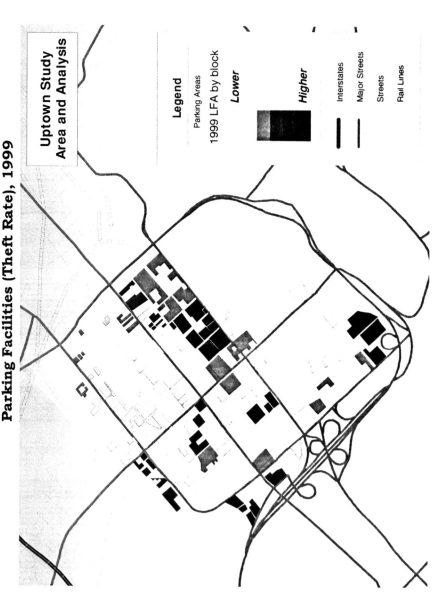

Uptown Study
Area and Analysis

Legend

Parking Areas

1999 LFA by block

Lower

Higher

Interstates

Major Streets

Streets

Rail Lines

People are sometimes fearful in garages and decks, especially when they are out of view of attendants and nobody else is around. They often assume therefore that their persons and their cars are more vulnerable to crime. That fewer thefts were found to occur in decks than lots would probably surprise them. In fact, the same result was obtained in research undertaken in London where it was explained in terms of the lack of security in many lots (Webb et al., 1992). Few lots have an attendant, they often lack adequate lighting, and many lack natural surveillance from passers-by or nearby buildings. They also tend to be more open to offenders on foot than decks. Pedestrian movement in and out of decks is restricted to elevators and stairwells, so that a thief carrying stolen items may come into contact with others coming and going. Thieves in lots can make a quicker getaway through a route of their own choosing with greater certainty that they, and the items they are carrying, will not be seen.

The implications were far reaching of the large difference in theft rates between lots and decks. It suggested that decks could be eliminated from the project because they accounted for relatively few LFAs. It also suggested, however, that inadequate security of parking facilities — in both lots and decks — in the Uptown area could indeed be contributing to the LFA problem. If improvements in security were to be sought, these inadequacies needed to be documented. Recognition of this fact led to the next stage of the project — a survey of the security of Uptown's parking facilities, with the expectation that lessons could be learned from examining the decks, with their low rates of theft, as well as the lots.

The Security of the Uptown Decks and Lots

The first step in designing the survey was to review past research on theft in parking facilities. This could have proved a major undertaking, but Clarke's familiarity with this research[7] enabled him to contribute a quick summary of the findings most relevant to the Uptown situation:

- Center-city parking facilities tend to be at greater risk than those in other parts of a city. This may be due to the concentration of parking, making it easier for thieves to find attractive targets.

- Commuter lots where cars are left for long periods of the day have particularly high rates of theft.

- Parking facilities used around the clock tend to have higher rates of theft, if for no other reason than targets can always be found there.

- The availability of cash in pay-boxes, meters and pay-and-display ticket machines attracts thieves.

- For both decks and lots, the presence of attendants greatly reduces risks of theft.

- Closed-circuit television (CCTV) systems installed in parking facilities can be effective in reducing thefts in those facilities.

- Improved lighting can reduce crime in decks and underground garages, and in lots with evening or night use. (The research on this topic is limited.)

- Lots with pedestrian throughways experience higher rates of theft, and thefts have been reduced when pedestrian access is reduced.

- Improvements in perimeter security can reduce vehicle-related thefts. (Again, the research is limited.)

- Lots located near stores and shops have lower rates of theft because of the natural surveillance provided by shoppers and shop staff.

- No evaluations of electronic access systems to public parking facilities have been published, but these have been found effective in preventing theft from parking areas in housing complexes.

The research is far from comprehensive, much of it is small scale and exploratory, and most of it was conducted in the United Kingdom. Nevertheless, it consistently indicates that better-secured facilities (in terms of attendants, natural surveillance and access controls) have lower rates of crime, and it provided helpful guidance on what to include in the survey of Uptown's parking facilities.

This survey was not intended, of course, to meet the rigorous standards of an academic research study. This would have been beyond the resources available to the project. Even a detailed environmental survey of the kind undertaken for a Crime Prevention Through Environmental Design (CPTED) project was not practicable. The need was for a limited survey that: (1) would give a snapshot of the security in Uptown's facilities; (2) would provide pointers to improving security; and (3) could be undertaken quickly without occupying too much of the time of the officers and the crime analyst.

To meet this limited need, the officers and the analyst made a rough assessment of a small set of security variables that were under the control of each facility's operators. Some of the variables included were common to both decks and lots; others were specific to each kind of facility. The full list of data collected for the 38 decks and 167 lots was as follows:

For both decks and lots:

- Lighting (weak/moderate/strong).[8]

- Day-time attendant (yes/no).

- Night parking available (yes/no).

- Night-time attendant (yes/no).

- Passkey (yes/no).

For decks:

- Security guard service (yes/no).

For lots:

- Pay box (yes/no).

- Fence (none/partial/full).

Data were collected during the night shift when lighting levels could be assessed. Despite the survey's limited objectives, it represented a major data-gathering exercise, requiring an unusual commitment from officers Crawford and Foster.

Table 2: Security-related Features in Decks (N=38) and Lots (N=167), Charlotte Uptown

	Decks	Lots
% with:		
Moderate/strong lighting	77%	39%
Day attendant	74%	6%
Night parking	87%	46%
Night attendant	60%	4%
Pass keys	23%	15%
Security guard service	50%	N/A
No pay boxes	N/A	74%
Fully fenced	N/A	12%

Note: N/A signifies not available.

Once collected, the data yielded two sets of results for lots and decks: (1) simple counts of the distribution of the variables (Table 2), and (2) statistical relationships between these variables and LFAs, determined through analyses of variance undertaken by crime analyst Kristin Knight (Table 3).

Table 2 shows that, leaving aside night parking, the decks are generally more secure than the lots. The most important difference between them, however, probably accounting for most of the difference in risks of theft, is that decks generally have attendants (74% in the day and 60% at night), whereas lots generally do not (6% in the day and 4% at night).

The relationships between LFAs and security features were not strong (Table 3), and some of the variables appeared to be intercorrelated.[9] The results in Table 3 should therefore not be over-interpreted, but they suggest that:

(1) Security improvements are unlikely to reduce thefts in **decks** because there is no relationship between security features and the rate of LFAs. Most decks needing attendants may have them already and other security features appear to bring little added value.

(2) Reductions in thefts from parking **lots** would result from employing more attendants[10] and probably also from: (1) improving lighting and fencing and, (2) making greater use of passkeys and less use of pay boxes.

Table 3: Relationship between LFAs and Security Features in Decks (N=38) and Lots (N=167), Charlotte Uptown

Relationship between LFAs and:	Decks	Lots
Weak lighting	N.S.	F=1.698, p<0.02
No day attendant	N.S.	F=1.463, p<0.05
Night parking	N.S.	N.S.
No night attendant	N.S.	N.S.
"Security"	N.S.	N/A
Pay boxes present	N/A	F=2.602, p<0.01
No passkeys	N/A	F=1.671, p<0.015
Poor fencing	N/A	F=1.512, p<0.025

Notes:
(1) Relationships determined using analysis of variance.
(2) N.S. signifies not statistically significant; N/A signifies not available.

Together, the analyses in Tables 2 and 3 confirmed the decision to eliminate the decks from the project (their rates of theft were already low and it seemed unlikely they could be reduced further) and to concentrate efforts on improving the security of lots. Their rates of theft were much higher than of decks and there were many indications that if their security were to be improved, thefts could be reduced. Searching for the best ways to improve the security of the Uptown lots — the next stage of the project — occupied the project team for more than a year.

THE SEARCH FOR SOLUTIONS

The SARA model (Eck and Spelman, 1987), which teaches police the value of thinking sequentially about scanning, analysis, response and assessment, has been of great value in introducing police to problem-oriented policing. But it can also be misleading in suggesting the sequence of steps to be followed in any project. In fact, projects rarely follow a linear path from the initial scanning and analysis stages through the stages of response and assessment. Rather, the process is iterative, so that an unfolding analysis can result in refocusing of the project (as happened more than once in the present case), and questions about possible responses can lead to the need for fresh analyses. The longer and more complicated the project, the more iterations of this kind are likely to occur.

Understandably, at the beginning of the project, police continued to utilize the responses they had advocated in the past, and continued to pursue them while the analysis was proceeding. Furthermore, the pros and cons of some of the solutions that had earlier been proposed by the police, such as the closing down of liquor stores patronized by suspects and the relocating of the homeless shelter, were periodically reconsidered. But as the project progressed, these discussions differed markedly from the earlier discussions. They reflected a greater unity and focus in seeking solutions — a result, it appeared, of the exchanges among the participants, who brought different perspectives and experience to the table, and the gradual blending together of the growing findings and the street knowledge of the officers. It was becoming clearer that the heightened enforcement being pursued by officers was having little effect on the overall problem, since the numbers of LFAs in Uptown had risen from 513 in 1998 to 814 in 1999. In addition, having been directly involved in collecting the data on the parking facilities, the David One officers had acquired greater understanding of the part played by inadequate security in LFAs.

In March of 2000, arrangements were made for two David One officers, Sgt. Craig "Pete" Davis and Officer Crawford, and crime analyst White to visit Portland, Oregon. Steve Ward, the assistant district attorney participating in the project, had heard about Portland's success in preventing thefts from autos in the city's Lloyd District, a commercial and office district immediately adjacent to its downtown core. In an area about as large as and similar to Charlotte's Uptown, the number of LFAs had been reduced from about 900 per year in the early 90s to 200-300 per year after the program. Their visit served to support the exploration of new strategies by providing some specific examples of preventive measures that had been used by another police agency for reducing LFAs in addition to the traditional dependence on law enforcement.

The team sent to Portland reported back that the successful program in Portland had been implemented through a partnership of local businesses, private security companies, the police and the DA's office. The program was comprised of: (1) a streamlined legal process that resulted in more convictions and more severe penalties, with repeat offenders being more often sentenced to prison; (2) the installation of electronic single-arm gates at parking lot entrances (to deter thieves cruising in cars); (3) the closing down of camps near the parking facilities that had been illegally established by the homeless; (4) the reorganization of security services to provide a bike patrol covering all the lots; and (5) the provision of a direct radio link between the bike patrol and district police. All these measures were thought to have played a part in the reductions achieved, but the most effective was generally believed to be the bike patrol.

By this time the project team had acquired a sound understanding of the LFA problem and a broad knowledge of responses that had worked elsewhere or might work in Charlotte, given the specific nature of the problem in Uptown. They were now in a position to set about developing an intervention plan that would have an immediate impact on the problem as well as a sustained longer-term effect. Given the complex nature of the problem, it was clear that the plan, as in Portland, would involve several elements requiring partnerships with other agencies, including Uptown business interests, city departments, the parking lot operators and the DA's office. If it were to have any chance of being implemented, it could not be too costly and should anticipate likely bureaucratic and legal difficulties.

It was also accepted that some recommendations might be implemented quite quickly, but others would require a longer time scale, perhaps of two or three years. Accordingly, the plan should take account of anticipated changes in the city that might have an impact on LFAs. Several of these changes, related to the anticipated continuation in the expansion of the Uptown economy, seemed likely to make the problem worse. These included an expected growth in nighttime activity resulting from the construction of more office space, the building of more housing and hotels, and the opening of more clubs and restaurants. The proposal for construction of a new basketball arena and baseball stadium had been defeated in a recent referendum, but it was expected that these projects might be revived.

Other anticipated changes seemed likely to reduce LFAs. One of these was that more lots would gradually be converted to freestanding decks or to office buildings with garages, with the accompanying security those facilities generally experience. Shorter term, a new trolley service was scheduled to be introduced (in 2002) on the tracks currently used by the transients as a conduit through the city. This new service, with the activity and natural surveillance it would, as a byproduct, generate, would make it harder for the transients, were they inclined to engage in theft, to gain access to the parking lots from the trolley line. This relieved the project team of the need to pursue a response which would assuredly be controversial — the possibility of trying to re-site the shelter or soup kitchen to keep transients, who were thought by the police to be among those responsible for the LFAs, away from the Uptown lots.

A second imminent change was that an Uptown CCTV system was to become fully operational in the first half of 2001. This would be funded from the CMPD's block grant from the federal government and by contributions from business members of the Center City Crime Prevention Council, who made available locations for the cameras atop some of the tallest buildings in Uptown at no cost in exchange for a linkage to their security desks. The system would comprise nine cameras that would be monitored by the police from one central location for up to 10-12 hours per day. The precise proportion of the surface lots that would be subject to surveillance by the cameras was not established.[11] The police involved in the project roughly estimated that a majority of the lots would be under observation. But even if coverage were limited, the cameras might still provide a convincing deterrent to casual thieves.

In deciding upon the final group of measures to include in the intervention plan, the project team avoided blanket requirements for every lot to be illuminated to a particular standard, or to have full-time attendants. While such requirements could effectively reduce LFAs, they might not bring uniform crime prevention benefits for all lots and could also bankrupt the operators of the smaller ones. A more selective, cost-effective approach was sought. With these criteria in mind, the intervention plan that was developed included five distinct recommendations:

(1) The police and the DA's office would continue to develop aggressive policies of arresting offenders, seeking convictions, and seeking severe sentences for repeat offenders. This had always been a central aim of the police response in David One and was also an element of the successful Portland program.

(2) Parking lot operators would be asked to post the address of their lot at the entrance(s) to each lot. This would assist victims in reporting thefts, help police in responding to calls for assistance, and assist future analysis of LFAs by allowing these to be assigned to the specific lot in which the LFA occurred.

(3) Changes would be sought in the city's zoning ordinance that currently, requires, for aesthetic purposes, that all new lots be surrounded by screening (which in practice is usually a fence) that is no less than four feet in height and can have no more than 25% of its surface left open.[12] These fences, most often solid, have reduced surveillance of lots by passing motorists, pedestrians, and police officers on patrol. Furthermore, lots established before the ordinance came into effect in 1993 (and its amendment in 1995), which constitute a majority of all lots, were not required to have screening. The proposed new ordinance would require "see-through" fences to be erected for all new parking lots and, within a period of two or three years, for all existing lots.

(4) With the cooperation and agreement of lot operators, the police would seek to implement a rating scheme that would result in every lot being graded for its security on a number of variables. Grades would be determined by either the police or the building inspector and would be posted at the lot entrances, in the same way health inspection results are posted for Charlotte's restaurants. This rating scheme would be modeled on the "Secure Parking" scheme as originally proposed in the United Kingdom. Experience there has shown that the implementation of the proposal, with adjustments over time, provides a strong incentive for parking facility operators to improve security (VCRAT, 1999).

(5) Funds would be sought for a security bike patrol for the uptown lots similar to the successful patrol introduced in Portland. Such a patrol had also been found effective in rail commuter lots in Vancouver (Barclay et al., 1996). The patrol would be trained in what to look for, how to focus patrols for greatest effect, how to deal with suspicious persons, and when and how to call the police (their radios would be compatible

with police radios). The patrols would give the customers and employees of Uptown businesses the same type of security that private patrols give to customers and employees at large shopping malls.

SELLING THE SOLUTIONS

The recommendations for more aggressive legal pursuit of offenders and the posting of lot addresses were relatively uncontroversial. But it was thought that the others, particularly the changes in fencing, the grading system and the bicycle patrol, were likely to encounter resistance from lot operators because of the potential costs and, in the case of the grading system, the commonly expressed concern about increased government regulation. It was decided that a presentation should be put together which would be used in "selling" the intervention plan to lot operators and others. Crime analyst White undertook responsibility for developing the visuals on which the presentation would be based. These were refined over the ensuing months and eventually consisted of 50 PowerPoint slides that took nearly one hour to present. They covered the background to the project, the reasons for focusing on LFAs in parking facilities, the visit to Portland, the decision to study lot security, anticipated developments in Uptown, rejected solutions, the thinking behind the proposed intervention plan, and the next steps toward its implementation.

Considerable care was taken to report the findings of the analyses in a readily understandable form. The crime analyst spent many hours developing maps that clearly showed differential risks of LFAs throughout Uptown. In reporting the statistical relationships between LFAs and security features, he avoided correlation coefficients (which many people have difficulty interpreting) and, instead, made use of maps showing lots that were close to one another, but which differed in their levels of security and in their rates of theft. For example, he found adjacent lots that varied in lighting quality and which had quite different rates of LFA. Figure 4 shows the maps he made to illustrate the relationships between LFAs and lighting quality, fencing and the presence/absence of attendants.[13]

Figure 4: Relationships Between Security Features in Parking Lots and Rates of Theft in Those Lots, Uptown, 1999

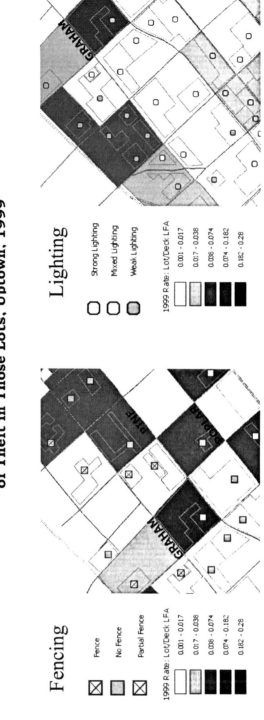

Figure 4 (continued)

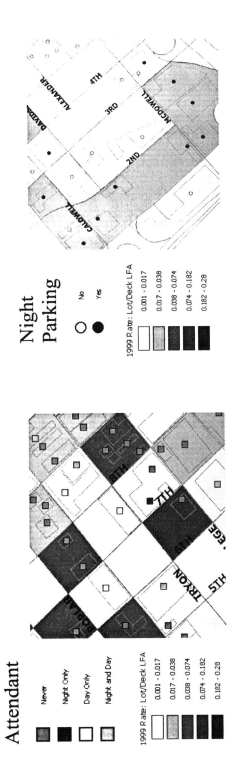

Night
Parking

Attendant

Also, in preparation for the meetings, two members of the David One team, Officers Crawford and Robert Vandergrift who were trained in Crime Prevention through Environmental Design, undertook surveys of three pairs of adjacent lots with widely differing LFA rates to identify the differences in the security of the lots. The striking results of these surveys were included in the presentation, together with photographs of the lots showing the differences between the two lots in each of the three pairs.

This presentation formed the basis of a report made on the project to Chief Darrel Stephens (who had recently succeeded Chief Nowicki) and senior officers of the CMPD. This meeting was helpful in refining the presentation, particularly concerning the likely benefits of the new CCTV system, but it also raised important issues regarding the proposed bike patrol and security grading system. Concerning the bike patrol, it was pointed out that the additional officers funded by Uptown businesses were already undertaking bike patrols and these patrols had gradually been extended into parking facilities, but these did not seem to be controlling the problem. To recommend that bike patrols be undertaken by additional security officers would likely provoke the question as to why these should be expected to succeed when police bike patrols had not. As for the grading system, the project team was instructed to undertake a careful study of the police capacity for undertaking these surveys, which would involve technical difficulties as well as requiring a considerable resource investment.

These comments resulted in a more cautious presentation, in which recommendations were phrased more tentatively with fuller discussion of the difficulties attached to each. Over the succeeding months, this presentation was made by Captain Sennett, assisted by the project team, to Uptown lot operators, to Charlotte's Center City Crime Prevention Council, and at a meeting with the city's planning department. The sequence of these meetings was carefully arranged so that agreement in principle to the intervention plan was obtained first from the parking lot operators, whose cooperation was vital, and that agreement was then conveyed to those with whom the team subsequently met.

The project team considered these meetings to be highly successful, which we can confirm having been present at the one with the Center City Crime Prevention Council. At least 80 people attended this meeting, representing a wide range of business and city interests, including the three largest parking lot operators (controlling among them 85% of the parking spaces in Uptown). Those present were clearly impressed by the professional nature of the presentation and by the wealth of detailed information presented about the problem. No criticism was voiced of the inability of police to control LFAs, and very little dissent was expressed concerning the recommendations. To the contrary, expressions of support and offers of help in implementing the plan were made from the floor.

During the period that these meetings were being held, the project team was undertaking work needed to advance the recommendations. Little new needed to be done about aggressive legal pursuit of offenders since this was already agreed policy, though David One officers now regularly request that a territorial exclusion order be part of the sentence imposed on an offender convicted on an LFA charge who is returned to the community under probation. The recommendation concerning the posting of lot addresses was quickly accepted and lot operators are already beginning to comply. Progress was initially slow in changing the fence ordinance, despite the endorsement of lot operators, and a letter of support written by Tim Crowe, a nationally-known expert in CPTED.[14] After the presentation at the planning department, however, the director of planning agreed to lend his support, considered vital, to the new ordinance. He also suggested that it should be extended to include requirements about adequate lighting and, at the time of writing, the revisions to the ordinance are being drafted and subjected to the approval of interested parties before being formally submitted to the City Council for its approval.

A security grading system that the police could administer is also being developed, again with the assistance of Tim Crowe. Lot operators made surprisingly few objections to the scheme. They asked only that: (1) they be given a preliminary "grade" (A, B, C or D) for each lot, which would only be made final after they have the opportunity to make necessary improvements, and (2) that they be given the opportunity to be re-graded whenever they make subsequent improvements. They also expressed reservations about the requirement for posting of grades at lot entrances. At the time of writing, these matters are still under discussion.

The lack of opposition to the proposed bike patrol might have been due to the absence of details about costs and who would bear these. Captain Sennett obtained proposals from two interested security companies for a patrol that would call for two persons to be on duty at any one time, augmented by another two at peak hours — requiring that, in all, eight persons be trained and available to fill this level of staffing. The costs of the proposals were similar and were comparable to the cost of hiring fully equipped CMPD officers on an off-duty basis. At the time of writing, Sennett is working with the Center City Crime Prevention Council to find ways of paying for the patrols. An alternative being considered is to combine the existing bike patrols provided by Bank of America for lots used by its employees[15] with similar patrols to be provided by another major Uptown bank.

Meanwhile, David One (with funds from the local Alcohol Beverage Control authority) has very recently implemented a new communications system that allows the Bank of America security officers and those of some other Uptown businesses to have direct radio contact with the on-duty David One field supervisor and the David One district office. This will enable greater advantage to be taken of the CCTV surveillance of lots undertaken by several of these security companies. It is also a further step in forging a crime prevention partnership between the police and the private security firms operating in Uptown.

An Unexpected Decline In Thefts

The work of selling and implementing the intervention plan spanned the end of 2000 and the beginning of 2001. It was during this period that it became evident that LFAs in Uptown were declining. In fact, the decline in 2000 was substantial (38%), the number having dropped from 814 in 1999 to 506 in 2000. Most of the decline took place in the lots and decks, not on the streets or on private property (see Table 4).[16]

Table 4: Location of LFAs in Charlotte Uptown 1998-2000

	1998	1999	2000	Reduction in 2000*
Decks	58	93	52	44%
Lots	292	510	269	47%
Elsewhere	163	211	185	12%
Totals	513	814	506	38%

*Compared with 1999.

Clearly, the decline was not due to the intervention plan, which had not yet been implemented. Nor was it due to the CCTV system, whose first cameras only became operational in November 2000. Finally, it does not appear to have been due to any greater success in arresting offenders in 2000. In that year, 11 LFA arrests were made in Uptown compared with 25 in 1999 and 16 in 1998.

The most likely explanation for the fall is that the lots began to attract more attention from police and security patrols in 2000, partly as the result of the project team's activities. This was argued in a report on the project made by David One to the COPS office in April 2001:

> Although not every David One District officer was directly involved in the project, many officers were aware of the District's heightened interest in larceny from auto in the District. As a result, officers became more aware of suspicious activity in surface parking lots as they traveled throughout the District. Because of this heightened awareness, officers stopped to talk to suspicious people who were in the parking lots. The prevention aspect of this interaction with suspicious persons should be credited to the project and to the level of attention the District Captain conveyed to his officers.

Another reason why the lots attracted more attention from police and security patrols was that on July 13, 1999, a woman employed by a law firm in Uptown was fatally stabbed while approaching her vehicle in one of the surface lots. This homicide resulted in a heightened sensitivity to the safety of the lots. It also resulted in an expansion of the coverage of the private bike patrols into the lots used by employees of the buildings maintaining those patrols.

The unprogrammed increase in the surveillance given to the surface lots by patrols does not account for the decline of LFAs in the decks, though this could have been the result of offenders being more generally "scared away" from the Uptown. If so, it would be another example of the diffusion of the benefits of crime prevention activity beyond the targets of intervention (Clarke and Weisburd, 1994).

The number of LFAs continued to drop precipitately in the first quarter of 2001, as shown in Table 5.[17] At this stage, a contributory factor could have been the CCTV system that gradually came into operation in the first quarter of 2001, accompanied by news stories about the system carried by the local papers and TV stations. While few arrests could be attributed to the CCTV cameras,[18] they helped alert officers to suspicious persons in the surface lots and they might have raised the fear of apprehension among potential thieves.

Furthermore, the decline of LFAs in Uptown did not result in displacement of LFAs to the rest of the David One District, where LFAs also declined from a total of 499 in 1999 to a total of 441 in 2000 (see Table 6).[19] This decline of 11.6% was somewhat greater than the 8.5% decline in LFAs reported for the CMPD as a whole (CMPD, 2000). If anything, this pattern suggests, once again, that there may have been some diffusion of benefits to the rest of David One from the Uptown reductions in surface lot LFAs.

Table 5: LFAs in Charlotte Uptown January-March, 1998-2001

1998	87
1999	201
2000	144
2001	68
% Reduction in 2001*	53%

*Compared with 2000.

Table 6: LFAs in David One District 1998-2000

	1998	**1999**	**2000**
Uptown	513	814	506
Rest of David One	498	499	441
Totals	1011	1313	947

This welcome decline has not removed the need for the measures in the intervention plan, which could help to turn what might otherwise be a short-term improvement into a permanent reduction in LFAs. Indeed, Captain Sennett has resolved to press on with the plan, including the more difficult elements such as the grading system and the bike patrol. Full implementation of the latter might wait however to see how the situation develops over the next year or two.

LESSONS OF THE CASE STUDY

As advocates of problem-oriented policing, we constantly ask ourselves why a concept that is so straightforward, and even commonsensical, is so difficult to put into practice. As explained in the introduction, this question is also repeatedly raised in the literature. Direct involvement in this case study in the CMPD, where the conditions for advancing problem-oriented policing are particularly favorable (e.g., overall reputation as a modern police agency; commitment to the concept; highly developed crime analysis operation; superior data retrieval and mapping capacities) produced a number of insights that inform the larger, broader efforts to implement problem-oriented policing elsewhere.

The most frequent explanation for the absence of a fuller implementation of problem-oriented policing is framed in terms of the difficulty that police experience in making the switch from their usual way of doing business. This conventional method of policing involves a quick "in-out" response to single incidents, commonly referred to as a "fire brigade" response, leaving officers free and ready to respond to the next, potentially more serious incident demanding their attention. The problem-oriented approach requires police to restrain the impulse to use traditional responses of questionable value and, instead, to undertake a slow, methodical analysis of classes of similar incidents so as to identify and implement longer-term, preventive measures. This process might take weeks or months, rather than the minutes or hours usually required for their normal method of responding. It could be characterized as demanding patience at the beginning of a project and persistence at the end. It requires not just a fundamental change of attitudes by individual officers and their supervisors, but also a radical change in police organization and management.[20] In most cases, even when they have embarked enthusiastically on a project, police find these changes difficult to sustain in the environment in which they operate. This is why analyses are so often superficial, responses are uncreative and assessments are perfunctory or absent.

While some of these difficulties were experienced even in the present project,[21] it is still underway after more than two years of continuous work and, despite the unexpected decline in LFAs, it remains focused on achieving the longer-term changes designed to prevent a resurgence of the problem. This degree of persistence is well beyond that which is normally reported. The absence of persistence, sometimes labeled lack of commitment, is frequently cited as the primary reason in explaining the failure to implement problem-oriented policing. But, in our opinion, the much stronger reason for the lack of progress, reinforced by our experience working on this project (and the other CMPD projects in which we were involved) is the sheer difficulty of undertaking problem-oriented policing. It is both administratively and technically difficult and, unless these difficulties are addressed, there is little prospect of the problem-oriented approach becoming a standard policing method.

As problem-oriented policing was initially conceptualized, it was never contemplated that the primary burden for implementing the concept would rest on line police officers. Around the country, police officers have been introduced to problem-oriented policing through a variety of short-term training programs. Line officers have repeatedly demonstrated that they are among the most committed, from among the ranks and staffs of police agencies, to grasp the concept, conduct studies, and implement new responses. But the most skilled and committed among them will acknowledge that, when it comes to an ambitious, in-depth study of the type undertaken in this case study, there is little in their police training — relating to the analysis of data and, more generally, in research skills — that equips them to carry out such a study on their own. The specialized training and skills needed are more likely found in a crime analysis unit, and the primary responsibility for *analysis*, which is at the heart of problem-oriented policing, must be placed there.[22] Heavy dependence, however, must continue to be placed on officers — for their important role in contributing their knowledge of problems as they exist on the street, in aiding in the collection and interpretation of data, in helping to weigh the merits of alternative responses, and, most importantly, in working on the implementation of new strategies. An appropriate blend of talents must be achieved. Just as it is unlikely that police officers could, by themselves, carry out a problem-oriented policing project, so a crime analysis unit cannot implement problem-oriented policing without the involvement of both line police officers and police leadership.

These assumptions were confirmed in the David One project. The officers had been introduced to problem-oriented policing, but had no training or prior experience in researching, in the required depth, a problem of this magnitude and complexity. With guidance, they responded with growing enthusiasm to the need for collecting information, acquiring information from elsewhere, and conducting surveys. The captain of David One took the lead in presenting the results of the study and negotiating with potential partners in implementing the new strategies. The crime analysts, with no prior experience working on a problem-oriented policing project that was this ambitious and that probed a problem in such depth, demonstrated that, with guidance, they could use the tools and data readily available to them to take their usual work to a new and higher level.

While a problem-oriented policing project will always compete with the many urgent matters that arise in a police agency, the time consumed in carrying out a project can be greatly reduced. Our limited involvement was not enough to pick up on tasks required doing or to coordinate matters on site in ways that might have sped up the project. The numerous tasks fell to an otherwise busy team of people. Among the lessons of this project was the realization that continued involvement in ambitious problem-oriented policing projects, to be accomplished in a timely manner, requires more on-site, in-house coordination of the various component efforts. The commitment and enthusiasm of the officers and crime analysts involved in this project could have been even more effectively channeled with the sustained attention of a full-time coordinator who could have stayed on top of things, and who could thereby have brought the project to a speedier conclusion.[23] A coordinator could, for example, most likely have sped up the David One project by: (1) expediting the collection of data on parking facilities and parking spaces; (2) assisting the crime analyst in identifying questions for study; (3) searching for other relevant experience in dealing with LFAs; (4) relieving the police of acquiring certain information (e.g., about the costs of fencing and private patrols) and making some contacts (e.g., such as initial explorations with lot operators, the planning department and other partners); (5) assuring follow-up on the many points and questions raised at periodic meetings; and (6) undertaking a host of other essential tasks that fell to individual team members to perform along with their regular work. The need for such coordination, in any project meeting the definition of problem-oriented policing, is a fact that must be faced by departments seriously committed to the approach.

Without substantial and continuous involvement in research, it is not easy for officers engaged in problem-oriented policing to conduct a "literature review" to identify relevant studies and relevant prior experience in dealing with similar problems. And even if they are experienced in conducting a search, they confront other problems. The nature of the literature is such that they may learn about titles, but have difficulty finding copies of actual documents. Specialized libraries that are most likely to have the fullest collection of such materials are few in number and not conveniently located to all agencies. And without familiarity with this body of literature, it is often difficult to judge the quality of the research reported so as to decide what is worth focusing on.

The Internet has helped some police deal with these difficulties, but, for this type of search, computers, too, have their limitations.

While we were able to meet the need for literature review in the present project, ways of helping police everywhere to profit from the available literature must be found. The forthcoming publication of the *Problem-Oriented Guides for Police*, a project developed under a grant from the COPS office, constitutes a substantial step in this direction. These guides, of which 20 have been prepared, seek to present in a synthesized, readable form the lessons that have emerged from the experience of police and others in dealing with specific problems, such as that addressed in the LFA project.[24] Another approach would be to expand the responsibilities of crime analysts, and give them appropriate training, so that they could be expected on request to undertake and report the results of focused literature reviews.

Lastly, the project illustrated the difficulties faced by members of a police agency — both officers and crime analysts — in obtaining the considerable amounts of information needed to guide each stage of a project. They must decide what information is needed, they must identify sources and persuade those holding the information to release it, and they must then analyze and interpret it. The following brief list of the information collected for the present (incomplete) project will illustrate the scope of the work that will often be required:

(1) At the *scanning* stage, data about vehicle-related thefts in the David One area were examined to determine the relative proportions of auto thefts and LFAs occurring in the parking facilities and elsewhere. The hot spot mapping undertaken by the crime analyst facilitated this examination.

(2) At the *analysis* stage, maps of the Uptown area showing individual lots and decks had to be updated from planning records, from aerial photographs and from physical checks made of facilities. The number of spaces in each parking facility had to be recorded and in many cases counted. Security surveys had to be undertaken of the 206 separate parking facilities identified. These data had to be subjected to correlational analysis and significance testing. Rates of LFAs had to be calculated for each block in the city. Computer maps of Uptown showing the distribution of rates of LFAs had to be constructed.

(3) At the *response* stage (still incomplete at the time of writing), cost data were obtained for employing full-time attendants, for installing various kinds of fencing and for the projected bike patrol. Information was obtained about the projected new trolley line. CPTED surveys were undertaken of three parking facilities. Studies were designed (but not carried out because

of lack of resources) to measure the surveillance given to each lot by the CCTV system and from the windows of overlooking buildings. Computer maps were made showing LFAs in adjacent lots with and without attendants and with different levels of lighting and fencing. A detailed grading scheme for lot security was developed with the assistance of Tim Crowe. LFA data for Uptown and the remainder of David One had to be analyzed for 2000/2001 to document the unexpected decline in thefts and to see whether displacement had occurred.

The need for these data draws attention to the vital roles of both crime analysts and line officers in problem-oriented policing. But given the expectation that has built up about officer involvement, the examples emphasize the importance of giving more attention to the role of the crime analysts. Strong and engaged as the analysts were in this case study, and we know of none better, they had, prior to this project, no occasion to get deeply immersed in problem-oriented policing or situational prevention. If this were true in the CMPD, with its unusual investment in crime analysis, it must hold with even greater force elsewhere. This means that, if problem-oriented policing is to be properly implemented, ways will have to be found to provide a greater pool of those who can furnish the necessary analytic support. This will require two questions to be addressed:

(1) How can enough people with the appropriate blend of interests and basic research skills, and the appropriate computer skills, be recruited for these positions, when — especially with regard to the computer skills — they are in such great demand in the more highly-paid, private sector?

(2) How can crime analysts be given a form of specialized training, designed to expand their capacities, that would draw heavily on what is known about problem-oriented policing, situational crime prevention, and the relatively new specialty of environmental criminology?

The first question lies outside our competence and might require a national plan to be formulated. As for the second, narrower question, we should note that the U.S. National Institute of Justice and the COPS Office have both played a useful role in drawing police attention to the capacities of the new mapping software and in providing training to analysts and officers in crime mapping.[25] However, neither agency has invested in training designed to provide crime analysts with the skills and knowledge needed if they are to provide support for problem-oriented policing. Attempting to do so would expose a shortage of expertise and a lack of training materials, which is a situation that needs to be urgently addressed.

SUMMARY AND CONCLUSIONS

The purpose of the project was threefold: (1) to illustrate, within the context of the CMPD, what is involved in a full implementation of problem-oriented policing by taking on a comprehensive, in-depth effort to address a specific piece of police business; (2) having focused on the problem of theft from vehicles, to develop specific strategies designed to increase the effectiveness of the CMPD in dealing with that problem; and (3) more broadly, to gain new insights into the complexities of introducing problem-oriented policing into a police agency.

It is difficult to measure the degree to which the first objective has been achieved. The project has touched many members of the CMPD. Descriptions of it have been incorporated in some of the agency's training. Presentations have been made to management. And perhaps most importantly, those in a position to encourage new ways of thinking about policing now have, by virtue of their familiarity with this and a companion project on theft from constructions sites (Clarke and Goldstein, 2002), a better understanding of what problem-oriented policing entails.

With regard to the problem of theft from vehicles, the project has produced several specific strategies, grounded in detailed study, that are targeted at reducing such thefts in the uptown area of Charlotte. The most promising proposals have yet to be implemented, but work is proceeding on putting them in place. In the interim, an unexpected decline has occurred in LFAs. No hard evidence is available to explain the decline, but the police involved feel that the project may have indirectly contributed to the decline through the attention focused on the problem. Police regularly assigned to the area appear to have intensified surveillance of the surface parking lots in Uptown. It is anticipated that full implementation of the newly devised strategies will contribute to a long-term, permanent reduction in LFAs.

A major benefit of the project (apart from an anticipated long-term reduction in LFAs) has been the deeper understanding acquired of the administrative and technical difficulties encountered by police in implementing problem-oriented policing. The project abundantly illustrated just how complex it is to examine a large problem that, though commonly confronted by the police throughout this nation and abroad, has rarely been put under such an intensive microscope. And this is just one of the many problems routinely handled by police which have not been similarly examined. The project confirmed that, in its most ambitious form, problem-oriented policing is indeed, contrary to the frequent claim, a complex process that requires much patience at its beginning, and much persistence in blasting through to the end. It is an iterative process, not lockstep, in which the gradual acquisition of data and information informs the project, leading to more questions, to redefinition, and even to changes in focus as it moves along. And the cycle repeats itself several times as more knowledge is acquired and possible strategies are explored and ideally tested. It cannot simply be introduced alongside other activities without an allocation of sufficient staff time, without special training, and without other adjustments in the management and organization of a police agency. It requires that police have improved access to information about prior experience dealing with the problems being addressed. And if it is to be adopted more widely by police agencies, it requires a substantially expanded and better-trained cadre of crime analysts to support the initiatives and efforts of career police. Ways of meeting these needs must be found if problem-oriented policing is to achieve its prime objective, which is to enable police agencies to engage in-house in the kind of analysis that helps them to improve their effectiveness in dealing with the problems that the public expects them to handle, and to share the results of their efforts with police elsewhere.

Address correspondence to: Ronald V. Clarke, Rutgers University School of Criminal Justice, 123 Washington Street, Newark, NJ 07102-3192, USA. E-mail: <RVGClarke@aol.com>.

Acknowledgments: This project was completed under a grant 970CWX0060 made to the Charlotte-Mecklenburg Police Department by the Office of Community Oriented Policing Services, U.S. Department of Justice.

Because the integration, analysis, and mapping of data constituted such an important part of this exploration, the project leaned heavily on the crime analyst assigned to the David One district, Matthew White. He also prepared the maps included in this report. In the data collection stage, crime analysts Monica Nguyen and Michael Humphrey lent a hand and, later, Kristin Knight, assisted in some of the statistical analysis.

It was the captain of David One, Jerry Sennett, who initially proposed the project as a case study in problem-oriented policing. He subsequently participated in the various meetings at which the data were analyzed and possible solutions discussed, made the connections to the various groups that would be important in carrying out new strategies, and also took the lead in the several presentations of the study's findings. Captain Sennett assigned a member of his staff to monitor the project and to acquire some needed information — first Sergeant Craig "Pete" Davis and, more recently, Sergeant Harold Medlock. A team of two police officers, Anthony Crawford and Veronica Foster, carried out the enormous task of acquiring, through on-site inspections, the detailed information on existing parking facilities, including the counting of the number of parking spaces in each facility. Subsequently, Officers Crawford and Robert Vandergrift conducted CPTED analyses of selected parking facilities used in the PowerPoint presentation.

Steve Ward, a senior district attorney who is (in a unique arrangement in American policing) assigned full time to working as an adviser within the CMPD, participated in all of the meetings held over the life of the project, and in formulating the recommendations for earlier intervention.

Dennis Nowicki, the former chief of the CMPD, initially suggested taking on several case studies in problem-oriented policing as a way of illustrating what was involved in a comprehensive carrying out of the concept. From the time of his appointment, shortly after the project got underway, the project has received strong support from the current chief, Darrel Stephens. The former Director of Research and Planning, Dr. Richard Lumb, was generous in his arrangements for the allocation and scheduling of his staff's time, as was current Acting Director, John Couchell. This report on the project was greatly facilitated by detailed notes taken on early project meetings by Officer Lisa Carriker. Finally, James LeBeau of Southern Illinois University provided us with valuable statistical advice.

REFERENCES

Barclay, P., J. Buckley, P.J. Brantingham, P.L. Brantingham and T. Whinn-Yates (1996). "Preventing Auto Theft in Suburban Vancouver Commuter Lots: Effects of a Bike Patrol." In: R.V. Clarke (ed.), *Preventing Mass Transit Crime.* (Crime Prevention Studies, vol. 6.) Monsey, NY: Criminal Justice Press.

Barthe, E. (2000). Unpublished Ph.D. prospectus, School of Criminal Justice, Rutgers, The State University of New Jersey.

Burrows, J. and K. Heal (1980). "Police Car Security Campaigns." In: R.V.G. Clarke and P. Mayhew (eds.), *Designing Out Crime.* London, UK: Her Majesty's Stationery Office.

Charlotte-Mecklenburg Police Department (2000). "Annual Summary." Unpublished report.

Clarke, R.V. (2002). *Theft of and from Cars in Parking Facilities.* (Problem-Oriented Guides for Police series No. 10.) Washington, DC: Office of Community Oriented Policing Services, U.S. Department of Justice.

—— (1998). "Defining Police Strategies: Problem Solving, Problem-Oriented Policing and Community-Oriented Policing." In: T. O'Connor Shelley and A.C. Grant (eds.), *Problem-Oriented Policing: Crime-Specific Problems and Critical Issues and Making POP Work*, vol. 1. Washington, DC: Police Executive Research Forum.

—— (1997). "Problem-Oriented Policing and the Potential Contribution of Criminology." Unpublished Report to the National Institute of Justice (Grant # 95-IJ-CX-0021).

—— and H. Goldstein (2002). "Reducing Theft at Construction Sites: Lessons from a Problem-oriented Project." In: N. Tilley (ed.), *Analysis for Crime Prevention.* (Crime Prevention Studies, vol. 13.) Monsey, NY: Criminal Justice Press.

—— and P. Mayhew (1998). "Preventing Crime in Parking Lots: What We Know and Need to Know." In: M. Felson and R.B. Peiser (eds.), *Reducing Crime Through Real Estate Development and Planning.* Washington, DC: Urban Land Institute.

—— and D. Weisburd (1994). "Diffusion of Crime Control Benefits: Observations on the Reverse of Displacement." In: R.V. Clarke (ed.), *Crime Prevention Studies,* vol. 2. Monsey, NY: Criminal Justice Press.

—— and P. Harris (1992). "Auto Theft and Its Prevention." In: M. Tonry (ed.), *Crime and Justice: A Review of Research,* vol. 16. Chicago, IL: University of Chicago Press.

Crowe, T. (1991). *Crime Prevention through Environmental Design: Applications of Architectural Design and Space Management Concepts.* Boston, MA: Butterworth-Heinemann.

Eck, J.E. and W. Spelman (1987). *Problem-Solving. Problem-Oriented Policing in Newport News.* Washington, DC: Police Executive Research Forum. and the U.S. National Institute of Justice.

Frank, A. (2000). "Police Shut Holes at Newark Airport." *The Star-Ledger,* March 22.

Geason, S. and P. Wilson (1990). *Preventing Car Theft and Crime in Car Parks.* Canberra, AUS: Australian Institute of Criminology.

Gladstone, F. (1980) *Co-ordinating Crime Prevention Efforts.* (Home Office Research Study No. 47.) London, UK: Her Majesty's Stationery Office.

Goldstein, H. (1996a). *Problem-Oriented Policing: The Rationale, the Concept, and Reflections on Its Implementation.* London, UK: Police Research Group, Home Office.

—— (1996b). "Problem-Oriented Policing." An address to the summer conference of the Association of Chief Police Officers, Manchester, England, July 3, 1996.

—— (1994a). "Examining the Current Status of Problem-Oriented Policing and Thinking Through an Agenda for Research and Technical Support for the Concept." Unpublished memorandum addressed to Craig Uchida, Office of Community Oriented Policing Services in the United States Department of Justice, July 11, 1994.

—— (1994b). "Suggestions for Inclusion in the National Institute of Justice Research Agenda Relating to the Police." Unpublished memorandum addressed to Jeremy Travis, Director of the National Institute of Justice, September 29, 1994.

—— (1990). *Problem-Oriented Policing.* New York: McGraw Hill.

—— (1979). "Improving Policing: A Problem-Oriented Approach." *Crime & Delinquency* 25(2):234–58.

Harries, K. (1999) *Mapping Crime: Principle and Practice.* Washington, DC: National Institute of Justice, U.S. Department of Justice.

Hesseling, R. (1995) "Theft From Cars: Reduced or Displaced." *European Journal of Criminal Policy and Research* 3:79-92.

Laycock, G. and N. Tilley (1995). "Implementing Crime Prevention." In: M. Tonry and D.P. Farrington (eds.), *Building a Safer Society: Approaches to Crime Prevention.* (Crime and Justice: A Review of Research, vol. 19.) Chicago, IL: University of Chicago Press.

—— and C. Austin. (1992). "Crime Prevention in Parking Facilities." *Security Journal* 3(3):154-160.

Mancini, A.N. and R. Jain (1987). "Commuter Parking Lots: Vandalism and Deterrence." *Transportation Quarterly* 41:539-53.

Meredith, C. and C. Paquette (1992). "Crime Prevention in High-Rise Rental Apartments: Findings of a Demonstration Project." *Security Journal* 3(3):161-167.

Phillips, C. (1999). "A Review of CCTV Evaluations: Crime Reduction Effects and Attitudes Towards Its Use." In: K. Painter and N. Tilley (eds.), *Surveillance of Public Space: CCTV, Street Lighting and Crime Prevention.* (Crime Prevention Studies, vol. 10.) Monsey, NY: Criminal Justice Press.

Poyner, B. (1991). "Situational Crime Prevention in Two Car Parks." *Security Journal* 2:96-101.

Read, T. and Tilley, N. (2000). *Not Rocket Science? Problem-Solving and Crime Reduction.* (Crime Reduction Research Series Paper 6.) London, UK: Home Office, Police Research Group.

Riley, D. (1980). "An Evaluation of a Campaign to Reduce Car Thefts." In: R.V.G. Clarke and P. Mayhew (eds.), *Designing Out Crime.* London, UK: Her Majesty's Stationery Office.

Sallybanks, J. and R. Brown (1999). *Vehicle Crime Reduction: Turning the Corner.* (Police Research Series Paper 119.) London, UK: Policing and Reducing Crime Unit, Home Office.

Sandby-Thomas, M. (1992). *Preventive Strategies to Reduce Car Theft in Northern Ireland.* Report No. 2. Belfast: Extern Organization.

Scott, M.S. (2000). *Problem-Oriented Policing. Reflections on the First 20 Years.* Washington, DC: Office of Community Oriented Policing Services, U.S. Department of Justice.

—— and R.V. Clarke (2000). "A Review of Submissions for the Herman Goldstein Award for Excellence in Problem-oriented Policing." In: C. Sole Brito and E.E. Gatto (eds.), *Problem-Oriented Policing: Crime-Specific Problems, Critical Issues and Making POP Work,* vol. 3. Washington, DC: Police Executive Research Forum.

Smith, M.S. (1996). *Crime Prevention through Environmental Design in Parking Facilities.* (Research In Brief series, National Institute of Justice.) Washington, DC: U.S. Department of Justice.

Spelman, W. and J. Eck (1989). "Sitting Ducks, Ravenous Wolves, and Helping Hands: New Approaches to Urban Policing." *Public Affairs Comment,* vol. 35, no. 2. Lyndon Johnson School of Public Affairs, University of Texas at Austin.

Tilley, N. (1993). *Understanding Car Parks, Crime and CCTV: Evaluation Lessons from Safer Cities.* London, UK: Police Research Group, Home Office.

VCRAT (Vehicle Crime Reduction Action Team) (1999). *Tackling Vehicle Crime: A Five Year Strategy.* (Communication Directorate.) London, UK: Home Office.

Webb, B., B. Brown and K. Bennett (1992). *Preventing Car Crime in Car Parks.* (Crime Prevention Unit Series, Paper 34.) London, UK: Home Office.

NOTES

1. This is particularly true when situational prevention projects are included in the count. When practiced by police, situational prevention is indistinguishable from problem-oriented policing (Clarke, 1997).

2. The David One District (one of 12 CMPD districts) is split roughly into two parts — the northern part consisting of Charlotte's Uptown, and a larger inner city area to the west and south consisting of mixed residential and industrial development.

3. At the same time, Clarke and Goldstein also served as consultants to problem-oriented projects in other units of the CMPD.

4. The center-city businesses have provided funds that enable the CMPD to assign 10 officers to foot and bike patrol that are in addition to the number that would otherwise have been assigned based on the county-wide standards for allocating police personnel.

5. For the purposes of this study, decks are either freestanding multilevel parking structures or parking garages/parking floors belonging to multi-level office buildings. Lots are open, surface-level parking facilities.

6. We were supported in this latter argument by Steve Ward.

7. For example: Clarke, 2002; Clarke and Harris, 1992; Clarke and Mayhew, 1998; Eck and Spelman, 1987; Frank, 2000; Geason and Wilson, 1990; Laycock and Austin, 1992; Mancini and Jain, 1987; Meredith and Paquette, 1992; Poyner, 1991; Phillips, 1999; Sallybanks and Brown, 1999; Sandby–Thomas, 1992; Smith, 1996; Tilley, 1993; and VCRAT, 1999.

8. Definitions were as follows: weak means more than half the facility is dark or shadowed; moderate means less than half the facility is dark or shadowed; strong means none of the facility is dark/shadowed.

9. More refined statistical analyses of these relationships would not have been justified given the limitations of the data-gathering methods.

10. Three reasons permit this to be confidently asserted: (1) the relationship in Table 2 between attendants in lots and LFAs was nearly significant, even though so few lots had attendants; (2) the primary factor in the reduced risks in decks was the presence of attendants; and (3) the previous research consistently indicates that the presence of attendants reduces theft.

11. A plan to undertake such a study, together with a study of the amount of surveillance given lots from surrounding buildings, was abandoned because of lack of time and resources.

12. Section 12.303 of the City Code.

13. While not entirely defensible on scientific grounds, it was an effective way of showing these relationships.

14. Tim Crowe is author of the principal text on CPTED (Crowe, 1991) and had been engaged by Chief Stephens to provide CPTED training for the department.

15. Bank of America has maintained foot patrols since 1996 and bike patrols since 1998. These operate from 6 am to midnight, with 2-6 security officers on duty at any one time.

16. There is a significant difference in LFA locations across the years (observed Chi-Square 17.49; degrees of freedom 4; Critical Value 13.27; Alpha=0.01).

17. There is significant drop in LFAs across the years as shown by a one-way Goodness of Fit test (observed Chi- Square 86.64; degrees of freedom 3; Critical Value 16.26; Alpha 0.001).

18. In the four months until the end of April, only 4 LFA arrests were made in Uptown and it is not known in how many of these the cameras played a role.

19. There is a significant difference in LFAs in David One across the years (observed Chi-Square 33.037; degrees of freedom 2; Critical Value 9.21; Alpha 0.01).

20. These changes are spelled out in detail in chapter 9 (pp. 148-175) in Goldstein (1990).

21. At its beginning, some of the officers were anxious to "get-going" and expressed some frustration when initial efforts were made to extend the analysis and the search for proposed solutions. Without the periodic deadlines imposed by the regularly scheduled meetings between ourselves and team members, it is likely that progress on the project would have been even more delayed by the press of other business. Likewise, our involvement as consultants helped to ensure that problem analysis and the search for alternative responses were pursued further than might otherwise have been the case.

22. This observation may conjure up an impossible burden for police administrators who are so often strapped for resources. But it is not contemplated that any one police agency would invest, at any one time, in an in-depth analysis of a large number of problems. Rather, precisely because resources and staff are so scarce, a single police agency such as the CMPD might not be able to examine more than two or three such problems in a year. Ideally, the development of a department-wide commitment to creating an atmosphere in which all members of the department think in terms of identifying and addressing problems at all levels of the agency — a process that should not be abandoned — will not only increase police effectiveness regarding more discrete beat-level problems. It would also serve as the means for nominating problems that are potentially good candidates for more in-depth inquiry. Moreover, if police departments that can afford the minimum staff commitment conducted

even one such study and shared the results with others, the police field in general would enormously benefit.

23. This same conclusion has been reached by others in reviewing efforts to implement situational crime prevention (e.g., Gladstone, 1980; Laycock and Tilley, 1995).

24. These guides can be downloaded from the COPS web site: http://www.usdoj.gov/cops.

25. For example, the Crime Mapping Research Center at the NIJ (http://www.ojp.usdoj.government/crmc/) holds an annual mapping conference and has published an important text on crime mapping (Harries, 1999), while COPS has sponsored training in mapping by the Regional Community Policing Institutes. (The Carolina Institute for Community Policing, in which the CMPD is heavily involved, has Geographic Information Systems as its major focus area. The Institute has provided much training over the course of its existence.)